THE FC
BOOK OF

To Joan,

  From Mom & Dad.

Looking forward to
reading your Sermon
in due course.

The Fourth *Times*
Book of Best Sermons

Edited and Introduced by
RUTH GLEDHILL

Foreword by
RABBI DR JONATHAN ROMAIN

CASSELL

Cassell
Wellington House
125 Strand
London WC2R 0BB

370 Lexington Avenue
New York
NY 10017-6550

www.cassell.co.uk

First published 1999

British Library Cataloguing-in-Publication Data
A catalogue record for this book is available from the British Library.

ISBN 0-304-70467-9

The sculpture on the cover appears by courtesy of Ros Stracey.
Cover photograph by Michael Powell.

Typeset by Kenneth Burnley, Wirral, Cheshire.
Printed and bound in Great Britain by Biddles Ltd, Guildford and King's Lynn.

Contents

CONTENTS

Foreword

RABBI DR JONATHAN ROMAIN
Maidenhead Synagogue

I F THERE is not already a patron saint for preachers, then I hereby
nominate Thomas Carlyle. It was he who declared 'Who, having
been called to be a preacher, would stoop to be a king?'

It is a remarkable privilege to be given the opportunity to communicate that which one likes to think is the word of God. It is also a
rare boon to do so in an undisturbed slot, knowing we will not be
interrupted when guilty of hesitation, deviation, repetition or even
nonsense.

It is inevitable that over the centuries there has been a percentage of
preachers who have failed to live up to their task. It was they who led
W. E. Sangster to declare 'It is one of the tragic curiosities of preaching
that some men commissioned to give this message seem to have no
message to give.'

Often preachers do have a message, but can sometimes lose sight of
it. There is the story of a congregant who had to leave church early. As
he went out, another person rushed in late and breathlessly asked
'Have I missed the sermon?' 'Yes and no', he replied. 'The sermon is
over, but the minister is still talking.' Even the best preacher can have
an off-day, with as great an orator as St Paul once causing a member of
his audience to fall asleep (Acts 20:7–12).

Another problem can be the mode of delivery. A wonderful theme
can be spoilt through monotone pronunciation or lack of eye-contact.
A preacher should be an actor manqué: master of the dramatic pause,
able to span both tragedy and comedy, turn dry eyes wet and then
cheer them up again, and occasionally use the full force of his/her body
to emphasize a point.

We can all sympathize with the warden who listened to a visiting
preacher read out his sermon, never lifting his eyes from a carefully
typed-out script, and afterwards complained to the minister 'How do
you expect me to remember your sermon when you cannot?'

Still, stories about incompetent preachers are like mother-in-law
jokes. They give us a good laugh, even though we know many fine
examples who are the exact opposite. Perhaps this is one of the reasons
why the institution of preaching has survived so long.

Other reasons are the fact that in an age before mass-printing and a general absence of books, the sermon was the only method of education. It also served as one of the few sources of public entertainment. Yet even today, with instant access to electronic knowledge and with a vast leisure industry, sermons offer a unique level of personal intimacy and emotional power that can move a listener.

The sermon also has an important liturgical function. With most services following a set text that is largely the same every week, it is the sermon that differentiates one service from another. When someone at home asks the returning worshipper 'How was the service today?', what they really mean is 'What was the sermon like?'

At its best, a sermon can change lives. Many a person can attest to hearing a sermon that led them to give up a particular vice, adopt a positive course of action, rectify a damaged relationship or pursue a new career through hearing a message that touched something deep inside them. No doubt they had been edging that way, but it was the preacher that was the catalyst for change and who turned subterranean thoughts into direct action.

By way of example, I shall never forget John, a good-looking 40-year-old man, tall, with jet-black hair. We had a pleasant chat after the service, although I noticed he was a little pensive. I was shocked to see him in the High Street two weeks later: his hair had turned completely grey. When I gently commented on the change in his appearance, he said: 'It was your sermon, rabbi, when you said we should put aside the pretences in our lives and the false identities we hide behind. My hair went grey long ago, but I dyed it and nobody knew. But I always felt awkward about it, as if I was cheating people. Your sermon made me decide to be myself and get rid of the hype.'

It may be a relatively trivial incident, but for John it was a major turning point, and it typifies the process of change that a sermon can engender. It also highlights the fact that sermons should talk not only about the glories of God but also the problems of humanity. No subject should be alien to the pulpit. Sermons should span the ABC of everyday life: alcoholism, battery of spouses, cancer, divorce etc. and speak openly about the issues that most people bring secretly into the service with them.

Of course, the preacher may have an agenda that is different from that of the congregation. But he/she has to start from where they are at, address their concerns, command their attention and then take them to where he is at. The best sermon is a journey that brings them to a point they might otherwise not have reached and deposits them safely down at the end.

As a regular preacher myself, one of my formative experiences was going as a child to an open-air show on the beach in Eastbourne. It started to rain and some people began leaving. 'Never mind the rain', called out the presenter, anxious to reassure those of us left, 'the show will go on. Even if there is only one man and his dog in the audience, I keep going. And if the man goes to the loo and leaves the dog, I'll still carry on.'

That sense of mission and determination has inspired me ever since, although thankfully I have never been put to that particular test.

Introduction

RUTH GLEDHILL

WHEN *The Times* agreed to sponsor the first Preacher of the Year Award in 1995, the College of Preachers, then our partners in the venture, stipulated that the award should be open to Christians only. At the time, because the college was an exclusively Christian body and was the organizer of the competition, we agreed. However, in the first year we received at least one entry from a rabbi, which we sadly had to return. In the successive three years, we received mounting numbers of entries from the Jewish community, all of which had to be returned.

At the same time, the entries from the Christian community were in decline, in terms of both quantity and quality. We were not sure why this was, although we suspected it might have something to do with our withdrawal of the monetary prize of £1,000 for the winner and £200 for the runners-up after the first year. We had taken this decision after criticism was voiced in the Christian community about our offering money to reward preachers for speaking the word of God. We are certainly not in the business of giving money away where it is not wanted, so we desisted immediately from doing so. Nevertheless, we were dismayed when, having responded to what we understood to be a demand from our constituency in withdrawing the prize money, the number of entries from Christian preachers fell by half, from more than 500 to barely more than 250. Meanwhile, entries from rabbis continued to grow, and I continued having to return them, much to my regret.

As a result, in 1998 we decided both to reintroduce the prize money, and to invite entries from the Jewish community. The College of Preachers decided that it was unable to accommodate rabbis within the remit of the competition, and withdrew all co-operation. As a significant number of entries had in previous years come in through publicity generated by the College in various publications, this was a sad loss. However, the number of entries we lost was more than made up for by the number of rabbis who submitted sermons, more than 30 in total, from the Liberal, Reform and right through to the Orthodox communities. And to our delight, the quality of the sermons this year was also lifted to the highest level yet, partly as a result of the exceptional homiletics of these rabbis. In addition, we were delighted that Dr Peter Graves, superintendent minister at Methodist Central Hall at Westminster, London, stepped in to fill the gap left by the College. Without his support and assistance, in offering us Central Hall as a venue for the final and in using his network of Methodist preachers to assist with the judging process, there would have been no preaching competition and no sermons book this year. We are also grateful for the support of Premier Christian Radio, and hope to develop our connection with them in future years, in both promoting and publicizing the competition. In particular, all of us at *The Times* were stunned and amazed by the astonishing generosity of the American millionaire Grainger Weston, who this year offered free holidays at his resort, Frenchman's Cove in Jamaica, with flights, accommodation and spending money included, to the 30 preachers shortlisted in the 1995 competition and their spouses. Some declined the offer, which had as its one condition that they should preach a sermon in Jamaica, but those who did go have since reported back that it was truly 'paradise on earth'.

I was now able to take control of the assessment system by which the sermons were judged. Although not a judge myself, I decided a different system was needed from that used in previous years, when I had watched dozens of high-quality sermons come in as entries past my desk at Wapping, and then for some reason seen some of the best fail to make the shortlist of 30. Lacking the resources of the College, which had sent the sermons out for assessment to various of its members who marked them accordingly, I instead instituted a Booker-style system of initial assessment. Judges who are leading communicators in their respective fields were invited to take part. All the men we asked agreed, none of the women did. So it was not for want of trying that we ended up with an entirely male panel. We also asked last year's winner, the Rev. Paul Walker, whose winning sermon appears at the end of the book, to join the panel. All the judges were sent the entire 250-plus sermons to read at their leisure, after which we met over lunch in a private room at the Reform Club, and attempted to dissect, analyse and choose the top 30 sermons in no more than 80 minutes.

The process worked surprisingly well. Each of the five judges had been asked to choose their top 30 sermons. Two sermons had five marks, in that they were chosen by five judges. Twelve had four, six had three and fifteen had two. So we had to lose five. Some heated discussion followed, but eventually the judges made their choices. Every Jewish sermon submitted had at least one mark – in most cases awarded by one of the Christian judges. One of the sermons with five marks was Jewish, one was Christian.

Our one Jewish assessor, Rabbi Dr Jonathan Romain, author of this year's Foreword and minister of Maidenhead Synagogue in Berkshire, enlivened the proceedings from the start with a succession of Jewish preaching jokes, which he has given me permission to reproduce here.

'A new rabbi was hired by the synagogue council and they all attended his first service, keen to see how he would preach', he began. 'It was a brilliant sermon and they all left inspired. On the next sabbath they were all very expectant as to how he would follow up his initial success, and so they were very surprised when he gave exactly the same sermon. "Perhaps he picked up the wrong notes as he left home", they thought, and went away somewhat puzzled. On the third week he gave exactly the same sermon. This was too much, so a delegation went to the rabbi and demanded to know why he kept on preaching the same sermon. The rabbi seemed unperturbed and simply said: "Just remind me, what did I say in the sermon?" The chairman paused and looked confused. "I can't remember", he said in some embarrassment and, turning to the others present, he said: "Can anyone else recall what the rabbi said?" None could. "That's the point", said the rabbi. "And so I shall continue giving that sermon until you do remember!"

'A young rabbi had just been ordained and was giving his first sermon to the congregation who had just appointed him. He was rather nervous, but was delighted that at the end of the sermon, everyone shouted: "Encore, encore!" Bowing to their wishes, he gave the sermon again, and was amazed when once more he was greeted with shouts of: "Encore, encore!" Blushing deeply, he said: "No, I could not possibly give it a third time." At which point a member of the congregation stood up and said: "Young man, you will continue giving it until you get it right!"

'The rabbi was about to leave home to preach at the synagogue when his wife, who was unwell and unable to go that day, asks him what he is preaching on. He is planning to give a sermon on the Jewish attitude to sex but is embarrassed to tell her this, so instead refers to their recent holiday and says: "Water skiing." She thinks: "How boring." The following week she is shopping in town when she bumps into a fellow congregant, who tells her what a marvellous, riveting sermon her husband preached. "That is very odd", says the rabbi's wife. "He doesn't know much about it, he's only ever done it twice, and he fell off both times!"'

The ice thus broken, and after lively argument and discussion when much time was spent bewailing the lack of quality of preaching generally, while admitting we couldn't do much better ourselves, we ended up with 22 Christian sermons and eight Jewish sermons in the short-list of 30 and thus for publication in this book. Of the rabbis, two are Orthodox, three Reform, one is Liberal and two Progressive. There is one woman rabbi, Dr Margaret Jacobi, from Birmingham, who is also a highly-qualified doctor of medicine. Some of the rabbis have impressively-long rabbinic ancestries, and can trace their families back through many generations of rabbis. Of the Christians, there is one Seventh-day Adventist, one United Reformed Church minister and two Baptists. The majority, as in previous years, are Anglicans and Methodists, both lay and ordained. Sadly, this year there were few Roman Catholic entries and none in the final 30. An enthusiastic worshipper at Westminster Cathedral sent in a sermon by Cardinal Basil Hume, Archbishop of Westminster, that some of the judges would have liked to include, but one of our rules is that no entries can be accepted without the permission of the preacher, and Cardinal Hume requested that his be withdrawn. For the first time, we have included comments in the book submitted by some of the judges. Nine criteria were used in the initial judging process. They were as follows:

1. Was there a clear message?
2. Was attention held throughout?
3. Did the sermon engage both the mind and the emotions?
4. Were illustrations used effectively?
5. Was there a balance of theology and application?
6. Was the personality of the preacher engaged by the sermon?
7. Did the message have identifiably biblical values?
8. Did the sermon evoke a positive response?
9. Was there a sense of God speaking through the preacher?

For the final, this year at Methodist Central Hall in Westminster, when five preachers take part in a service of worship and prayer, a tenth criterion is added: Was the voice used effectively? For obvious reasons, it was not possible to use this tenth criterion at the initial stage, when judges had only texts to work from. If it was practicable to visit every church to listen to each entrant, we would. But we simply do not have the resources to arrange this. However, the final five have been chosen over the summer in a careful process where each of the 30 shortlisted preachers was visited and listened to by an assessor, who is either one of the five original judges, or a Methodist minister who has offered to help through the offices of Dr Graves. Besides Dr Graves, Dr Romain and Mr Walker, the judges at the initial assessment included Mgr Kieran Conry, head of the communications arm of the Roman Catholic Church in England and Wales, the Catholic Media Office in London, and the Rev. Dr Bill Beaver, Director of Communications for the Church of England. Peter Kerridge of Premier Christian Radio, who along with the others will be a judge at the final, also helped, through written assessments, with selecting the shortlist of 30. And at the final, at the request of the editor of *The Times*, Peter Stothard, there will be an atheist, who will assess the believability quotient or otherwise of the five finalists. He is Andrew Brown, who prefers to describe himself as a 'lapsed agnostic'. He was formerly the award-winning religious affairs correspondent of the *Independent* newspaper, and is currently a freelance journalist who is a contributor to the *New York Review of Books, Granta* magazine, *Prospect, New Statesman* and many other journals and newspapers. His brief history of the selfish gene, *The Darwin Wars*, will be published by Simon and Schuster in February 1999.

'There is still a place for preaching', he says, 'even though it does have to compete with so many other forms of communication. I have preached twice myself, once at Wadham College, Oxford, when I gave a sermon on the author Terry Pratchett, and once at Guildford when I realized halfway through I had lost my diary and should have been at that moment doing an interview at LBC. I have heard a lot of sermons. Too many in fact. I got to a point where I started to avoid them because I was so often savagely disappointed. They too often consisted of people with not much to say, and taking too long to say it.'

But he does, finally, confess to some interest and enjoyment. 'The sermon is a public performance', he says. 'I remember hearing Jesse Jackson preach once. It was absolutely beautiful. It was 50 per cent incomprehensible, and 50 per cent to be disagreed with. But it was great. I remember what he said then, when I can remember nothing else of that trip to the States, and certainly nothing that I saw on television.'

Many rabbis take the concept of the Millennium almost as seriously as, if not more so than, their Christian brethren, according to our survey of the views of the 30 shortlisted preachers in *The Times* Preacher of the Year Award 1998. For both Jewish and Christian preachers, the Millennium is linked almost inextricably with the death of Diana, Princess of Wales, and with what she represented in society, both in life and death. We sought the views of the preachers on both these issues and have reproduced them here, along with their views on the value of preaching, in the separate introductions to each sermon.

Ruth Gledhill is the Religion Correspondent of The Times.

Acknowledgements

The editor and publishers are grateful to the following for permissions:

Centre for Black and White Christian Partnership for Ian Sweeney's sermon (p. 147);

Faber and Faber for the extract from T. S. Eliot, *Murder in the Cathedral* (p. 159);

Victor Gollancz for the extract from W. H. Reed, *Elgar As I Knew Him* (p. 79);

Keston Institute for the letter extract on p. 154 and the translation of the passage from *The Unknown Homeland* on p. 156.

The publishers have been unable to trace the holder of copyright for the lines by John Oxenham on p. 69, but will gladly make appropriate acknowledgement in any reprint if contacted.

Special thanks to Karen Wright, the specialists' secretary at *The Times*, and to Melanie Garfield, of *The Times'* publicists THP, without whose help this competition could not have taken place. To Dr Peter Graves of Methodist Central Hall for the same reason. Special thanks also to Peter Stothard, Editor of *The Times*, and Graham Duffill, home news editor, for their moral and practical support in enabling the competition to take place for a fourth year. Thanks also to Ruth McCurry, Diana Smallshaw and Fiona McKenzie at Cassell, and to my agent, Mike Shaw, for their support, help and advice.

Relative Values

RABBI DR MARGARET JACOBI

Sermon given at Birmingham Progressive Synagogue, Shabbat Vayetze 5757, on 23 November 1996.

Rabbi Dr Margaret Jacobi, 40, was recently married to David Ehrlich, a research optometrist. Dr Jacobi's own father is currently the rabbi at a congregation in Amersham, Bucks and she was the first girl to have a bat mitzvah when her father was rabbi at Southgate Progressive Synagogue in north London. She qualified in medicine at Birmingham University in 1982 and went on to do a PhD at St George's Medical School in London, specializing in respiration. She followed this with two years' post-doctoral research in St Louis, Missouri into respiratory physiology. 'Then I decided to become a rabbi', she says.

'Jewish people tend not to talk about callings and vocations in the way that Christian people do', she says. 'But I had a strong feeling that it was what I wanted to do. I had a similar feeling in my teens but I felt it was not something I should do without some experience in life. My career as a medic was very good because I met all sorts of people and developed all sorts of skills. But after I had done my post-doc I felt ready to become a rabbi. I realized I was much more interested in Jewish study and organizing Jewish events than in my research, even though I enjoyed that too.'

She studied for two years at the Reconstructionist Rabbinical College and then went to the Leo Baeck College at the Sternberg Centre in north London. She was ordained in 1994, and has been at the Birmingham Progressive Synagogue since then. Her congregation of about 300 households is stable, neither growing nor declining, in spite of recent research published by the Board of Deputies of British Jews which indicated a fall of 25 per cent in the Jewish population of Birmingham.

'Preaching has different uses', she says. 'Sometimes it can help people to think about their lives. Sometimes it can give consolation and strength to people. Sometimes it is informative and more of a teaching tool. I preach on topical issues sometimes, although that has to be done carefully. In a sermon I want to make people think, to challenge them, to help them with their problems. I don't have strong views on the Millennium because I think it is fundamentally a Christian event, but it is an opportunity to stop and think about where we are going. If you live in the Western world, you can't really avoid the Millennium.'

Dr Jacobi actually got married on the day Princess Diana died. 'I woke up to get ready for the wedding and I heard something about Tony Blair preparing to say something. In the end I just had to put it to the back of my mind, because personal events were really more important to me on the day. We did have a moment's silence at the reception.'

She found the reaction to the Princess's death extraordinary. 'I cannot really understand why it was so powerful. I think it brought up a lot of emotions in people. She was someone so prominent, dying so young. It was certainly a tragedy, but it seemed to trigger something deeper than the event itself. For me it highlighted the fact that I have someone, and that it is possible to lose someone so easily. It made me realize how much we should all treasure what we have.'

Text: Genesis 29:9–12.

And it came to pass, when Jacob saw Rachel, the daughter of Laban his mother's brother, and the sheep of Laban his mother's brother, that Jacob went near and rolled the stone from the well's mouth and watered the flock of Laban, his mother's brother. And Jacob kissed Rachel and lifted up his voice and wept. And Jacob told Rachel that he was her father's brother and that he was Rebecca's son, and she ran and told her father.

THE narrator of the story of Jacob seems to be preoccupied with relationships. Everyone is described as the relative of someone else. Last week we read that when Jacob was leaving his father's house his mother told him to go to Laban her brother. Isaac repeated her instruction, telling Jacob: 'Go to the house of Bethuel your mother's father.'

When Jacob meets Rachel, he tells her that he is her father's brother and that he is Rebecca's son. Rachel in turn is described as the daughter of Laban, his mother's brother. Position in the family is equally emphasized. Twice in last week's Sidra, we were told that Esau was the elder and Jacob the younger brother. This week, the parallel is drawn with Leah the older daugher and Rachel the younger daughter.

Either the narrator is keen to ensure that we know who is related to whom, which is quite possible since the relationships are quite complicated, or we are supposed to learn something else from this emphasis. We cannot be sure what the narrator intended us to understand. The Midrash has plenty of suggestions, but it is up to us to find our own meaning as well.

Perhaps one thing that we can learn is that relationships are significant. Nobody exists in isolation. If we are told that Jacob was Laban's brother and Rebecca's son, that is telling us something about him. The Midrash suggests Jacob is saying: 'Should your father wish to deceive me, I am his brother in deceit. Should he treat me fairly, I am Rebecca's son and will know how to reciprocate.' There are parts of Jacob that are probably like his cousin and parts that are like his mother. We might disagree with the details of the Midrash – for example we might think that he had inherited the ability to deceive from his mother Rebecca. But what is clear is that each person carries something of their relatives within them. So Rachel, who is described as the daughter of Laban, also inherited her father's ability to deceive. Like Jacob, she deceives her own father, when she steals his household goods and evades detection.

There are further parallels between Rachel and Jacob. Each is the younger. Jacob steals his older brother's birthright. Rachel, intentionally or not, steals the place in Jacob's heart which should have been Leah's as the first wife. Jacob and Esau, Leah and Rachel; both pairs of siblings are engaged in perpetual rivalry. Their position in the family determines what should happen to them, but it also determines their reaction to it and their unwillingness to accept things as they are.

Like Jacob and Rachel, who we are is determined by who our parents are. We inherit their genes and what is not determined genetically in our character is determined by our upbringing. As we grow up, we develop characteristic mannerisms which mirror deeper behaviour patterns which we have either inherited or learnt from our parents. Psychologists have done endless studies to determine the relative contributions of genes and environment. But where we are brought up by our biological parents, nature and nurture are intertwined. Our looks and our behaviour are determined by the two.

Psychologists have also discovered how our personality is determined by our position in the family. Thus, the oldest child usually has a greater sense of responsibility which is shown, for example, in a tendency to enter the caring professions. The youngest tends to feel more secure and be more independent.

But there is a part of us that is mysterious. It cannot be traced to either parent, it is something quite unique and unexpected. There is in every person that which cannot be attributed to nature or nurture and which cannot be rationally explained. This is the part of our personality which makes each of us unique.

To discover in ourselves that uniqueness, that part of ourselves which is not our parents, not our upbringing but our true selves, is a lifetime's work. Part of the power of the Jacob narrative is that we see how he becomes himself. Jacob starts off very much as Rebecca's son. He is under her influence. He barely thinks for himself. Forced to leave his home, he begins to become independent, to think for himself. For the first time, Jacob receives a blessing from God in his own right. Now he is the inheritor of God's promise not because he is Isaac's son and Abraham's grandson but because he is Jacob. Then he comes to the well and rolls away the stone at its opening, with a strength he probably did not know he possessed. The commentators suggest he is able to

3

do this because he had just fallen in love with Rachel; certainly the two events are linked. In any case, Jacob has just experienced another momentous event: falling in love. It is a new and defining experience for him. Not only does he end up working for Laban for fourteen years as a result, but more importantly, falling in love for the first time is, as it always is, a formative event in his becoming a man. Shortly after this, he starts working for a living, for the first time in his life.

It takes Jacob fourteen years to earn Rachel as a wife. In this time, he develops his own identity, so that when he finally leaves Laban, he is ready to take on a name of his own. As he is about to cross the River Jabok and meet his brother Esau once again, he is given a new name, the name of Israel. The name means 'who has struggled with God and human beings and prevailed'. Jacob was a young man who grew up in tents, living a sheltered existence. But he had to learn to struggle, and in the struggle he discovered who he truly was. He remained the son of Isaac and Rebecca, he was never completely Israel, and even after he is renamed, he is still referred to as Jacob sometimes. But he knew what it meant to be himself, to be Israel, who has struggled.

Like Jacob, we all struggle to determine who we are. We can spend our whole life in the search for ourselves. Some never embark or progress very far. Others get so lost in the search that they lose sight not only of who they are, but of what their purpose is. Jacob managed to succeed. But he did so by engaging in the world. He did not go into retreat. He discovered who he was by responding to life's experiences. He fell in love, he worked for a living, he faced his brother's wrath. So we, too, may find ourselves as we engage in the world. As we face difficulties we discover our potential; find strength we never knew we had in order to face life's trial; learn our ability to love and be loved, to help others and to look after ourselves.

The more we discover about ourselves, the more we are able to return home, as Jacob did. To return home is to feel at home, to be at ease with ourselves and with our families. When we discover who we are, we are also able to accept those parts of us that come from our parents. We learn that we are that part of us which is ours alone and also that part which comes from them. We come home when we are able to integrate all those parts of ourselves and feel a sense of wholeness. It may be a long journey. But just as Jacob was assured that God would be with him as he left his home and went into exile and found a new life, so we may feel God's presence with us as we struggle with the circumstances of life, and in the process find ourselves. May we, like Jacob, be assured that God is with us and may the promise that God gave to Jacob as he set out on his way be fulfilled for us.

And behold, I am with you and will keep you wherever you go and will bring you back to this land, for I will not leave you until I have done what I have spoken.

Amen.

Comments

Paul Walker: *'I was delighted to read this sermon and finished it wanting to scream, yes, absolutely. We seem constantly to be told that each one of us is some mysterious combination of our upbringing and our genes. We can assent to this to a certain extent but I for one always want to say, yes, but what about me? I was delighted that Margaret Jacobi talks about that bit of Jacob, that bit of me that neither geneticist nor psychologist can explain.'*

Peter Graves: *'Perceptive blend of biblical exegesis and psychology, crisply developed.'*

A Thief in the Night

DR ARNOLD KELLETT

Dr Arnold Kellett, a Methodist lay preacher, and his wife, Pat, have four children and fourteen grandchildren. He has had many books published, and is an acknowledged expert on Yorkshire dialect and a frequently-published poet. His latest book is On Ikla Mooar baht 'at – *the story of the song, which was originally a Methodist hymn-tune.*

Dr Kellett, whose eldest daughter Ruth Ward is training for the Methodist ministry, was head of modern languages at King James's School, Knaresborough until 1983. He has been Mayor of Knaresborough twice. He was first captivated by preaching as a teenager in Wibsey, Bradford.

Dr Kellett, a former finalist who was a close runner-up to the winner of the 1996 Preacher of the Year Award, says: 'The essence of preaching is communicating the good news about the coming, the dying and the rising again of Jesus Christ. The sermon should be like a spiritual take-away, so people have something to remember, not merely for the rest of the day but for the rest of the week. A sermon has to make a lasting impression. People remembered what Jesus preached. That is why we have the Gospels.

'Preaching in the final at Southwark was a tense and at the same time an exhilarating experience. We were all close and it was very difficult to judge between us.' He has since become engaged in the ongoing debate in the churches, prompted by the award, of whether preaching should indeed be the subject of a competition. He even wrote in defence of the award to a fellow-Methodist who criticized it in The Methodist Recorder. *He was persuaded to enter again by his wife.*

He is reasonably sanguine about the Millennium. 'It is only an approximate date for the anniversary of the birth of Christ. I don't believe in magic numbers. Nevertheless, it is a chance for the Church to celebrate 2,000 years of Christianity and the vast contribution Christianity has made to the betterment of the world.

'Of course I would not defend the Inquisition and all the rest of the horrors perpetrated in the name of Christianity, but when we look at hospitals, education, social welfare, as well as preaching the Gospel, the Christian record is pretty good. I would think it is better than the record of atheist systems such as communism or fascism, which are fundamentally anti-Christian. Christianity speaks of another world and another dimension of reality. It is the contribution it makes in terms of people's hopes and

lives that is important. The contribution is a spiritual one, and not just a social one.'

He was 'incredibly moved' by the death of Diana. 'I think she was an altruistic and caring person.' One of the poems he has written about her is included in his book Kellett's Christmas. *'Someone in her position need not have bothered, but she did bother', he says. 'She was genuine in her concern about landmines, one of the most wicked things human beings have ever devised. If nothing else, she will go down in history for her work on that alone.'*

He adds: 'The interesting thing about her death will be to see whether it has any lasting religious impact, for example, whether churchgoing increases, or charitable giving goes up. It is so difficult to distinguish between sentimentality and genuine religious feeling. But I do think the reaction was a hopeful sign in our society. There were one or two sceptics around, but most people seemed to think the grief was genuine. It was like a Greek tragedy, but one happening in real life.'

Text: 1 Thessalonians 5:1.

About dates and times, my friends, there is no need to write to you, for you know perfectly well that the day of the Lord comes like a thief in the night.

S T PAUL is talking about the Second Coming, the dramatic return of Christ in supernatural glory. His first coming was humiliation, rejection, crucifixion. This time he will come as the righteous Judge of all the earth, the triumphant King of Kings and Lord of Lords. Watch out! The Day of the Lord is about to dawn, the day when he winds up the affairs of the world and ushers in the Kingdom of Heaven.

Now, this is not some cranky charismatic notion spin-doctored by St Paul to put new heart into the struggling Christians of Thessalonika. Strange though the doctrine may be to modern minds, it is rooted in the Gospels, and Paul was simply referring to what Jesus himself had taught, in particular quoting his teaching that the Second Advent would occur with the shocking unexpectedness of a burglary. In exactly the same way, said Jesus, 'The Son of Man will come – at the time you least expect him' (Luke 12:40).

Yet, in spite of the fact that Paul accepts this unpredictability, and says he is not going to suggest dates and times, it is clear from his letter that he believes the Day of Judgement will be very soon, within his own lifetime. And he urges his readers – because they could be called to account at any moment – to be on their very best behaviour. To sharpen the sense of urgency he adds to the image of a thief in the night another vivid illustration. Even expectant mothers, he reminds us, can be taken by surprise – by the sudden onset of labour pains . . . But there was no burglary, and no birth. Paul was wrong. Indeed, far from the imminent dawning of a brave new world, there was soon to be an increase in persecution and a gradual descent into what historians call the Dark Ages.

Bible commentators have described Paul's misapprehension as 'the Thessalonian mistake'. And yet this is, in a sense, everybody's mistake. All down the centuries Christians have kept making forecasts about the end of the world, especially the millenarian movements, from the Montanists of the second century to the Jehovah's Witnesses who so persistently turn up on our contemporary doorsteps. We have heard it all before. As in the legend of the boy who cried 'Wolf!', we have grown so accustomed to the discredited prophets of doom that the doctrine of the Day of Judgement is in danger of falling into neglect and ridicule.

But the approach of the year 2000 has changed the picture. Suddenly there is a revival of interest in the Day of the Lord. Fundamentalist Christians everywhere are busily thumbing through the prophecies in Daniel and Revelation, many confidently predicting the return of Christ at the completion of the second millennium – and some have even enlisted the impenetrable prognostications of the nebulous Nostradamus. In more extreme sects, talk of the Second Coming has become an obsession, gathering momentum as the Millennium approaches. There are American television stations exclusively devoted to it, one beaming out its alarmist propaganda to 160 countries.

Most of this, of course, is romantic nonsense, easily dispelled by a little scholarly reflection. In the first place, there is no biblical justification for linking the Second Coming with the year 2000. The idea seems to go back to the apocryphal *Epistle of Barnabas*, and is little more than a superstition about impressive figures, as was the case with the year 1000, which in many parts of Europe was seen by panic-stricken penitents as the year the world would end.

In the second place, even if the Second Coming were to occur exactly two millennia after the birth of Christ, it would hardly be in the year 2000 or 2001. According to Matthew's Gospel, the infant Christ could have been as old as two when Herod attempted to kill him. Since it is generally agreed that Herod died in 4 BC, this gives us a date for the birth of Jesus as early as 6 BC. So if we want – unlike St Paul – to talk about 'dates and times', the Millennium has already taken place. We should have been celebrating it in 1994.

Millenarian prophets of doom, however, argue that the imminence of the Lord's Return is confirmed by the 'signs of the times'. Both the state of society and the state of the natural world (earthquakes, volcanoes, hurricanes, pestilence, famine) make it plain – so they tell us – that the end is nigh . . . Well, though we cannot possibly be happy about the state of the world – in particular the atrocious starvation of the Sudanese and terrorist bombings – things have been worse. Hitler's

Holocaust or Pol Pot's genocide made them ideal candidates, I would have thought, for the role of the Anti-Christ. It is true, of course, that there are signs that time is running out – global warming, environmental pollution, the exhaustion of resources, new viruses and bacteria capable of wiping out whole populations . . . Yet, however pessimistic we are, the end of the world as we know it still seems some way ahead.

Does this mean, then, that we can dismiss Paul's reference to the coming Day of the Lord as a first-century curiosity with no relevance to our own lives? Certainly not. It has a practical application for every one of us. Remember that it was Jesus, not Paul, who first taught that we would all be called to the strictest account on the Day of Judgement, and that we should therefore always give our very best, spiritually, morally and in the practical outreach that Jesus himself demonstrated. What an example he set us, this Man of Action! Always on the move, tramping the dusty roads of Palestine, healing the sick, cleansing the lepers, casting out demons, feeding the hungry, preaching, teaching, debating – always with a sense of urgency. 'The night is coming', he said, 'when we can no longer work!' – a text written above his desk by Kipling's grandfather, a Methodist minister, to keep him on his toes.

We have plenty of evidence that this kind of exhortation has a salutary effect – provided there is this sense of judgement being just round the corner. A modern equivalent might be the way a whole school is galvanized into better standards by the prospect of an Ofsted inspection! In this case, the school is given due notice of the date of the inspection. Suppose it were told that the Ofsted inspection would certainly take place, but that the date would not be announced beforehand. This could work both ways. It could have the effect of keeping standards permanently improved in readiness for the inspection. On the other hand, as time went on, it would become easier and easier to assume that it might never take place at all.

Similarly, Christians can fall into the trap of assuming that the Day of the Lord – because it seems so far off – is not to be taken seriously. Yes. It's in the creeds, in the Te Deum, part of the traditional teaching of the Church, but it is so remote, something at the very end of history. Even so, there is a sense in which the Day of the Lord will come to us – every one of us – and catch us unprepared, far sooner than we expect.

Running parallel to all the biblical preoccupation with the end of the age – what you might call global eschatology – there is the theme of individual eschatology. It is not simply that the world will come to an end. You and I will come to an end. *That* is our immediate problem. No matter what is to happen in the history still to be unfolded, to all intents and purposes the Day of the Lord is the day we die. It is then that we are switched from time into eternity, and – since time now no longer exists – the Day of Judgement is instantly upon us.

I have always found a nice irony in the fact that millions of millenarians, spending their lives in the tense expectation of the Day of Judgement, have already encountered it, simply by dying. Death, too, so frequently comes upon us as the thief in the night – with little or no warning. We have a rough idea of our life-span – 75 years for men in the developed countries, a little longer for women. But, again and again, we are pulled up short by the brutal unexpectedness of the death of someone we have taken for granted – as in the phenomenal reaction to the death of Princess Diana at the age of 36.

Preachers in the tradition of St Paul still remind their congregations, from time to time, of the frailty of human existence, using it as a spur to greater endeavour in the pursuit of holiness and righteousness. The logic is flawless. Since we do not know how much time we have left, we should act on the assumption that *this* could be our last day. How often Bishop Thomas Ken has roused us out of our lethargy with his sparkling morning hymn:

> Redeem thy misspent moments past,
> And live this day as if thy last;
> Improve thy talent with due care;
> For the great day thyself prepare!

The 'great day', the Day of the Lord, when as Paul put it, 'we must all stand before the Judgement Seat of Christ'. A sobering thought, but not a terrifying one – for Christians. Paul's doctrine of moral accountability is always in the context of the grace – the undeserved generosity – of God in Christ, reconciling the world to himself. The Jesus who is our Judge is also our Saviour.

The sophisticated wizardry of medication and surgery nowadays prolongs our lives and helps to cushion us from the stark reality of death. If we speak of it at all, it's in circumlocution. 'This watch is for thee, lad', said the Yorkshire grandfather, 'when 'owt 'appens ter me.' His little grandson eagerly ran up to him on the next visit, asking 'Grandad? Grandad? 'Owt 'appened yet?'

We shrink from talking about our death, yet far from being morbid and depressing, facing up to it can be a tonic – in two ways. First, it can encourage us to make a virtue out of uncertainty, and get on with the job of living life to the full, as committed Christians. There's so much to do – for others – and so little time left in which to do it. Another of Paul's sound-bites is written above the clock on the ancient tower of our parish church at Knaresborough – 'Redeeming the time' – make the very most of the time you have left.

Secondly, the greatest tonic of all is when we glimpse just a fraction of the glory which lies beyond death. When I first started teaching, the school gave a church performance of Bach's wonderful Cantata *Gottes Zeit ist die allerbeste Zeit* – 'God's time is the best time of all' – a meditation on the certainty and unexpectedness of death . . . And yet the music was so cheerful and lively and heart-warming that it made me want to get up and dance down the aisles. It was not just the incomparable melodies of Bach, but the words. 'Set your house in order!' sang the male voices, almost teasingly reminding us that it really is always later than we think . . . Then the sopranos gilding the individual's death with the words 'Yes! The Lord Jesus is coming!' Finally, the warm reassurance of the bass who sings Jesus: 'This day you will be with me in Paradise.'

I remember particularly noticing one of the violinists, a music teacher at the school. Shortly after that performance, he collapsed and died of a heart attack . . . Death had come like a thief in the night. Yet he could not have played himself out in any better way. Oh for the balanced harmony between these two themes! A realistic acceptance of the precarious nature of life – and a simple trust in the compassion of Christ, who will surely come again, however and whenever that may be. So I end, as the Bible itself ends, with the prayer: 'Even so, come, Lord Jesus!'

Comments

Jonathan Romain: *'By using at the very end of the sermon the phrase that began it – like a thief in the night – the preacher wraps up the sermon neatly and reminds us of the message that had been explored thoroughly in between.'*

Peter Graves: *'Helpful consideration of an important but difficult theme. Well-argued and illustrated.'*

Paul Walker: *'Although slightly flawed by the use of theological jargon like millenarianism and eschatology, this was a timely sermon for a unique time.'*

Passover: Liberation from the Cage of Human Nature

RABBI SHMULEY BOTEACH

Shmuley Boteach, 31, who with his wife Debbie has six children, works with her for the L'Chaim Society, a Jewish-based organization that seeks to promote and create values-based leadership. The controversy surrounding his recent book Kosher Sex *led to him resigning as minister of an Orthodox congregation in Willesden, north-west London. L'Chaim, which has premises in Oxford, London and Cambridge and is highly active among the Oxford student population, is currently in the process of purchasing a new building in Willesden which will serve as the base of a new congregation.*

Rabbi Boteach, who comes out of the Lubavitch movement in Judaism, a vigorous Orthodox educational movement, was ordained in America before coming to Britain with his family to set up L'Chaim.

He believes preaching can be an extremely valuable tool, if its purpose is properly understood. 'The purpose of the sermon is not to inform', he says. 'That is what a class or a lecture is for. The sermon cannot be a substitute for the study of scripture or texts.

'But once a week we need to stop, take a step back and look at life from a truthful, spiritual perspective. We need to approach a subject, be it God, the family or gossip, and provide the inspiration and impetus for people to want to better themselves. The trouble with inspiration is it can be a fleeting emotion. So it must lead to a basis for action. The best sermons are when a preacher is preaching for himself, and looking for his own path through the labyrinth of life.

'But this is why in Britain, sermons are so often ineffective. Since clerics are expected to exude perfection rather than humanity, preachers here can never be honest about their own malicious tongues, or about how they are threatened by the gossip of a colleague. This makes their sermons ineffective. A sermon is really about a rabbi speaking to himself, inspiring himself and letting other people listen in. But if you preach in order to impress, your words will not penetrate in the same way. This is why I disagree with the term "preacher". The word "guide" would be a better one to use.'

He is one of the few preachers in the country who succeeds in provoking his congregation to interrupt. 'Often someone will throw in a one-liner while I am speaking', he says. 'Once I was quoting from scripture and I forgot the verse. Someone stood up and quoted the whole verse. I asked him to come up and take over. He started walking to the front! In Oxford the students are not used to the idea of a sermon. Often I will be preaching on a contentious issue, such as the place of women in religion. These young American Rhodes scholars will stand up and tell me I am talking a load of rubbish. I enjoy getting a response where people laugh or cry, but it is equally important to touch a raw nerve occasionally. The purpose of religion is not to answer all the questions in life, but to make people think about these questions.'

He has strong views on the Millennium. 'I have been reading about how the world was affected by the approach of the year 1000. The Millennium is still primarily a Christian celebration in that it celebrates 2,000 years after the birth of Christ. Having said that, all of us have adopted the Gregorian calendar, although the Jews use the Lunar calendar as well, when the Millennium will be the year 5760. So I accept that the Millennium will be a very important milestone.' He says that the Millennium can have a very positive impact on humanity if it is treated like the Jewish Sabbath. 'People need time for introspection and reflection in order to determine the direction of their lives. We need to step back.'

He said rabbis should insist on being relevant to the Millennium. 'I am a great fan of Billy Graham, for no other reason than that he makes religion relevant, and has become a great icon of the twentieth century.'

He describes the death of Diana as 'a great human tragedy'. He says: 'For me, she became an icon for people who have everything, and yet have nothing at the same time. We are the most prosperous generation of all time, yet happiness remains so elusive. She was the poor, rich princess. That is why we all identified with her so much. She was truly a tragic figure. People did not cry over her, they cried for themselves, and for all the people who never manage to maximize their potential, or achieve their dreams.'

CONVEYING the contemporary relevance of Passover to a Western audience, all of whom have grown up in thriving liberal democracies, is fraught with difficulty. Thank God, the most severe form of oppression that we who have been raised in England and the United States experience is perhaps paying taxes and getting speeding tickets. When Jews speak of incarceration, imprisonment, torture or terror, our minds immediately flash back to our ancestors in the Spanish Inquisition and the Chemielnicki massacres. Similarly, we conjure up images of Maidanek, Grossrosen, Buchenwald and Auschwitz. But we who live in the aftermath of the Holocaust are free. What message does Passover have for our generation? I remember how, when I first arrived in Oxford, the students organized vast Passover meals – throughout the year – to support imprisoned refuseniks of the Soviet Union. But now, even with their thankful release, how can Passover be anything but a simple tale of an event that transpired long ago?

To be sure, we can indeed look at Passover as nothing more than the retelling of an ancient saga of bondage and liberation. The Jews were enslaved to their Egyptian taskmasters, and the Almighty, through spectacular acts of intervention – the ten plagues, the splitting of the

Red Sea – redeemed them from servitude. Yet, the ancient rabbis stated that 'in every generation, a Jew is obligated to see him or herself as having been personally liberated from Egypt'. Similarly, the Passover Seder night, highlight of the Jewish calendar, is not merely about retelling, but *reliving* the exodus from Egypt. The Jew is enjoined to taste of salt water and bitter herbs, and thus to re-experience his forebears' tears and suffering in Egypt; to eat matzo, the poor man's bread, thereby re-experiencing a taste of servitude; and finally to drink four cups of wine, with which to experience the elation of redemption. What possible relevance does this message of bondage and servitude have for this, the free-est, most prosperous Jewish generation of all time?

Surely, it is this: while we think we are free, we are still servants. We who grow up in the West amid phenomenal pressures to conform, to own a bigger house, to work all hours of the day and night so that we have no time for family, community or religion, are perhaps the most enslaved generation of all. Think of all the millions enslaved to a superficial definition of success, which will laud a man who becomes chairman of his company, even though he has no reputation for integrity, is on his third marriage, and is estranged from his children. Think of all those who are enslaved to the pursuit of pleasure at the expense of obligation and duty. Growing up in Miami Beach, America's largest retirement city, I watched tens of thousands of elderly people relegated to old-age homes by children who felt that the burden of caring for an elderly parent would interfere with the pleasures which they owed themselves.

Young Jews who feel intimidated and out of place in the overarching Gentile society are imprisoned by its culture and its mores. I have witnessed all too many Jewish students in Oxford whose very first action upon arriving at the University is to remove their *kippot* so that they may better blend into their new surroundings. Giving rationalizations of their actions, they lack even the courage to admit that they too are bondsmen of the prevailing culture into which they are submerged. One Orthodox student even told me that he would be far more effective denying his Judaism since he had never been afforded an opportunity to serve God amid temptation. 'Besides, when I wear my *kippa*, the students in my year think I'm a Mossad agent.'

And what of the many women who diet themselves into oblivion as they receive yet another copy of *Cosmopolitan* magazine? Are they not slaves to an image of 'the perfect woman' which makes them feel inadequate? Young women today are enslaved to a culture which teaches them to experience far greater regret for some extra calories gained rather than for close friendships lost. And what of the millions who are enslaved to the shallow images of television, who literally cannot summon the willpower to turn the TV off and pull out a book which will bring them knowledge and enlightenment?

We humans tend to think of imprisonment only in external terms.

If an outside party superimposes their will upon us, we then feel restrained and oppressed. If Jews cannot emigrate from an Arab country like Syria, a clarion call goes out through the Jewish world: let my people go! What we forget, however, is that the most ruthless form of duress is the restrictions imposed upon us by our own intrinsic natures. We are all prisoners to human nature. And the central message of Judaism, as embodied in the Passover festival, is that man is not an animal. Man can transcend instinct and impulse to lead a glorious life suffused with altruism and concern for others. Man has an innate yearning to leave Egypt and be free.

There are essentially two forms of slavery, which need not coincide. The first is juridical slavery, a political state of enslavement, in which one man becomes the prisoner of another man. This state reduces humans to a chattel, an object to be bought and sold, a thing serving as the private property of an owner. The slave's productivity – even his very being – belongs to his master. He is exploited and humiliated by a political system that so degrades his status. But there is still a light at the end of the tunnel. He can still one day be freed and be restored to his full dignity as a free and responsible human being.

But the second type of slavery, while far less overtly discomfiting, is actually far more severe. For this slavery is typological, a mental state of servility rather than a physically imposed enslavement. There are people whose will has been broken and whose ego has been effaced, to the extent that they think, feel and act in a distinctively docile manner which suggests that their initiative has been broken. Their internal freedom – their ability to think and react as liberated men – has been constricted and manipulated. Dreams and ambitions which they once cherished have dissipated and their hopes for the future have been crushed. They are disinclined to take responsibility for their actions and they submerge their individuality beneath that of another, be it a person, a company, or the state. This slave mentality can be found even among politically liberated peoples. Witness the fact that after Moses had redeemed the Jewish people from Egypt and sent a group of slaves to spy out the land and determine the most efficient way to conquer it, they returned with a dispiriting report: 'The Land is filled with Anakim – giants, and we were in their sight as grasshoppers, and so we appeared to ourselves as well.'

Such feelings of inferiority would not have allowed for the conquering of the land, and thus the Almighty decided to wait 40 more years until that entire generation had died out, before allowing Jews to enter the land and attempt to acquire it. The terrible and unjustified low self-esteem and lack of self-confidence, which so infects modern man, is the ultimate form of enslavement. We are subtly trained to look across at our neighbour and his success – to constantly compare ourselves and our spouses to others, rather than being satisfied with our lot, which the Talmud teaches is the ultimate form of riches.

Typological slavery is far worse than juridical because it is much easier to take the man out of prison than it is to take the prison out of man. While the former is enslavement of the body, the latter is the enslavement of the mind.

One of the saddest things that can ever happen to a human being is to reach an age – say 40 or 50 – to look into a mirror, and discover that you have become something you never planned; that your life resembles a thermometer rather than a thermostat. Rather than create and control your environment, you are moulded and shaped by capricious, external events. Being a child of divorce, I remember promising myself on countless occasions that I would not make the same mistakes my parents made to undermine their marriage. Now, every time I find myself becoming upset over trifles in marriage, and being unable for a short time to overcome it, I acknowledge just how imprisoned I am.

I spoke last week with two brothers who were once inseparable but have since fallen out over a financial dispute. I beseeched the older of the two to apologize to his sibling so as to reawaken their dormant love. 'I simply cannot. He was wrong and he should apologize.' 'But that's not the point', I told him. 'What is more important? To be right, or to have a brother? Here you have the opportunity to have your brother back. All it takes is a phone call. But you seem more interested in justice than you are in basking in the pleasure of sibling love, truly one of life's richest blessings.' But he just could not bring himself to lift the telephone receiver. He was imprisoned by his own stubbornness. I related to him how Passover will soon be upon us and that his goal this year in celebrating the festival must be to liberate himself of his incarcerating nature and become a better person.

My duties as director of the L'Chaim Society necessitate that I fundraise, and I have seen first-hand how difficult it is for individuals to contribute 10 per cent of their earnings to charity. One of the most unnatural activities known to man is to simply give away one's hard-earned remuneration. The message of Passover is that we can be liberated from our nature and lead unique and glorious lives suffused with holiness and compassion for others.

One of the unfortunate by-products of the otherwise constructive nature-wave which swept through the Western world over the past two decades – replete with its lust for exercise and all things healthy and its simultaneous rejection of all things artificial as unhearty and unrobust – was the concomitant belief that it is a sin to do anything which violates nature, both human and otherwise. From this was born the preposterous notion that whenever man attempts to transcend or act in contradiction to his nature, he scars himself internally. Freud was the High Priest of this school of thought, and made us all believe that more than anything else it is the suppression of our intrinsic natures which leads to neurosis and psychosis. So if you're angry, don't bottle it in. It's unhealthy to repress natural emotion. And if you feel stifled in marriage, get out and be liberated. Man must accommodate, or at the very least find an outlet for, his every urge. The festival of Passover, however, demands that we go out of Mitzrayim, which means 'Egypt', but also translates as 'natural limitations'. Man is not a prisoner to his nature. Rather, far more powerful than human nature is innate human will. Each of us is endowed with the capacity to be and do whatever we wish, modern-day genetic research notwithstanding. Scientists now claim to have identified a promiscuous gene, but Judaism says that amid this predisposition, the man or woman who is unfaithful in marriage is no more than a weak fool.

Whether man becomes an angel or an animal is completely dependent upon his choice and free will. We are all accountable for our actions. Nobody has the excuse that they cannot overcome their natural inclinations and predispositions. This is why Judaism is most distinguished from other faiths by its doctrine of personal accountability. Man is held responsible for his actions both for exaltation and damnation. Because notwithstanding the power of his passions, they do not ultimately hold sway over him, and every human is the sole arbiter over their own destiny; that is, so long as we are prepared to exit Mitzrayim, our instinctive constraints.

It was Hitler who proclaimed in *Mein Kampf* that 'Going against nature brings ruin to man . . . and is a sin against the will of the Eternal Creator. It is only Jewish impudence which demands that we go against nature.' But Jews, and all others who subscribe to a holy way of life, cannot partake of such an easy escape. The very definition of holiness is something which transcends normative human experience, and man becomes holy when he acts in a fashion that is loftier than where his nature would have led him. This ultimately is the definition of altruism.

With this we might understand the very enigmatic statement of the great Talmudic sage Rabbi Yehoshua ben Levi, recorded in Avos (Ethics of Our Fathers) 6: 'There is no free man except one who occupies himself with the study of the Torah.' How misguided and inaccurate the statement appears! Judaism is perhaps the most demanding of all religions. It tells us what to do upon awakening, and what our last utterances must be before retiring to bed. It dictates what we may eat and when we may engage in marital relations. It tells us when to feel elated, and when we must mourn. Is there any greater prison than this? How could a wise rabbi proclaim that it is specifically a life preoccupied with the study and observance of the Torah which sets man free?

The answer surely is this: possessed within man is an innermost will which above all else desires to be decent and holy. Deep down, every single one of us would like to be a compassionate, kind and caring human being. We would like to have lofty and spiritual values in place of indulging in materialism and devoting our lives to the pursuit of money, power and celebrity. We crave to be the kinds of individuals who, upon leaving a gathering of friends, can feel confident that our peers have only kind things to speak of us.

What we really want to be is charitable, offering compliments freely and showing appreciation to family and friends, rather than being envious of their success. We wish to be totally devoted to our spouse, and the finest parents that the world has ever seen. We seek to be diplomatic and gracious in all social interactions, never losing our temper or offering an unkind word or opinion. Is there anyone reading this essay whose life's aspirations do not include all the above? One day when you have passed from this earth, do you wish to be remembered as successful, or charitable? Does anyone care to be eulogized by a rabbi as having owned ten apartment blocks, or having had time for everyone in need? And if we want this so badly, why doesn't it just happen? Because we are slaves to our nature. It is not natural for us to put others before ourselves. Neither is it natural for someone to hear that a colleague has won the lottery and not experience a burning pang of jealousy. We cannot become what we truly desire, because to a great extent we are still fettered by the Pharaoh inside of us which constitutes our very nature and selves.

But when a man or a woman is bound by the tenets of Jewish law which bids them to always show sensitivity and love to the orphan and the poor; when one is forced to give a significant percentage of one's salary away to the needy; when one is enjoined into observing the sabbath and thus putting family and friends before going to the cinema, when one is commanded to offer a blessing before and after every meal, thereby teaching them gratitude and appreciation for what they possess – then they acclimatize with the desire of their irreducible essence, namely, to be good and holy individuals who enjoy an unblemished relationship with their God and their fellow-man. Thus, Judaism does not imprison us so much as allow us to manifest our most innate yearning and calling: to be angels of mercy on earth and harbingers of redemption to humankind. A life in accordance with God's law as recorded in our Torah is a life which allows us to become a blessing both to ourselves and to others.

May this be the last Passover we spend in bondage to our natures, and the last which the Jewish nation spends in exile.

Comments

Peter Graves: *'Well-argued sermon, written in arresting style.'*

Paul Walker: *'I didn't think I was familiar with a Jewish style of preaching but such a use of stories reminded me of another Jewish preacher, Jesus of Nazareth.'*

Jonathan Romain: *'What a marvellous tapestry of words, weaving in and out modern history, ancient truths, comic stories and bursts of insight. A breath-taking tour-de-force of ideas and anecdotes.'*

Kieran Conry: *'Rather technical but the use of stories is effective.'*

The Challenge of the Martyrs

REV. MIKE STARKEY

Sermon preached at All Saints, Margaret Street, London on 22 March 1998.

The Rev. Mike Starkey, 35, and his wife Naomi, a commissioning editor at the Bible Reading Fellowship, have two children. He has been at his present church in Finsbury Park, north London for three years after serving for three years as a curate in a large evangelical parish in Ealing. He was ordained in 1993 after working as a newsreader and reporter on a commercial radio station in Cambridge, Q103.

'I was brought up in a Methodist home but it did not become very meaningful until my mid-teens. There were various steps towards a deepening faith during my late teens and early twenties.'

His faith was transformed when, during his modern languages degree at Lady Margaret Hall in Oxford, he spent a year teaching in the Loire valley in France. 'France is a very secularized country', he says. 'It really knocked my faith for six and I went through a real period of crisis, and of wondering whether my faith was just based on my friendships, and on being in a church youth group. After that, I went through a slow, painful process of reassembling things.'

During his time at Oxford, he found most satisfaction in editing college magazines. 'I always enjoyed communicating, and it is still the part of my ministry that I find most fulfilling.' After leaving university he worked for the music and religious press for a year, went to the Jubilee Centre in Cambridge as press officer, campaigning against Sunday trading, and from there to the radio station.

'The thing that changed my life, and turned me away from journalism and towards the priesthood, was a serious car crash I had. I was driving from home in a little village near Newmarket to the radio station, where I was meant to be reading the news on the breakfast show. I was late for work, and the road was wet. I was skidding round some little country lanes when the car left the road, bounced on its roof and ended up completely smashed up in a field after turning somersaults in the air. The car was a write-off, but I emerged completely unhurt. Up until that point, even though I had a faith, I had never considered the ministry. That was something other people did. But after that accident, my sense of calling changed. From being a Christian

working in the media, I felt called to use my journalism and communication skills within the Church. I suppose I felt that God had saved me for a purpose, like John Wesley felt when he had that experience of being pulled from a burning house.'

He also felt that reporting on other people's troubles was no longer enough. 'I wanted to be in the thick of it, and to be there, offering people help.'

He regards preaching as almost a form of journalism. 'It is an extension of journalism, in that it is communicating with people at a very earthy level. I know we live in a multi-media age, but I think there is still an important role for the sermon as a teaching medium. I don't think the ways that sermons have always been done in the past will necessarily continue, especially with regard to the long, expository sermon, where the shape of the text determines the shape of the sermon. I think that particular form of preaching may have had its day. The challenge for me is to write sermons in the same way that I write features for magazines. The homework needs to be done in the priest's study before the sermon can be written. The trick is to use arresting, short, punchy sentences and illuminating illustrations to bring a sermon alive.'

There is little tradition of churchgoing in his parish, where a small, modern church has replaced a huge Victorian edifice that was knocked down about seven years ago. Residents consist of young professionals in large houses converted into flats. There was no established congregation used to listening to long, complex sermons. When he arrived there, the congregation numbered around a dozen people. 'So the one thing I cannot be is boring', he says. 'In fact I was in two minds about taking it on. Going from a large evangelical parish to a tiny church in an Anglo-Catholic tradition was a bit of a culture shock. What we have ended up with is evangelical Catholicism. About 50 people come now each week. A fair number of them have no churchgoing background at all. They are people in their twenties and thirties, living in flats, on their first or second jobs in London.'

As he rightly says, this is the missing generation for most churches today. 'So we are on the front line of making contact with that generation.' His experience prompted him to write a book, God, Sex and Generation X (SPCK, 1997), about how the Church can connect with this lost generation. This followed success with an earlier book, Fashion and Style (Monarch, 1995), where he called for Christians to dress more fashionably.

He does not have strong views on the Millennium. 'It is not a major theme in what I am doing', he says. But the response to the death of Diana affirmed what he had already suspected. 'This was that most people have strong spiritual yearnings and instincts. It is just that they do not know which peg to hang them on. If you look at church attendance statistics, you would conclude that people are no longer interested in God and spirituality. But quite the opposite is the case. I just think people are disillusioned with the mainstream churches. The challenge for the churches is to connect with these sorts of instincts. That was borne out by the Diana phenomenon. Suddenly, the lid came off the pot, and the only way people could cope with their grief was to revert to religious language. We opened up our church, and people came in and spent the evening there and brought flowers. I do not believe for a moment that we are living in a secular age. But whether people can connect with what they find in some of our churches is another matter entirely.'

Texts: Isaiah 40:27 – 41:13; 2 Timothy 4:1–18.

I MUST have been about 23 at the time. I was a newly-trained jour- nalist, working on a magazine. One day the editor called me in and asked me to go and interview somebody I'd never heard of, about a subject I knew nothing about.

I was to go to a London hotel to meet a man named Festo Kivengere, a Ugandan bishop who'd come to London for some emergency med- ical treatment. I didn't know it at the time, but Bishop Festo didn't have long to live. We spoke for nearly two hours about the Church in his home country, Uganda, and about some of the atrocities it had suf- fered during the previous twenty years. For me it was another world, a world far removed from small-town Warwickshire where I'd grown up.

A name that came up repeatedly during our interview was that of his Archbishop, Janani Luwum – another person I'd never heard of. So I asked him to tell me more about Archbishop Janani. And this is what he told me.

Janani Luwum was born in East Acholi, Uganda, to poor parents. He originally trained as a teacher but after his conversion to Christianity in 1948 he studied for the Anglican priesthood, and was ordained in 1955. After three years as a parish priest, he came to England to study at the London College of Divinity.

Later, he returned to his former theological college in Uganda as its principal. In 1969 he was made Bishop of Northern Uganda. Just two years into his episcopacy an army general named Idi Amin came to power after a violent coup. Uganda was 70 per cent Christian, but Amin set about trying to convert the nation forcibly to his own brand of Islam. Amin presided over a reign of terror, in which thousands of people were massacred. Christians in particular suffered.

When Luwum was appointed Archbishop of Uganda in 1974, he felt he had to use his influence to confront Amin. In 1977 Luwum and his bishops wrote a stiff letter to Amin, protesting against the evils com- mitted by the regime. He knew he was putting his own life on the line. One girl told him she'd overheard people say he was on Amin's hit list, and he should escape Uganda. His reply was: 'I am the Archbishop. I must stay.' Amin did see the bishops' letter as a personal attack, and evidence of a plot to overthrow him. In February 1977, Radio Uganda reported that the Archbishop had been killed in a car crash. The reality was far worse. In one of Amin's torture-cells, the President had told Luwum to sign a confession, admitting to plotting his overthrow.

But the Archbishop refused. Instead, he prayed for Amin and his men. In front of a 'kangaroo court' of soldiers, the President ordered a soldier to strip the Archbishop and whip him. He then hit the Archbishop, forced a soldier to carry out degraded sexual acts with him, and finally pulled out his own revolver and shot him twice through the heart. Archbishop Luwum was aged 55. No memorial service was allowed.

Another Ugandan Christian who managed to leave the country at that time was a young high court judge called John Sentamu, who'd deliberately been putting innocent people in prison because he knew that there they'd be out of the reach of Amin and relatively safe. He'd applied for a stay in Cambridge to study theology, and his trip to England saved his life. He's now the Area Bishop of Stepney, and a good friend and colleague to many of us.

Since he died, Janani Luwum has become known as one of the most courageous Christian martyrs this century. Our new Lectionary remembers him on 17 February every year.

But the question that stayed with me from my interview with Bishop Festo was: 'Why? How is it possible to make sense of a death like that?' Everything inside me wanted to say: 'What a tragic waste of life. If you're faced with a lunatic, just humour him and keep your head down. Don't challenge him or he'll kill you. And then there'll be fewer good guys left in the world.'

It was a gut response. In the same kind of way, I'd probably have wanted to say to the Christian martyrs in Rome: 'Listen! What's a bit of incense offered to a statue of the Emperor? You know and I know he's not really a god. It's all a sham, for the sake of the unity of the Empire. Say with your mouth that Caesar's divine, offer the incense, then get back to your home, family and church and put it all behind you.

'And keep one more Christian alive to witness to the faith.'

Martyrdom is a waste of the finest people the Church has. And what about those glorious promises about God vindicating the cause of his righteous people?

> All who rage against you will surely be ashamed and disgraced; those who oppose you will be as nothing and perish. Though you search for your enemies, you will not find them. Those who wage war against you will be as nothing at all.
>
> Isaiah 41:11–12

Well, that's fine and comforting – for people who're already fine and comfortable. But what if it's the evil dictator who survives, and you and your friends who are 'as nothing and perish'? I realized that little in my experience had prepared me for making sense of martyrdom.

But the blood of the martyrs cries out down the Christian centuries, challenging our complacency, and maybe our theology too. A third of all Christians worldwide still have to meet in secret, under the threat of persecution or even elimination. The shadow of Caesar – the shadow of Amin – is a long shadow. And it's a shadow that will probably remain long and dark, until it is swallowed up in the glorious radiance of the new heavens and the new earth.

So what is the challenge from the martyrs? What do they say to us today? As we read the writings of Christian martyrs – and more significantly, as we read their lives – I believe two challenges stand out. One is the challenge that there's more to life than life. The other is that we don't have the full story, until we've extended it into eternity.

Let me explain what I mean. Firstly, there's more to life than life. The quest for long life and eternal youth has never been more prevalent. From the countless anti-ageing creams on sale in department stores just around the corner from here, to Walt Disney, whose dead body even now lies suspended in cryogenic fluid, waiting for the day when science has discovered how to resuscitate him. We live in a culture where death is denied. It's entirely possible to reach your forties and never have been to a funeral or seen a dead body. An untimely death, whether it's a child or a princess, comes like lightning from a clear sky. And we have a range of clichés which reassure us that the most important thing in life is simply staying alive: 'Where there's life . . . there's hope.'

But the unsettling challenge from the martyrs is that there are more important things in life than staying alive. Two months before he died, Archbishop Janani said this:

'I live as though there will be no tomorrow. I face daily being picked up by the soldiers. While the opportunity is there, I preach the Gospel with all my might, and my conscience is clear before God that I have not sided with the present government, which is utterly self-seeking. I have been threatened many times. Whenever I have the opportunity, I have told the President the things the churches disapprove of. God is my witness.' He's saying there are at least three things which are worse than death: a failure to preach the Gospel, siding with an evil system, and the refusal to speak out against injustice. To fail on any one of these three counts is for Janani Luwum a loss more acute than the loss of one's own life. Luwum's final words to his fellow-bishops as he was led away to his death were: 'I can see the hand of the Lord in this.' He knew himself called by God to a calling more significant than life or death.

Our New Testament reading, from 2 Timothy, is also written by a man who ended up dying a martyr's death. Not in Uganda, but in Italy, centuries earlier. In the section just before our reading, he talks about the persecutions he himself has gone through for the sake of the Gospel. But for Paul, too, the loss of life is a lesser evil than the loss of zeal for Christ. The motto of the London College of Divinity, where Janani Luwum studied, was a phrase from St Paul: 'Woe to me if I do not proclaim the Gospel.' For both men, that woe is a greater woe even than the loss of life itself. For the Christian martyrs, there's more to life than life.

Secondly, the martyrs remind us that we don't have the full story until we've extended it into eternity. And I was reminded of that as I sat down to plan this year's services for Lent and Holy Week. In the tradition many of us were raised in, we didn't bother with Holy Week. You went from Palm Sunday one week to Easter Sunday the next. From triumphal entry to resurrection, with none of the mess in between. And that was fine by me. Why dwell on the depressing bits in the run-up to Easter?

In the same way, the idea of giving things up for Lent always used to strike me as quaint and archaic. But I have to say, I no longer feel that way. In recent years Lent has become for me one of the key parts of the Christian year.

I've begun to see how Lent is about entering the drama of the Gospel story, becoming a participant in the movement from patient expectation to joyful fulfilment. I love its roots in that period of preparation before the joy of baptism. I love its echoes of the 40 days of the flood before the joys of dry land, and 40 years wandering in the wilderness before the joy of entering the promised land. I love its overtones of Jesus' 40 patient days in the desert, winning the battle in here before he could win the battle out there. I find myself moved by its air of penitence and preparation. It's a symbolic entering into death, which makes the power of resurrection all the more stark and dazzling by contrast. Renunciation is not just a pointless doing without something. It's a liberating discipline which teaches us that some things are so good, you've got to wait patiently for them. And that they're all the more special for the wait. It's a concept not well understood in a world where the credit card and the condom have made the idea of delayed gratification quite alien.

Lent and Holy Week don't make sense in isolation. They only make sense in the light of what comes afterwards: the joy of Easter morning, the transforming glory of resurrection. In other words, this season of the Christian year only makes sense if it's read backwards. The joy of Easter gives meaning to the season of penitence and preparation which precedes it.

The martyr is the person who knows that history too only makes sense if it's read backwards. The martyr is the person in whom the vision of resurrection in a new heavens and a new earth is a solid hope. And that hope sustains them through the Lenten period which is their earthly life. In our reading, Paul says to Timothy:

THE CHALLENGE OF THE MARTYRS

For I am already being poured out like a drink offering, and the time has come for my departure. I have fought the good fight, I have finished the race, I have kept the faith. Now there is in store for me the crown of righteousness, which the Lord, the righteous Judge, will award to me on that day – and not only to me, but also to all who have longed for his appearing.

2 Timothy 4:6–8

A crown of righteousness. The martyr is the person who's had a vision of the end of the story, and has learned to read the plot backwards. Their life only makes sense if it's seen as a larger story which extends into eternity.

On 15 September 1963, a funeral was held at Sixteenth Street Baptist Church in Birmingham, Alabama, for some young children who'd been killed by a bomb as they attended Sunday School. The preacher was Martin Luther King, Jr. And at that funeral he spoke powerfully of how death was not the end. Not long after that funeral, he himself was dead. To read the life of the martyrs – a Martin Luther King, a Janani Luwum, a St Paul – is to be reminded that for the Christian, there's more to life than life itself. And it's to be reminded that we can't see the full story until we've extended our horizon into eternity. May we who read their words and their lives, be fired with the same hope, the same blazing vision.

Comments

Peter Graves: *'Excellent, profound, beautifully ilustrated and clearly developed with good use of biblical material.'*

Paul Walker: *'Many preachers seem either to romanticize the notion of life after death or ignore it. This sermon, it seems to me, deals intelligently with the issue.'*

Kieran Conry: *'Excellent and engaging, full of personal experience, a well-told story. Clear, articulate and full of conviction.'*

Jonathan Romain: *'Here we have the priest as story-teller. The strong ending left the listeners uplifted and feeling that we, too, wanted to be part of the heroic process described.'*

Finding Life Amid Death

REV. DR JOLYON MITCHELL

Sermon preached at Christ Church, Edinburgh on 8 March 1998.

Dr Jolyon Mitchell, 34, is married to Clare, who teaches English as a foreign language and is also an aromatherapist. Dr Mitchell runs a media and theology project at Edinburgh University, where he is a full-time lecturer and teaches areas related to communication, religion and media ethics, and has taught homiletics. His doctorate, from Edinburgh University, was on what preachers can learn from radio broadcasters and from this he has written a book, Visually Speaking, *to be published by T. & T. Clark in 1999. He was ordained into the Scottish Episcopal Church after working as a journalist and producer with the BBC World Service and BBC Radio 4. He studied theology at Selwyn, Cambridge and went on to do a Master's at Durham, where he specialized in twentieth-century church history.*

'When I was 15 I became a Christian through a youth group', he says. 'I was also inspired by studying RE at A level. While I was at university I thought I wanted to help the media understand the church better, and the church understand the media. I went to America to have a look at television evangelism and was shocked by what I saw, especially the way that young, committed preachers were seduced and corrupted by television. I wanted both to understand the media, and to help people think critically about media theology. I later postponed ordination and went into the media first because I had a passion about what makes good radio. I had to see if the media bug was part of my system. It was.'

Although he is attached to Christ Church in Edinburgh, where he preaches occasionally, he sees his primary calling as being ordained to work as a teacher within an academic setting.

'I would argue that preaching is experiencing a renaissance but is also in crisis', he says. 'The length of sermons is going down, and there is a loss of confidence among many preachers about their preaching. Preachers are no longer the centre of a town or village's learning as they were in the medieval period. There are now so many forms of communication. Standing up there on your own to preach is quite a bizarre form.'

He does however detect a growth of interest in homiletics, and believes preachers are faced with a number of different options. 'One is simply to give up preaching, but I do not buy that one. Another option for preachers is to put our heads in the sand like ostriches, and go on as we always have, without change. The third option is to adapt to our communicative environment and to take seriously the fact that we live in a media-saturated age. It is vital for preaching that we take this third option.'

He has not given much thought to the Millennium. 'For preaching, it is a good moment to take stock and think about where we go in the next hundred years.'

When the Princess of Wales died, he was about a mile away from Kensington Gardens, with friends whose baby was being baptized. 'I went to Kensington Gardens just twelve hours after the accident. I went as a mere spectator. I will never forget the flowers, the people, the teddy bears, the smell of the candles, the crying. I found myself changing from being a spectator to being a participant, and was very moved. It made a much greater impact than I had expected. Listening to different people, what struck me was the diverse meanings her death had for so many. For some it was clearly a spiritual moment. For others it was a catalyst for their own grief. And for others, it was something to tell their grandchildren about.'

Text: John 11:33–44.

EARLIER this morning I went for a walk.

On the way round The Meadows a girl stopped me:

'Excuse me, would you like to come to church?' Given what I was to do later this morning, it was a tempting offer but I just managed to decline: 'Sorry, I've got to preach at church today. Thanks for the invite.'

As you'll perhaps remember, Jim, the Rector, has asked a number of us to talk a bit about something we've found a help in tough times. Today I'd like to concentrate on the story we've just heard: the story of Lazarus, from the Gospel of John.

I will never forget sitting on an old wooden balcony,
sipping a cup of tea, and reading this story.
I was trying to escape the grief of a recent loss.
It had caused much pain.
This story of Lazarus then made a huge impression.
It was a word in a bleak season.
It's been interesting a few years on to ask: Why?
Why it spoke so clearly then.

There's a head answer:
on an intellectual level.
I was intrigued how it worked in John's Gospel.
Think of an eagle – John's Gospel is often linked with an eagle.
On one wing, there's the Book of Signs, chapters 1 to 10.

On the other wing, there's the Book of Glory, chapters 13 to 20.

Then there's the body of the eagle, chapters 11 and 12.
This includes this story of Lazarus.
It takes us to the heart of the eagle,
to the heart of the Gospel of John.

Now it was interesting to notice that this final and seventh sign in John's Gospel was a pivotal interlude between the Book of Signs and the Book of Glory, but it wasn't that which touched me. What grabbed me were two tiny phrases.

The first was the shortest verse in the Bible. It resonated with my own recent experience.

As a radio producer and journalist I spent much time reading, covering or watching stories of sorrow.

A father bravely holding back tears at a press conference following the death of his daughter.

A mother crying at the graveside of her son in Bosnia.

Two of many examples of sorrow we touched on.
But it was easy to become anaesthetized to grief.
On the one hand, I had become intimate with others' suffering.
On the other, I had been distanced by a stop-watch culture:
Most days we had to move on.
Move to a new story for the next day's programme.
Now I'd rather not go into gruesome detail, but through my own loss, something broke through, took me beyond the pictures and sound-bites; touched me not only here in the mind, but here in the heart.

Some people talk about numbness, anger and a sense of isolation. Others the 'long dark night of the soul'.

My sense of loss felt like being trapped in grief.

It felt a little like being locked in a dark room without a light switch.

Borrowing C. S. Lewis's metaphor from *A Grief Observed*:

In that dark room words that mean to help, such as 'Suffering is God's megaphone in a noisy world', brought me little comfort. Instead they made me want to stamp my feet and shout: 'You don't know what you're talking about!'

But then I read:

When Jesus saw her weeping, and the Jews who had come along with her also weeping, he was deeply moved in spirit and troubled. (v. 33)

Some translate 'deeply moved' as 'groaned in spirit'.

In other words, some think that as Jesus faced death and loss he was angry: was it because he saw death as an aberration, an enemy?

Here then, were some words that spoke to me:

Jesus, once more deeply moved, came to the tomb. (v. 38)

I vividly remember standing at a friend's funeral. Watching as they lowered the coffin in. Just 18 and tragically killed in a car crash. Two others had died. It wasn't their fault either. I found myself wondering 'Why?' and 'Why them, God?' And there was no answer but the windy rain, the smart black shoes squelching in the mud, and parents holding each other as they sobbed.

This story in John takes us into the midst of such grief and loss. And we're met. Met not by a God who folds his arms, and puts on a serene and distant smile; rather by a God who has made himself vulnerable, a God who has experienced grief, anger and loss.

Jesus wept. (v. 35)

Jesus cried at least once over the death of a friend and once over a city. We're not dealing here with a 007-style super-hero, who in a crisis merely adjusts his tie. No, his response is to be deeply moved: *Jesus wept*.

Those two simple words continue to make an impact, but then, two other words spoke even more powerfully to me:

Come forth! (v. 43)

Part of why this story made such an impact on that wooden balcony in Harare was because of a book by Gerard Hughes, called *Oh God Why*. He talked about this story and about the different tombs we can build for ourselves.

This may sound a bit crazy, but at the time I was wondering and praying whether to leave a basement flat in London, so I thought perhaps this was a sign. Here was the tomb I should move out of!

But then I thought more deeply about tombs, the many tombs that we build for ourselves.

A tomb of regret: 'If only. If only I hadn't said, done, or been like that.' Such lines can become like a tape, going round and round.

A tomb of resentment or bitterness: 'How could they do this to me?' Or: 'I'm hurt and I want to get my own back.'

It's too easy to become comfortable and enjoy this tomb.

I wondered what other tombs we build for ourselves?

A tomb of isolation:

This, a windowless tomb, often echoes with voices:

'We're alone in this Universe.'

'We have to face loss, disappointment, grief on our own.'

'We must face up to that fact bravely, for death is the end.'

A tomb of worry:

Like many people my age, I work on a series of rolling short-term contracts.

These pressures can create a tomb of short-term worry: 'What will we do if . . . ?'

A tomb of false dreams:

Often supported by endless and gripping soap stories, which may provide an escape from one tomb but take us into another where the story goes on and on and on, but rarely raises questions about the next life.

Or fast-moving, beautifully filmed adverts which entice us to dream of a better life, eternal youth, constant sex appeal if we purchase, if we diet. The simple message whispered, shouted, fired at us from many directions is: 'This life is all that there is.'

But this story in John puts a question mark over such tombs.

Christ, I believe, calls us out of our tombs: *Come forth!*

But it may take a lifetime, and death itself, to unwrap all the grave clothes; It was interesting how this story moved me from:

Jesus wept to *Come forth!*:

I found myself wondering: what's the author of John trying to encourage the audience to do?

Choose Life.

In the midst of grief, disappointment, loss and tears – Choose Life.

Not running away from the tears, from the anger. Facing it, naming the shadows; a little like that 9-year-old girl, Catherine Hamill, who told Bill Clinton and the rest of the world about the saddest day of her life – her daddy's death in Belfast:

'I like having peace and quiet for a change instead of people shooting and killing.'

Choose Life.

In our tombs of regret, of anger, of bitterness, of worry, Christ calls: Come forth out of the dark, dank-smelling stone into the bright sunshine. This story made me blink and hear in a new way those words read at the funeral service:

I am the Resurrection and the Life.

Choose life not because I say so, but because the sign-maker, wine-changer, bread-bringer, storm-calmer, story-teller, death-breaker and life-giver, calls:

Come forth and choose Life.

Let's pray.

Dear Lord,
Thank you that you weep with us in our losses, Thank you that you cry with us in our grief. Help us to hear your voice, as you call us to come forth. Help us to choose life. In the name of your Son and our Life-bringer Jesus Christ.

Amen.

Comments

Peter Graves: *'Shows deep pastoral sensitivity. Thoroughly biblical, clearly related to life and well illustrated.'*

Kieran Conry: *'After a curious and rather detached introduction this becomes a very effective look at death and relates the scriptures well to ordinary experience. After perhaps too many personal references, homily moves to straightforward, central exposition that might have been developed even further.'*

Jonathan Romain: *'Conventional slow beginning and build-up. Good ending that comes to a climax on an inspirational note.'*

Theological Blindness Versus Openness

REV. MARTIN CAMROUX

Sermon preached Sunday 14 September 1997 at the morning service at Immanuel United Reformed Church, Swindon.

Martin Camroux, 50, and his wife Margaret, a former secretary who still does occasional temping, have two children. Mr Camroux was a sociology lecturer at a Birmingham college until he was ordained in 1975, aged 28. His French name is a sign of his Huguenot ancestry. His ancestors fled to Spitalfields in London after Louis XIV revoked the Edict of Nantes in 1685.

'I have been a Christian for as long as I can remember', he says. 'When I was 16 I went to see my moderator to discuss being a minister. He told me to go to university and do something else first. I have been preaching since I was 15.'

He now preaches twice each Sunday at his church, Immanuel United Reformed in Swindon, before a morning congregation of up to 180, including about 50 children. He moved there seven years ago, from Birkenhead.

'Sometimes I deal with political questions in my sermons. I believe it is important that preachers address social and political questions as well as personal ones. If the Christian Gospel is relevant to the whole of life, it must address political questions. Biblically, this is inescapable. For example, last Sunday I preached on arms control. That comes from the Gospel imperative to be peace-makers. I approach such questions from Christian values, not in the interests of any political party. Only once in 34 years of preaching has anyone ever walked out on a sermon for political reasons and that was in reaction to a sermon on apartheid.'

He believes effective preaching is more difficult today. 'People find it harder to take in than they used to', he says. 'The ability to sit and listen for 20 minutes is rarer than it was, and this creates problems for preaching today. But where else can people get intellectually and spiritually challenged, if not in the sermon? Preaching has been the most important way of communicating the Gospel for 2,000 years, and I don't see how the Church can live without good preaching.'

He attaches no particular significance to the Millennium. 'I do not think that 2,000 years after Jesus is any more significant than 1,999 years or 2,001 years. Apart from encouraging some of the more loony people in society, I don't think the Millennium will lead to any great reflection about our

Christian heritage or where we should be going as a nation. I might be proved
wrong, but as far as I am concerned it is a rather meaningless jamboree.'

Text: Matthew 5:21–22, 33–43.

THE other day I went to visit one of our church members in
hospital. She'd had her hip replaced but we ended up discussing
the General Assembly's debate on homosexuality. Before I knew it, the
whole ward was caught up in the debate! Another visitor chimed in,
pointing out to me that Paul said a man should not lie with a man.
That was true, I said, but didn't we have to ask if in the last 2,000 years
there were any insights into homosexuality which might lead us to
modify that judgement? She was not convinced.

'Take another question', I said. 'Paul says wives should be submissive
to their husbands. Are you?' At that moment a passing nurse heard me
and zoomed in furiously. What did I mean, should women be submissive? Hadn't I read the Bible? Did Paul say wives should be submissive
to their husbands or did he not? Either you believed the Bible 100 per
cent or you didn't believe it all. It was clear which group she thought I
was in.

Last summer I came across a theological slogan that was new to me:
'The Bible says it. I believe it. That settles it.' That was obviously how
she felt. The Bible had said it. She believed it. That settled it.

I could not resist. 'Tell me', I said, 'do you keep your head covered
when you go to church?' No, she didn't think that necessary. 'Does
Paul say women should keep their heads covered or does he not?' 'Yes
he does, but times have changed since then.' So the Bible said it. She
didn't believe. It didn't settle it.

That of course was exactly the point I was trying to make. Whatever
view we may take about homosexuality or about male–female relationships we do need to recognize that 'time makes ancient good
uncouth', as Fosdick used to say. What is appropriate in the world
2,000 years ago may not always be appropriate now.

Firstly and most fundamentally, this is because ours is a living God.
Therefore he has always new light and truth waiting for his people.
There is an old Gospel song which says: 'If it was good enough for
Moses, it's good enough for me.'

To anyone who believes in a living God, greater nonsense was never
written. Do we believe in animal sacrifice today? Do we believe the
world is flat? Do we believe there is no real life after death? Do we
believe the enemies of Israel should be taken and slaughtered one by
one? It is of the nature of God to lead us into new truth.

In our day for example there has been new truth about the unity of
the Church. In 1956 Derek Worlock was private secretary to the Archbishop of Westminster. In this capacity he went to see the Archbishop

of Canterbury, Geoffrey Fisher, about an interdenominational meeting which was to be held in the Albert Hall. Of course there could be no act of worship but perhaps the Lord's Prayer could be said together. But if so, what form of the Lord's Prayer should be used – the one normally used by Catholics or the one normally used by Anglicans? To try and solve the dilemma, Worlock asked Fisher if it might be said in silence. Fisher exploded. This was monstrous. 'Haven't you Romans lived in this country long enough', he demanded, 'to know that we are the establishment and you must toe the line?'

Worlock rose and asked to withdraw, and as he left to go down the Lambeth Palace stairs he heard Fisher shouting after him: 'Aggression! It's Papal Aggression!' That was just 40 years ago. How much new truth and light God has led us into since then.

Or take other examples. How much new truth there has been from science, how much new truth about the equality of women, how much new truth about caring for God's creation, and the way the world is one. For anyone to dismiss all of this with the cry: 'Give me that old-time religion – if they didn't believe it 100 years ago we don't need it now' would be a kind of practical atheism, as if God no longer did or said anything. Truth is never settled once and for all – always there needs to be openness to what God may be showing us.

Then, secondly, trying to put a full stop after what we believe, and saying 'That's it' is contrary to the practice of Jesus. We heard today parts of that fifth chapter of Matthew. Did you notice there was almost a refrain running through it? *'You have heard that it was said to those of ancient times – but what I say to you is this.'* On retribution, on divorce, on anger, on loving, Jesus keeps on saying it. They used to believe this. But today I'm telling you something new. Should 'If it's good enough for Moses it's good enough for me' be true, that rules Jesus out as a false prophet.

This willingness to change makes Jesus a controversial figure. Look at his clashes with the Pharisees. They have the truth all settled and clear. Six days you worked. On the seventh day you rested. End of story. The Torah said it. They believed it. That settled it. But not for Jesus. 'It is permitted to do good on the sabbath', he said. And he broke their law and outraged them.

Jesus is an innovator. A disturber. For him the truth is never settled in an old mould. When the Holy Spirit comes, he says, he will lead us into all truth. For him this was the mark of his disciples – that they were open to new truth.

Thirdly, our faith has to be open because otherwise we limit our view to what we already believe. Back in the days when they had horses pulling carriages, the horses used to wear blinkers. In America they called them 'blinders', which is an even more vivid and descriptive word. The point of blinkers or blinders was quite simple. They gave the horse tunnel vision. It could see the way ahead but it couldn't see what was at the side. If the horse was pulling a carriage that was important. If it caught sight of something interesting or frightening by the side of the road you had problems. It might career off or turn. You needed the horse to have limited vision. So you put the blinkers or the blinders on it.

Some people go round in life with the equivalent of blinkers or blinders on. They have theological tunnel vision. They know exactly what the truth is. Anything outside their little view of truth they're not interested in. They are right and others are wrong and that is all there is to it.

When I was in Birkenhead a new church opened in our area. It had no notice-board or name. As I was chairman of the local ecumenical group I thought I must find out who they were and offer friendship and welcome. So I put a letter through the door. 'Dear Pastor, on behalf of the local churches I'd like to welcome you to the area. Perhaps there may be some things about which we disagree but I hope we can share together in Christian fellowship.' After a few weeks I got a reply. 'Firstly, we have no pastor because scripture makes it quite clear that the Church needs no such person. Secondly, we already have fellowship with all the Christians in this area.' That put me in my place.

There they were with their blinkers on. For them the whole Christian Church came down to their tiny little sect, and the only truth that was worth having they already knew. How sad and diminished a view of truth.

Let me give you an alternative story. When the Pilgrim Fathers left for America, their minister in Holland, John Robinson, remained behind. In his last sermon to the departing Pilgrims he said this.

We are now ere long to part asunder, and the Lord knoweth whether he should live to see their faces again. But whether the Lord had appointed or not he charged us before God and his holy angels to follow him no further than he followed Christ, and if God should reveal anything to us by any other instrument of his, to be as ready to receive it, as ever we were to receive any truth by his ministry. For I am very confident that the Lord hath yet more light and truth to break forth out of his holy word.

There you have the very opposite of tunnel vision, the Open Church, the Pilgrim people. That I am convinced is what God wants us to be.

Comments

Paul Walker: *'In many ways this sermon was banging a theological drum. Yet this drum does have to be beaten by those of us who wish to demonstrate that faith is possible without literalist interpretations of the Bible.'*

Jonathan Romain: *'A simple theme – that religious truth is open to change – taken and developed carefully and single-mindedly, with a rich variety of illustrations. One slight defect is that it does not differentiate between those parts of the Bible which are eternal and always to be kept, and those which are time-bound and are no longer applicable.'*

Kieran Conry: *'It might have been better to have more time to explore the implications of the stories. I would have welcomed a longer homily with the point driven home with a personal message for me.'*

Out of Death Comes Life

REV. JOAN PROUT

Sermon preached on Sunday 24 March 1996 at St Nicholas, Baydon, near Marlborough, Wiltshire.

The Rev. Joan Prout, 56, has three children and two grandchildren. She was ordained deacon in January 1997 and is hoping to be priested in December 1998 as a local non-stipendiary minister in the Church of England. She took early retirement from her job as a primary schoolteacher and although she is unpaid, works full time for the Church. She has pastoral care of St Nicholas, Baydon, which is in the Whitton team where she works with the Rev. Peter Hyson.

'I thought I was a Christian all my life', she says, 'but I did not become a really committed Christian until my forties. I came through a period of deep depression, when everything more or less fell apart and I discovered God in the middle of that. I found faith in the blackness. From that point I began to get better.'

The catalyst was a spiritual experience she still recalls vividly.

'I had driven to this place and stopped the car. I had been quite upset. I did not want to go home, so I sat in a glade and it was as though, suddenly and unexpectedly, someone took blinkers off my eyes. I had never seen anything properly before. I was filled with this wonderful sense of peace and joy. As I looked around me, everything seemed to change. It all became really beautiful, as though God was in everything. That inner peace and joy has never left me, even when things are difficult.'

She soon felt a sense of calling, and after training as a Reader, offered herself for the priesthood. Part of her training has been learning to preach. 'I soon recognized that if my preaching was to be effective, I had to find a way of enabling people to relate to what I was saying. The sermon has to be rooted in real experience. If a sermon is relevant to life today, and to people's experience, they will respond. It was the same when I was teaching young children. If I gave them some personal details they would sit up and listen.'

She says, for example, that she grew up in a Yorkshire family where true grit was prized above all else. When a task was begun it had to be finished, in accordance with Luke 9, 'No man having put his hand to the plough and looking back is fit for the kingdom of God'. When she was about 40 she real-

ized that this was a bondage, and it was permissible to reject a book and not feel obliged to read it doggedly to the end.

She believes the Millennium should be a festival which celebrates Christ's birth. 'If we are not careful, we will all get caught up in the secular celebrations. These are important, but as Christians we should also make sure we remember exactly what event the Millennium is commemorating. I also believe in the Jubilee 2000 campaign to cancel world debt. This should apply not just to other parts of the world but to our own country as well. There are people all around us who are suffering because they have got into debt.'

She said special prayers in church on the morning of the funeral of the Princess of Wales, and placed a sign in the village shop saying the church was open should anyone want to drop in. 'A lot of young people came and they brought children carrying flowers. I created a prayer time for the children to come and put the flowers on the altar. It was totally spontaneous. The death of Diana seemed to give a lot of them permission to release their own grief. It showed that the Church is there for the nation, not just for those who come each Sunday. We are there to serve the people when they need it. There is a great interest among young people in spirituality, but it is not Christ or God they can't stand, it is the Church. If we look at churches where there are a lot of young people, there is a terrific sense of renewal. Instead of singing about God, they are singing to him.'

Text: John 12:24.

I tell you the truth, unless a kernel of wheat falls to the ground and dies it remains only a single seed. But if it dies it produces many seeds.

I WAS in our local village school the other day, talking to the youngest children. We were sharing the amazing fact that everything required to grow a great oak tree is packed inside a single acorn. They thought it was very funny to try to imagine the process reversed – supposing you could squash down the oak tree to get it back into the acorn.

I understand the idea that life is contained in little seeds. What amazes me is that the life will rest there, seemingly dormant, until the seed is allowed to rot down. I have found seeds that have been forgotten in an old drawer for years, thrown them in the ground and like little miracles the vegetables or flowers have grown. One member of my congregation was telling me that when he and his wife visited Israel, there had been freak rains in the desert. Suddenly the desert blossomed with the most beautiful flowers from seeds that had lain dormant for years and years.

Jesus used the idea of this fascinating ability of seeds when he said: 'Unless the seed falls to the ground and dies, it remains only a single seed.' It seems strange that the seed goes through the process of all its life seemingly departing, before its burst of new life is triggered. In this passage, of course, Jesus is referring to his coming death. The hour is now come and he faces the reality of his Agony. For a moment, he knows the temptation of saying 'Father, save me from this hour.' Even though his whole life has been leading up to this point he is faced, in his humanity, with extreme horror. Then he says: 'No, it was for this very reason I came to this hour. Father, glorify your name.'

Jesus went through an agonizing death, but it was from that death that the new life sprang. Without Good Friday there could be no Easter Sunday. Easter Sunday was so much more than one seed returned. In one sense, before this, Christ, as a human being, could only be in one place at one time. After his death, the Risen Christ was able to be in the hearts of all who love him and that represents millions and millions of seeds.

So how does this theme of living through dying apply to us?

If we look closely its theme runs through our Christian lives.

When we become committed to God and make a conscious decision to live a life of service for him, we have to let our old lives die. Many things that we did without thinking are just not compatible with being a Christian. Even at the moment during Lent we are being challenged to root out those things in life that stand between us and God. Sometimes we need to throw out things from the past so that we can walk out refreshed, into a new life. This is one aspect of our baptism. We baptize with water to symbolically clean away the old. In other words, we die to our old life and begin a new life in Christ

When I was a child in Yorkshire, we made a great deal of this at Whitsuntide. On Whit Sunday, every child wore new clothes from head to toe, including underwear and shoes. Even the poorest families would go into debt rather than leave their children without having everything new. This was to celebrate the new life in the coming of the Holy Spirit. On Whit Monday, we all wore white – dresses for girls, and shirts for boys – and we had great processions through the streets to the local parks, carrying church banners. Hundreds gathered to hear the Whitsuntide hymns, all with the theme of old things being washed away and everything becoming new, as one of the hymns declared.

Living through dying for a good Christian means dying to self.

This is probably harder for us than for any past generation. We live now in a society that promotes 'self' more than ever before. We are encouraged to be self-aware, self-assertive and to promote self-interests. We are bombarded with advertisements begging us to pamper ourselves, spoil ourselves and if all else fails to indulge in self-pity. We aren't even stunned anymore when we hear of a mother who leaves her children to pursue her own happiness. How often do we hear that phrase: 'It's my life and I have to do what is best for me.'

That is not the Christian way. It is in dying to self or losing self in something greater that we find happiness.

As we travel on our Christian journey, we learn to submit more and more to our Father's will. The whole life of Jesus demonstrated this complete obedience to that will. Jesus also said: 'Whoever serves me must follow me; and where I am my servant will be also.' As we walk with Christ and die to self, we begin to change. We learn to look at life with his eyes; to reach out to others with his compassion; to love others with his love and gradually we find ourselves being shaped into becoming the children of God.

Comments

Peter Graves: *'A clear and simple presentation, written in a pleasing style with well-developed ideas.'*

Paul Walker: *'The metaphor of seeds has been rather overworked, but the sermon was partly redeemed for me by bringing home the difficulty of "dying to oneself" in the modern world.'*

Jonathan Romain: *'Some good points, such as the emphasis on self-interest that is contrary to the Christian view of selflessness.'*

Relationships

GORDON WENHAM

A sermon preached at Holy Trinity, Platt, Manchester on 8 February 1998.

Dr Gordon Wenham, 55, a lay reader in the Church of England, is married to Lynne and they have four children. He attends St Mary's, Charlton Kings in Gloucestershire and preaches about once a month.

Dr Wenham, who is a lecturer in Old Testament theology and who gained his PhD on the Book of Deuteronomy, was brought up in a Christian family. He had a period of serious doubt in his teens, but after reading a book written by an agnostic which examined different possible interpretations of the resurrection (F. Morison, Who Moved the Stone?*), he found his faith was restored and he has been a regular churchgoer ever since. A lecturer at Cheltenham and Gloucester College of Higher Education, he gained his first degree at Cambridge and subsequently studied at the Ecole Biblique in Jerusalem, and at London and Harvard Universities. He also taught at Queen's University, Belfast.*

'The purpose of preaching is basically to encourage people to live in a Christ-like way', he says. 'My aim is to show how the ancient text of the Bible applies to the modern world. As a preacher you never really know if you have been successful. You only ever get feedback from those who like it. I do think that a lot of what I say in sermons goes in one ear and out the next. Educationally, preaching is not a very good way of getting ideas across. It is said that people remember 10 per cent of what they hear, 30 per cent of what they see and 70 per cent of what they do.'

However, he still believes the sermon is important, even if people rarely remember what they hear. 'If you go to a liturgical church, much of the service is expected and known in advance. The sermon is then the icing on the solid cake of worship and prayer. If the sermon is a good one, people will therefore go away with the idea that the service was a good one. Although they may forget the specifics of the sermon, it will still flavour their memory of the service.'

He wishes the Millennium was more of an overtly Christian celebration. 'It just seems to be a great jamboree. There do seem to be a number of people around with weird expectations about the end of the world. I ran a course at our college entitled "Apocalypse 2000". It was on the Book of Revelation. A lot of people turned up who were interested in such questions. But personally I do not feel 2000 has anything but historical significance. It is 2,000 years since the coming of Christ, and even that is not accurate. So it is really more symbolic than anything else.'

He was also interested in the public response to the late Princess of Wales. 'I felt great surprise at the reaction to her death. I find it intriguing to think of why she aroused such great interest. But I don't have strong views on her otherwise.'

Text: Genesis 2 and 3.

TODAY I have been asked to look at the topic of relationships as they are set out in Genesis 2 and 3. Sometimes, listening to sermons, you feel the preacher is using a text to ride his hobby-horse rather than let it speak for itself, but I hope this is not true here. Jesus himself appealed to Genesis to back up his own view of marriage. Challenged by the Pharisees, he replied:

> Have you not read that he who made them from the beginning made them male and female, and said, 'For this reason a man shall leave his father and mother and be joined to his wife and the two shall become one.'
>
> Matthew 19:4–5

In other words, Jesus appeals to Genesis 1:27 and 2:24 to support his views on marriage. So sermons based on the opening chapters of Genesis are well justified. Like Jesus, I would like to say something about Genesis 1 before focusing on chapters 2 and 3.

Genesis 1 gives us a wide-angle view of creation, culminating in the making of man in God's image, whereas chapters 2 and 3 zoom in to give us a close-up of the relationship between the sexes and their relationship to God.

We are probably too familiar with Genesis 1 to realize just how surprising its ideas were to its first readers. If you had been brought up in ancient Babylon or Egypt and for some reason you came to Jerusalem to study, you would have been astonished by the story of creation told there. You would of course be surprised that there was only one God, but when it comes to the creation of mankind three points would have struck you.

First, the creation of man was not an afterthought, but the climax of all God's creative activity.

Second, in Babylon man was created to feed the great gods by offering sacrifice and other offerings. The Atrahasis epic tells how the lesser gods had gone on strike because it was too hard growing food for the gods. So to break the strike the great gods created seven human couples to provide them with food.

The third striking thing about Genesis 1 is the command given to the human race: 'Be fruitful and multiply and fill the earth.'

In Babylon, however, they were worried about the population explosion. According to them the gods sent the flood because there were too many human beings around disturbing the peace of heaven. And after the flood the gods tried to discourage human reproduction by decreeing that some women should suffer infertility or miscarriages, or children would die young. Genesis shows that God has a much more positive view of children than this. He wants the earth full of people made in his image. Traditional Jews have their own interpretation of this command in Genesis. They say that 'Be fruitful' means have a boy and a girl. 'And multiply' means have two boys and two girls. It is no good having a string of boys or a string of girls. You have to keep having children until you have two of both. Otherwise you have not fulfilled the first command in the Bible.

I was relieved to discover that your vicar passed this test! I would not have dared to tell this interpretation if he had not!!

It is of course far fetched, but it does remind us of God's very positive attitude to the human race in general and to its reproduction in particular. He created us in two sexes so that we could have children, a point that is sometimes ignored or played down in modern views of sexuality.

As we move into Genesis 2 other aspects of human relationships come into view. Here, even more clearly than in chapter 1, it is stressed that God is eager to provide for man's every need.

Here the Garden of Eden is portrayed as designed specially for Adam. It is described a bit like your perfect holiday island: trees and water in abundance, beautiful scenery and lots of food. Everything you could want.

Although Adam may not have realized that he needed anything, God did. He realized that Adam was lonely. So once again God sets about meeting that need. He sets about creating a help suitable for him – exactly matching him. The Hebrew here suggests complementarity: like two pieces of Lego or a jigsaw which click into each other. What Adam needs is not necessarily a helper identical with himself but someone who complements him, helps him in those areas where he needs it.

First of all God created the animals. Before the age of machines, animals were indispensable helpers of mankind in farming and transport. Now we city-dwellers tend to view them just as pets and food. But that is not the Genesis perspective: they are man's helpers. However, the animals did not exactly meet Adam's need: they did not match him. So God created Eve, who is of course just right, as Adam exclaims:

> This at last is bone of my bones
> and flesh of my flesh.
> She shall be called Woman
> because she was taken out of man.

God is here pictured as a man bringing his daughter to her future husband. In our culture this is done in the wedding service as the bride and her father walk into church together. In Old Testament society there was a procession from the bride's home to the groom's home. Here this idea is reflected in the comment: 'He brought her to the man.'

However, it is Adam's comments that matter most. Why does he say: 'This at last is bone of my bones and flesh of my flesh'? At one level the answer is quite obvious. Eve was created out of Adam's rib, therefore she was 'bone of his bone'. But this story is not simply about marriage in general. Genesis itself comments on Adam's exclamation. 'Therefore a man leaves his father and mother and cleaves . . . to his wife and they become one flesh', i.e. the story of Adam and Eve shows what happens in every marriage. The two become one flesh.

Modern readers may easily take the 'one flesh' idea rather superficially, not realizing what the OT means by the term. You are one flesh with your relatives. Laban said to Jacob his nephew 'You are my bone and my flesh.' We say our relatives are our blood relations. The OT says you are bone and flesh relations.

We easily think of our brothers, sisters, parents, children as our own flesh and blood. But what Genesis says is that your spouse, your husband or your wife, is your own flesh and blood. My wife is as it were my sister: I am as it were her brother. Notice how I qualified it by saying my wife is as it were my sister. We view such an idea as a mere figure of speech. But Genesis says: 'The Lord caused a deep sleep to fall upon Adam and while he slept took one of his ribs . . . and made it into a woman.' This is very realistic language. I think it is trying to make the point that man and wife are not just like brother and sister, they are just as intimately related to each other as brother and sister.

There has been a lot of discussion recently about the possibility of human cloning. This is the sort of idea Genesis is trying to get across: man and wife are as really and intimately related as if they were cloned: they are one flesh.

Some commentators have wondered whether there is any significance about God's choice of Adam's rib. Why did he not use Adam's finger or his toe, for example? I do not think we can be sure, but let me quote you what the much-loved commentator Matthew Henry said:

> Not out of his head to top him.,
> Not out of his feet to be trampled on by him
> but out of his side to be equal with him,
> under his arm to be protected,
> and near his heart to be beloved.

I suppose we might also ask why if God was really doing his best for Adam, he did not create several Eves for him. If one Eve was a good thing, would not Adam have been even happier with half a dozen Eves? Or why not another Adam or two?

It is important to recognize that these opening chapters of Genesis are just as much part of the Law as are the Ten Commandments in Exodus or the rules of Leviticus or Deuteronomy. In these stories of Genesis fundamental moral principles are being set out. The fact that God decided to create an Eve and not an Adam shows that heterosexuality is God's pattern. Even more obvious is God's decision to create only one Eve: this shows that God believes in monogamy not polygamy. One man, one wife; not one man, several wives. Yet, as you know, many a patriarch and king had more than one wife. Genesis 2 teaches that such behaviour was contrary to God's will.

The main thrust of Genesis is that man and wife become one flesh when they marry, that is, related like brother and sister, or parent and child. Now such relationships are not dependent on the behaviour of those involved. I may neglect my parents or ill-treat my children, but they are still my relatives. So Jesus argued against the Pharisees who had no fundamental objections to divorce, 'What God has joined together let no man put asunder.' If divorce does occur because the love between the parties has come to an end, then they are still biblically speaking man and wife. You can no more have an ex-wife or ex-husband than you can have an ex-father or an ex-sister.

Neither Old or New Testaments look for a mere formal relationship in marriage. I have already mentioned Jesus' use of Genesis 2:24, 'For this reason a man leaves his father and his mother and cleaves to his wife and they become one flesh.'

It sounds like a simple statement of fact. But it is saying much more. It is easy for modern Western readers to misunderstand 'leaving father and mother'. We suppose it refers to us leaving home when we marry and setting up home elsewhere out of the parents' interfering grasp! However, that was not what happened in OT times. The man continued to live in or near his parents' home. It was the bride who left home and lived with her husband.

What does Genesis mean then when it says the man leaves his father and his mother, if he actually continued to live near them?

It is speaking figuratively. When you marry, your priorities change. In traditional societies your most important duty is to your parents. You were expected to honour them throughout life and when they grew elderly to look after them. This was your most important social duty. Have you ever noticed that in the Ten Commandments 'Honour your father and mother' comes before 'You shall not kill'? But Genesis 2:24 says that when a man marries he leaves his parents and cleaves to his wife, for she is now his closest relative. Marriage is not an excuse for a man to neglect his parents, he must still honour them, but now his wife is even more important.

St Paul brought out the force of this remark well when he compared a husband's love for his wife to Christ's love for the church. In Ephesians 5:25 he writes 'Husbands, love your wives, as Christ loved the church and gave himself up for her.' In other words as husbands we should be ready to give everything for our wives, even to die for them if necessary.

What a picture of marital bliss! Adam with eyes for only one woman Eve, ready to do everything for her health and happiness. Eve on the other created for Adam as his perfect helper and complement. Totally at ease with each other, 'they were not ashamed'.

Unfortunately it all soon goes wrong. Instead of being the perfect helper of her husband Eve helps him to eat the forbidden fruit. I do not think Genesis puts all the blame on Eve: it holds Adam ultimately responsible for agreeing to eat the fruit. But certainly instead of working as a team together, they start to work against each other. They argue with each other and when God questions them they blame each other for their behaviour. 'The woman gave me to eat', says Adam. Their intimacy is lost: they make clothes of fig leaves and hide in the bushes hoping that God will not find them. What a ridiculous picture, as if God will not find them or fig leaves would cover their nakedness.

Whereas Genesis 2 gives a picture of relationships as they ought to be, Genesis 3 gives a picture of how they often are. God interrogated Adam and Eve, more as a detective to elicit their confession than as a way of finding out what they had done. Then as a judge he passes sentence. They are of course expelled from Eden where everything was just right. Now they have to fend for themselves. Adam will have the thankless task of dealing with thorns and thistles – how often do I think of this while weeding the garden on Saturdays!

Eve's greatest joy, her children, will be brought into the world with agonizing pain – 'I will greatly multiply your pain in childbearing.' There will often be conflict between them: Eve on the one hand seeking her independence, Adam on the other laying down the law. 'Your desire shall be for your husband but he shall rule over you.' Mutual love and support are replaced by self-interest and antagonism.

Thus God's design for mankind and for marriage in particular is shown by Genesis 3 to be destroyed by human disobedience. The rest of the Old Testament fills out the picture. There are husbands who do not look after their wives, they commit adultery or marry several wives. There are wives who betray their husbands or lead them into sin. The laws envisage divorce and remarriage as an option that could be followed when marriages failed.

However, Jesus saw these laws as a concession to human weakness. With his coming a new age began. God was creating afresh a new people of God and he challenged his disciples to live out the vision set out in Genesis 1 and 2. He said: 'For your hardness of heart Moses allowed you to divorce your wives, but from the beginning it was not so' (Matthew 19:8).

He therefore urged his followers to avoid divorce and remarriage and live as God intended. But he also pointed out that in the new age there was a role for the single and unmarried. In Old Testament society, everyone was expected to marry and have a family. But Jesus and Paul say that there is an important role for the single as well in God's purpose. Jesus talks of eunuchs for the kingdom of heaven, Paul says some people will be able to dedicate themselves more wholeheartedly for Christian work if they do not marry. And of course Jesus and Paul were single themselves.

Nevertheless, I think Jesus and Paul would agree that Genesis 1 and 2 represent God's pattern for most people. Singleness is a calling for the few, not the many. For most people, 'It is not good to be alone.'

But the pattern of relationships in Genesis 2 surely has much wider relevance than just marriage. The essence of a good marriage is living for the other. Eve was designed as a helper for Adam, matching him. The husband for his part is expected to make his wife's welfare his first priority, to leave his parents and cleave to his wife. They are expected to live not for themselves but for the other.

Our modern consumer society says just the opposite. It is an intensely self-centred society. Everyone is encouraged by advertising to make their own comfort and happiness their No. 1 priority. Self-fulfilment is the great goal of modern education and counselling. But Eve was expected to look after Adam, and Adam to care for Eve.

Our Lord Jesus was one who lived and died for others. He gave himself that we might live. And this is how we should live inside marriage and outside. In marriage we promise to love each other for better for worse, for richer for poorer, in sickness and in health, till death us do part. This commitment to others whatever the cost should surely characterize not just marriage but all our relationships. In the family we must love our children for better for worse, for richer for poorer (definitely the latter!), we must love our parents in sickness and in health. All our friendships may not be till death, but let us hope they will be long lasting. Church life needs to show these qualities too. 'By this shall men know that you are my disciples because you love one another.'

In our own strength we are unlikely to achieve these aims. Let us therefore end by praying that God will bring in his new creation and help us live as he intended.

Let us pray:
O God, forasmuch as without thee we are not able to please thee. Mercifully grant that thy Holy Spirit may in all things direct and rule our hearts, through Jesus Christ our Lord.

Amen.

Comments

Peter Graves: *'Fine biblical exegesis clearly related to marriage in our times. Possibly too much material for one sermon. Some non-biblical illustration would give more balance and so make the excellent content more accessible.'*

Paul Walker: *'Good use of text, looking at related mythology and drawing on contemporary experience. I disagreed with some of the conclusions, but that is inevitable with such a sensitive issue. Yet he effectively used his faith and mind, and connected with mine.'*

Listening to Jesus in a Busy Life

REV. HARRY YOUNG

Sermon first preached on Sunday 4 August 1996 at Oaklands Baptist Church, Surbiton, Surrey.

The Rev. Harry Young, 78, is the oldest of this year's shortlisted preachers. He and his wife Joyce have three sons and six grandchildren.

Brought up in the Open Brethren in Cumbria, a grouping similar to modern Baptists, he left school at 18 to train as a schoolmaster teaching English and history. He became a conscientious objector during the war and entered the non-combatant corps, and by the time the war ended was qualified as a lay pastor and a teacher. He was still working as a teacher when in 1955 he went to minister at the Surbiton Baptist Church in Surrey. The church was destroyed during the war, and his induction took place the day it re-opened. In the meantime, by 1963 he had become head of department in a comprehensive school. His next step was to read for a degree in English, history and theology, studying part-time at Birkbeck, London. When he graduated in 1966 he had moved to become associate minister at Duke Street Baptist Church, Richmond in Surrey.

In 1970 he was ordained and appointed part-time minister of Kingston Baptist Church in Surrey, while also working as a part-time lecturer. Ten years later he left education and became full-time minister at Kingston. Even though he retired in 1987, he remained active in the Baptist Church, working still as a minister at Richmond, Surbiton and Kingston.

Earlier this year, however, he and his wife moved to Westward Ho! in Devon, and are now members of Bideford Baptist Church. The publicity locally surrounding his being shortlisted has led to several invitations to preach in churches near his new home. 'I was sitting here moaning that I hadn't got any preaching to do when two friends persuaded me to enter', he says. 'I was amazed to be shortlisted.'

He believes preaching is a valuable educative tool. 'People love to be challenged and taught, and we need to do more and more of that', he says. 'We need to get to grips with the nitty-gritty of the Christian tradition. But people don't just need educating, they must also be inspired and uplifted. A sermon should also have aesthetic qualities. Many preachers fail because they are too colloquial, too spontaneous and impromptu.'

Preachers should also be self-effacing, he says. 'I am not there as an actor, to perform, but as an instrument through which God can communicate. A preacher needs to be clothed in a garment of humility, although personality and warmth must of course show through. People want and expect a measure of doctrine, but complex doctrine must be made simple. Simplicity is always the order of the day.'

He has strong views on the Millennium. *'It is time to start afresh, a new beginning. It is a time for everyone to acknowledge the contribution Christianity has made to the world. It is time, too, to acknowledge the divisions Christianity has caused. The Millennium is time for a re-dedication. A reformation of manners is desperately needed. We need a recovery of decency, of language, an end to the dumbing-down process. It is a time for a new beginning, with a touch of repentance.'*

He saw two sides to the death of Diana. He admired her work, and the way she was prepared to take up unpopular causes. *'Then there was the other side of her lifestyle that one could only – and I say this sympathetically – disapprove of. But I would rather stress the good side.'*

He has recently published a book, Understanding the Holy Spirit *(Autumn House), written in an easy-to-read style. The foreword is written by John Cole, formerly of the BBC.*

Texts: Luke 10:25–42; 11:1–4; John 12:1–8.

I N T H E brief paragraph in his Gospel, where St Luke features the two sisters, Mary and Martha, the 'beloved physician' has given us a splendid illustration of the way in which the love of God and the love of one's neighbour are always united. They represent the two sides of the spiritual life, that is, the active side of busyness and service, and the contemplative side of prayer and meditation, of working and listening.

From Aristotle onwards, scholars have usually regarded the contemplative side, rather than the active one, as the 'better part'. Now while it is true that the mind can be a great source of spiritual refreshment, St Luke sees these two sides as complementary and not contradictory: worship and service which go hand in hand.

This is how he does it:

First, he tells the story of one of our Lord's most popular and best-known parables, the Good Samaritan. A man lies sorely wounded by the roadside, half dead. The 'religious' – busy *en route* to their rituals of worship – pass by on the other side. Unlike the priest and Levite, the Samaritan forgets the animosity between Jews and Samaritans, to show concern by instant rescue of the unfortunate victim, giving care and compassion. The key words of Jesus in application are simply: 'Go and do likewise.' The lovely little cameo at Bethany follows, but then Luke tells us that Jesus was praying and the disciples asked him:

'Lord, teach us to pray.'

'Go and do' is a command to active service; 'Teach us to pray' is a call for instruction in the art of contemplation.

In between is this superb story of the two Bethany sisters. It was probably an unscheduled visit to their home where they lived with their brother, Lazarus – not far from Jerusalem. Martha receives Jesus, the first sign of her eager, active lifestyle. One can imagine her thoughts. 'Good grief, what can I give him to eat – not to mention his entourage?'

We know the feeling when unexpected guests arrive. Martha is a dynamo, and without delay she gets busy in the kitchen. She is the practical one. Meanwhile, and in vivid contrast, Mary simply sits down at Jesus' feet, absorbed by his teaching, not wanting to miss a word. Martha is fussing and fretting in the kitchen, striving to serve a three-course meal. She tries to catch Mary's eye, gives her a nudge or makes a gesture and then, containing herself no longer, she boils over. She is very cross indeed. 'Lord, don't you care that my sister has left me to serve alone – tell her to help me.' You can imagine how embarrassed Jesus was. He was thinking: 'Why is Martha going to all this trouble? I'd be perfectly satisfied with one course.'

He does not condemn Martha, only gently chiding her for her fretfulness, unnecessary worry, anxiety and trouble. 'Mary has chosen the good portion – only one thing is needful', he said.

With whom do your sympathies lie?

I love the story of the Desert Fathers of the fourth and fifth centuries. Brother Anthony, the most famous of those hermits, tells how a brother came to the Abbot Silvanus in the St Catherine's monastery at the foot of Mount Sinai. He saw the hermits working busily and exclaimed: 'Why do you work for the bread that perisheth? Mary chose the better part, namely to sit at the feet of Jesus without working.' The Abbot said to the disciple, Zachary, 'Give this brother a book. Put him in an empty cell and let him read.' At the ninth hour, the brother who was reading looked out of the cell to see if the Abbot was going to call him for dinner. Later still he went himself to the Abbot and said: 'Did the brothers not eat today, Father?'

'Oh yes, certainly, they have just had dinner.'

'Well', said the brother, 'why did you not call me?'

'You are a spiritual man', was the reply, 'we have to work, but you have chosen the better part. You don't need this food that perishes.'

Hearing these words, the brother said, meekly, 'Forgive me, Father.'

The elder replied 'Martha is necessary to Mary; it was because Martha worked that Mary was able to be praised!'

It is so easy to take sides in this wonderful character-drawing exercise, this clash of temperaments. On the one hand, service can be spoiled by self-pity, self-concern rather than self-forgetfulness, but on the other hand, to use an old cliché, it is hardly right to be so heavenly minded as to be of no earthly use. Jesus does not praise Mary to disparage Martha. Mary's phrase is 'Teach us to pray.' Martha's phrase is

'Go and do!' There should be sincerity in worship, simplicity in service. Indeed, the busier life is, the more urgent it is to listen to Jesus.

Further light is shed on these two sisters by the apostle John. 'Jesus loved Martha and her sister', we read (John 11:5). The active Martha went out to meet Jesus, while Mary sat in the house. Their brother, Lazarus, had died. Martha called her sister who was weeping, saying quietly 'The Master has come and is calling for you.' Later when celebrating the raising of Lazarus at supper, Mary turns contemplation into action. She had a pound of precious ointment to anoint the feet of Jesus. She had the intuition that it would be unnecessary to anoint him at his burial as he said he would rise again. Her act of devotion was both spiritual and practical, so beautifully brought together.

In our modern world, we are busier than ever, distracted by so much activity. The demands for practical service are unending and we cannot ignore them. Where do we get our strength to sustain us in our busyness? The answer is when we sit at Jesus' feet and say: 'Lord, teach us to pray.' It will not be long, however, before we hear a call for help or see a window of opportunity for service; not long before we hear the Master say 'Go and do!' Listening to Jesus, in private or corporate prayer, in worship, in scripture – all are necessary so that on the busy road of life, we may have the inner resources to respond to the challenge of service.

Comments

Jonathan Romain: *'The merit of a very good ending where he pulled the different threads together and gave listeners a task for everyday life.'*

Peter Graves: *'Good use of scripture, clearly applied and appropriately illustrated. Helpful and clear interpretation of an often-misunderstood story.'*

Paul Walker: *'Sometimes I'm a Mary and sometimes I'm a Martha. Sometimes I'm too busy and sometimes I feel lazy. He admits there are no easy answers. Sometimes we need to be busy and sometimes we need to stop and reflect. Perhaps best of all, we must not always feel guilty about it.'*

Coping with Cancer

RABBI COLIN EIMER

Rabbi Colin Eimer has been the rabbi at the Southgate and District Reform Synagogue in north London since 1977. He and his wife Dee, a stenciller in interior design, have two children. He was ordained in 1971 after a degree in geography at the London School of Economics and studying at the Leo Baeck College. He was brought up in an Orthodox, United Synagogue background and went to synagogue regularly.

'I was originally heading towards town and country planning', he says. 'My path was changed, partly by people I met such as Rabbi Lionel Blue and Rabbi Hugo Gryn, partly because of where I was heading intellectually and religiously, and partly because I rediscovered my desire to study Judaism.'

He switched from Orthodoxy to the Reform movement because he found it more intellectually acceptable. 'I could not do the mental gymnastics I felt Orthodoxy required', he says. 'I had to have something that could harmonize my secular and my religious education.'

Preaching, he says, represents the main opportunity for a rabbi or clergyman to raise questions, challenge and suggest possibilities to their people. The adrenalin comes into play when thinking of how to say something without hesitation and repetition, and how to interpret Jewish teaching in the light of the lives of my community and the world.

He feels a sermon has been a success 'when the congregation have laughed and cried in the right places'. He adds: 'It is however quite hard to judge a successful sermon. It is quite interesting what they take away with them and hold on to.' He is one of the few preachers ever to have received a standing ovation from his congregation, given to a sermon in 1982 during the war in Lebanon, when he preached on the massacre that took place in a Palestinian camp in Beirut. 'No one was quite clear what the Israeli involvement was, but there were a lot of questions people were asking', he says.

He has no views on the Millennium as such, although he has been reading about and making comparisons with fin de siècle thinking at the end of the last century. 'There is a sermon in it somewhere', he says.

He was puzzled by the emotional public response to the death of Diana, which he describes as 'mass hysteria'. 'I did wonder what that was all about', he says.

A FEW moments ago, among the prayers for the Royal Family, the State of Israel and the community, I also read one for those who are ill. For the past three or four years, I've been reading out their names, and you, too, have said out loud the names of family or friends for whom you wish a speedy recovery. There's something very powerful in that act of public naming.

In recent months, however, this has become an increasingly difficult and painful moment. Each week almost, there seems to be another name to add to the list. Because they're members of the community, they're known to many of us. Not only are new names being added to the list, but so many seem to be comparatively young, and to have been diagnosed with one form or another of cancer.

And so it is that many of you have been talking to me about this, using words like 'epidemic', 'plague' and so on. I think it's compounded by the fact that many are still grieving for a number of members of our congregation, such as Arthur Bergner, whose death in particular, from cancer, has had a great impact on many in the community.

It has raised fears and anxieties for many of us, posed theological questions for some about God's role or otherwise in this, created anger, consternation and puzzlement, made us all aware of our own mortality. In part, this is for obvious reasons. Cancer has an aura about it that marks it off from another . . . well, even finding the right word is difficult. It's not a disease, it's not an illness. Maybe we should simply use the word 'condition'. Those who have cancer often say they aren't ill, but that they're 'living with' cancer. It's a condition like, say, diabetes, hyperactivity or shortsightedness. You have it and you live with it. I'm not being naive – clearly, its effects and ravages are often much worse and it has the potential to kill. Its treatment is also often much more unpleasant than that for other conditions.

But cancer has also taken on a particular complexion, been 'hyped up' in a way that doesn't seem helpful to anybody. To find that you have cancer is not tantamount to being given an automatic death sentence.

Growing up in the 1950s, I remember how cancer was seldom mentioned by name. Obituaries simply spoke of somebody dying 'after a long illness'. In the media it was often referred to as 'the Big C' and if the word 'cancer' was used, it was in hushed, almost reverential tones, as if you were in the presence of the dead or nearly-dead – which just added to the mystique surrounding it, of course.

Things are considerably different now. Seldom a day passes when you don't open a newspaper, or switch on TV or radio, and hear somebody talking about it – how to deal with it, how to live with it, and so on.

But this openness might not be an unmitigated blessing. As Susan Sontag points out in an essay, 'Illness as metaphor', cancer has taken on a very particular range of meaning and implication. Cancer has become a metaphor for anything rotten – as in the phrase, 'a cancer in our society'. I don't think it's possible any longer to use the words 'malignant' or 'benign' without automatically evoking images of cancer.

But what does that way of using the word do to somebody living with it, or to others?

The imagery surrounding cancer is very militaristic. One talks of an 'invasion' of cancer cells against which the body must 'defend' itself; of 'aggressive' cancer and 'aggressive' treatment. Indeed, the vocabulary is that of chemical warfare – chemotherapy – or radiotherapy where the cells are 'bombarded'.

The problem with such words, as Sontag suggests, is that cancer comes to be seen as the 'enemy' – which, at one level, of course, it is. But talk of an 'enemy' implies a 'victim'. And a 'victim' suggests innocence. And innocence suggests guilt. And guilt evokes thoughts of 'punishment' or of 'fault'.

Countless theories purport to explain cancer – stress, a harmful diet, an inappropriate attitude to life and so on. But that in turn creates the impression that somehow it's the person's 'fault' if they have cancer – if only they'd lived differently, it suggests. And if there are so many theories, you can tie yourself in knots trying to respond appropriately to your 'chosen' one.

And what if it doesn't work? That then entails notions of success and failure. It becomes a vicious circle in which the person living with cancer has an additional burden of thoughts and feelings to carry. Yet no diabetic, epileptic or shortsighted person asks themselves, castigates themselves with how they might have brought about, or contributed to, their condition.

Until comparatively recently, there was almost some sort of stigma attached to having cancer. Stigma leads to isolation and the creation of what Erving Goffman, the sociologist, called 'spoiled identity'. People avoided those living with cancer, who often ended up feeling like pariahs – which, of course, simply added another level of anguish and difficulty to what they were already experiencing.

Sontag suggests that it's almost as if society has some need for an illness or condition that can be identified with evil, which creates 'victims' to whom 'blame' can be attached. In the nineteenth century, she suggests, it was TB, consumption. For much of the twentieth century, cancer has filled that role.

More recently that has begun to change, though, as a new killer disease has emerged – AIDS. It has brought with it all the same reactions, vocabulary, mystery and misinformation. It has entailed the same pain for those living with AIDS. There has clearly been enormous stigma and social isolation. In particular with AIDS there has been a real attribution of 'fault': 'If you have AIDS', it says, 'it's a deserved punishment for your wicked and sinful lifestyle.'

All of this raises a multitude of issues and questions for us. How do we view medicine and its role in our lives? Part of the surprise, the shock, the consternation about the amount of illness around is connected, surely, with the expectations we have developed of what medicine can do for us.

Since the 1970s, Western society has been going through a sort of cult of health. Look at the number of health clubs, marathons, joggers on our streets, David Lloyd Sports Centres, magazines, books and media attention devoted to healthy living and so on and so on.

It must be better to have a healthy body than not. But has it not become almost obsessive? What expectations does it engender about how long we will live?

But we aren't simply biological organisms. Has the health craze, by putting a disproportionate emphasis on our bodily well-being, not led us to pay less attention to the spiritual dimension of our existence? We human beings want to feel, need to feel, that there is purpose and meaning in our lives.

For is that not the real issue for us: how do we view life and death? Death is an eruption of chaos into our lives. Illness and suffering are also perceived as a similar outbreak of chaos. Everything appears to be ordered and normal in our existence, within our control. Then suddenly we find we have to live with cancer, or a tumour, or the effects of a stroke. Unless we have a view of life and death and their meaning for us, we will find it even more difficult to respond to the question 'What is the meaning of this event in my life?'

If we have focused primarily on developing our outer, physical, material resources for living, what has happened to the inner resources we will need when something happens to us physically? We might have a healthy balance at our bank on the High Street – but what resources will be available to us in our spiritual account?

The meaning of suffering in human existence is, perhaps, the central question facing religion. It has preoccupied religious thinkers since the beginning of time, and religion offers no easy, trite answers. We continue to struggle with the question, because suffering is so meaningless and absurd. Its very existence challenges our need, desire and urge to make sense of the world we live in and of our daily experience.

But it isn't just an intellectual problem. We do want to try and reconcile suffering with notions we might have about God's justice in the world. We can't 'blame' God for the suffering one human being causes another. But what we might address to God is the suffering which is beyond any human agency or control. We want to somehow assimilate that into a view of an ordered and sane world.

So it isn't merely an intellectual problem but an existential one, too.

We move beyond trying to explain and begin to respond humanly, I would say 'religiously'. Here we focus on how do we cope with suffering in our daily lives? How does the sufferer go on living in the face of pain? How must we, who are not suffering in that particular way, respond to the pain of human beings we know and love?

Not surprisingly, the intellectual responses offered by religious traditions to these crucial life questions are less than satisfying, if that is the appropriate word. But all religions do respond, at a human level, to the pain of the sufferer. In some ways, the more inadequate the intellectual response, the more important does the existential one become.

A synagogue can be, should be, a place of healing – not of the physical pains our bodies experience but of the anguish our spirits endure. They are not separate, of course – learning to cope with spiritual anguish can make the physical difficulties more bearable. In a phrase, we need to see how we can do more. More . . . to support those in our community who are in pain or in anxiety; more . . . to support members of their families, bearing so much of the suffering their loved ones are going through; more . . . to support each other as we cope with our own feelings at what we see going on around us.

This has been a difficult and painful sermon to write and to deliver. There are no answers – just a lot of questions, doubts and anxieties that many of us have at this time. If this sermon moves us to look together at what we can do – then *dayyenu*, it has been sufficient. I hope that it will.

Comments

Jonathan Romain: *'Full marks for dealing head-on with a subject from which other preachers might shy away. This is a reality in the lives of many listeners and causes anxieties and concerns that need addressing. Some might find the assertion that there are no answers disappointing and would have wanted the preacher to point at possible ways forward.'*

Peter Graves: *'A gallant and sensible attempt to deal with a difficult subject in an easily accessible and interesting way.'*

Paul Walker: *'All preachers tackle the problem of suffering. Colin Eimer admits there is a problem but, wonderfully, does not provide an answer. I wish more preachers would be brave enough to say "I don't know".'*

Liberal Jewish Belief

RABBI DAVID GOLDBERG

Rabbi David Goldberg, rabbi at the famous Liberal Jewish Synagogue, St John's Wood, opposite Lord's in north London, did postgraduate work in Hebrew and Semitic languages at Trinity College, Dublin after his BA from Oxford. His wife, Carole-Ann, is an astrologer in private practice. They have two children. Dr Goldberg's own father was also a rabbi, at the Jackson's Row Reform Synagogue in Manchester. His brother is the lawyer Jonathan Goldberg QC. Rabbi Goldberg is a Piscean but does not believe at all in astrology. 'When people ask how it feels to have an astrologer for a wife, I say it is no more irrational than believing in God', he says.

Asked why he became a rabbi, he says: 'It sounds flippant to say it is a family business, but it does go back a long way.' One of his ancestors was among the Grand Sanhedrin called by Napoleon in 1807 to deal with the situation of the French Jewish population. 'My family seems to go in for the law or the rabbinate', he says.

After attending Manchester Grammar School he went to Lincoln College, Oxford, then to Dublin, and finally to the Leo Baeck College in north London for his rabbinic ordination. He went first to Wembley and District Liberal Synagogue, but moved to St John's Wood in 1975.

'My persistent anxiety dream is being in the pulpit having lost my sermon and just standing there, with words not coming out', he says. 'After 25 years in the rabbinate, I still wake up in a sweat after having that dream. I take preaching very seriously, although with all due respect to The Times, *I don't take this competition very seriously. The one who wins will not necessarily be the best preacher in England. Week in and week out, the best preacher I know is my retired colleague, Rabbi John Rayner. This congregation at St John's Wood has always had a tradition of listening to sermons. You really see them settle down, cross their arms over their chest and start to listen.' He adds: 'The best piece of homiletics advice I was ever given was by an American rabbi, who told me: "If you don't strike oil after 15 minutes, then stop boring."'*

Sometimes he preaches to be educational, and other times to be supportive and consolatory. 'The most difficult, but also the most authentic, sermons are when you try to engage people on a human level. I try to be as honest as I can about my emotions, about life, the pain of life. I don't feel every sermon must be uplifting. I often find life very painful. There are so many "can do" books on the shelf. I would like to write a "can't do" book. All this stuff about focusing on your dreams to make them come true is nonsense. Think of the millions of people who focus on their dreams and they remain just that – dreams.'

On the Millennium, he says: 'I don't think it has been worked out clearly. I have every understanding for Christians wanting to celebrate the putative birth of Jesus, but the role of the other faith communities seems muddled. Are we all onlookers at someone else's party, or do we use the Millennium to make some sort of statement about a multi-cultural, multi-faith society?'

He confesses himself 'astonished' by the response to the death of Diana. 'We were in Boston at the time. Someone said "Your Princess has died." It was extraordinary to see the response of people there. People who attacked the Royal Family for being "dysfunctional" were way out of order, I thought. The flowers were extraordinary. The same thing happens if there is a crash on the motorway, people put flowers there. It is as if there is no other way for people to express their grief. This applies in Judaism as well. We are very good in Judaism at surrounding birth, marriage and death with symbolism. But I remember a time, when if a hearse passed, men would doff their hats and people stand in silence in the streets. Now I can take three funerals a day, and if I see a hearse on the way to Golders Green crematorium I hoot my horn and overtake it, because I am on the way there to take a funeral myself. The space for ritual over significant life events has been so eroded.'

IT has been said that the Church of England is so constituted that its members can really believe anything, but of course almost none of them do.

This always causes a nod of assent among the various bishops, deans, canons and vicars of my acquaintance, witty, urbane and civilized men one and all.

But because this is the time of the year when we hold up a mirror to judge ourselves, let us substitute a couple of words, and now try this sentence for size: 'Liberal Judaism is so constituted that its members can really believe anything, but of course almost none of them do.'

Suddenly, this is not so comfortable. There is a pointedness beneath the flippancy that we must reluctantly acknowledge and consider.

So let us ask: are there any irreducible beliefs that a Liberal Jew must subscribe to? Do we have the equivalent of a creed, a catechism, the Thirty-Nine Articles, which one can tick off and at the end of the quiz mark oneself 'Good Liberal Jew', 'Average Liberal Jew', or 'You really belong elsewhere'?

In one sense 'No', because as we never cease explaining, Judaism is a religion which demands only a single profession of faith; that there is One God. Beyond that, it is all a matter of formulation, interpretation and general consent. The Thirteen Principles of Faith by Maimonides, familiar to us in the *Yigdal* hymn, may be well known and have found their way into most prayer books; but not even in their own time were they universally recognized or accepted.

As Moses Mendelssohn, by modern standards a punctiliously observant Jew, expresses it in his philosophical work *Jerusalem*: 'Nowhere in the Torah is there a commandment to believe. Even the Ten Commandments themselves begin with a simple statement of fact: *I am the Lord your God . . .*'

For Mendelssohn, the law upon which Judaism is founded is called *Torah*, always meaning 'teaching' or 'knowledge', never 'faith' or 'belief', and while a Jew must not transgress any of the basic laws of Judaism, he need not believe in anything that is not compatible with his intelligence. If that was the position of a prince among observant Jews 200 years ago, how much more so would it apply to Liberal Judaism today.

But that is only a partial answer. There may be elasticity of belief in Judaism, but as we know, if you belong to the Conservative Party you subscribe to a certain set of political affirmations, if you belong to New Labour, you subscribe to . . . the same set of affirmations; if you are a Marxist, your economic vision is different from that of a capitalist. As it is with politics, so it is with religion. Someone who describes himself as an 'Orthodox' Jew is asserting that the Torah is the revealed will of God, which cannot be altered or modified in the light of changed social circumstances and advancing knowledge.

That is the most obvious difference between Orthodox and Liberal Judaism. But in itself it hardly makes up a manifesto. We come back to the original question: does Liberal Judaism have a core of irreducible, key beliefs? And if so, can we define them, so that people will be able to judge whether or not they are true Liberal Jews? Well, let us try.

Number 1: Liberal Judaism firmly believes in liberalism. That is to say, we stand four-square in support of liberal ideology which, since the Age of Enlightenment, has been distinguished by the importance it attaches to the civil and political rights of individuals, as well as substantial personal freedom, including freedom of conscience, speech, religion, association, occupation and sexuality, provided that those freedoms do not infringe upon the rights of others. That is a carefully thought-out and, I hope, accurate definition of liberalism. If you take exception to all or any part of it, you may worship in a Liberal synagogue, but you are not a Liberal Jew.

Number 2: Liberal Judaism, because it lays such stress on individual rights and personal liberty within the boundaries of the law, firmly believes in the autonomy of the informed conscience. The highest capacity that humans possess is to act as rational beings observing universal moral laws – what the philosopher Immanuel Kant called 'the categorical imperative'. Therefore we follow the teachings of Judaism not through coercion or fear, but by the voluntary consent of our educated conscience.

Number 3: Liberal Judaism firmly believes that Judaism is the best religion for all who are born Jews or wish to become Jews. Note, we do not say 'the best religion' *tout court*, because that would be to denigrate the personal choice of those who follow another religion, which is, presumably, the best for them as Judaism is the best for us. It is the best for us because, given our background, culture, upbringing, history, family ties and genetic inheritance, it is the religious system that most naturally provides us with the inspiration of a noble past, the fellowship of a living community, the pageantry of a colourful cycle of rituals, and a code of moral practice that, in the words of the Psalmist, delights the mind, enlightens the eyes, and revives the soul. Judaism is, for us, sufficient in itself when buttressed with the insights of modern knowledge. Therefore we regard messianic fringe sects, whether Jews For Jesus or Lubavitcher Chasidism, as unhealthy accretions; nor do we encourage attempts to syncretize Judaism with other religions.

Number 4: Liberal Judaism firmly believes that the child of one Jewish parent – irrespective of whether the Jewish parent is the father or the mother – that the child, if brought up as Jewish, should be recognized as Jewish. This, usually but somewhat misleadingly called 'the patrilineal principle', as though the father takes precedence, when in fact it is 'bilineal' or 'equalineal', is the single most important contribution that English Liberal and American Reform Judaism have made to contemporary Jewish life. We have welcomed, and given an entry back into their heritage to, thousands of people who otherwise would have been cut off from Judaism because their father, but not their mother, was Jewish.

Number 5: Liberal Judaism firmly believes that ethical conduct takes precedence over ritual observance. What comes out of the mouth is more important than what goes in. Ritual is meaningless, unless it directs the worshipper towards greater spiritual awareness. Therefore if you want to wear a head-covering all the time, or bow whenever the Ark is opened, then feel free to do so if it consciously directs your thoughts heavenwards. But if it is because everyone else seems to be doing it, so why not you, and every time they come back from a visit to Israel they've got a new little ritual, then recognize it for what it is – simply a folk custom, a sign of ethnic identity, and no more spiritually significant or Jewishly authentic than wearing an MCC tie or standing for the National Anthem.

Number 6: Liberal Judaism firmly believes in universalism above particularism, and that our responsibility to the Jewish people cannot be at the expense of our obligations to all of humanity. Throughout Jewish history there has always been this tension between the description by the biblical writer of Israel as 'a people that dwells alone', and Second Isaiah's vision of Israel as a people that shall be 'a light unto the nations'. Liberal Judaism unhesitatingly allies itself with Isaiah, as a natural corollary of our belief in liberalism. For us, the truth of Israel's message is: One humanity on earth, even as there is one God in heaven.

These, then, are six distinctive beliefs of Liberal Judaism, not shared with Orthodoxy, British Reform or the Masorti movement. Because they are all based on reason, rather than intuition, you might prefer the word 'convictions' or 'affirmations' to that of 'beliefs'. But the terminology is secondary. What counts is that our form of Judaism is liberal, but it is not woolly. It is rational, scholarly, respectful but not nostalgic about Jewish tradition, truthful but not sentimental about Jewish history, and setting honesty in word and deed at the pinnacle of religious observance.

If you wholeheartedly endorse these six beliefs, and share the general approach I have outlined, then you are a Liberal Jew by conviction, not by chance. *B'ruchim ha-ba-im*, welcome to the club, and together let us make it our resolution for the new year to introduce others to the beauties of our heritage as it is lived, taught and practised by Liberal Judaism.

Comments

Jonathan Romain: *'Remarkably provocative sermon asserting the six definitions of Liberal Judaism, not something the listener can walk away from. One of the hallmarks of a good sermon is that it challenges us – perhaps also surprises us or even infuriates us – but it demands a response.'*

Peter Graves: *'A clarion call for Liberal Judaism, clearly and interestingly communicated.'*

Paul Walker: *'Attractive and persuasive definition of Liberal Judaism. Perhaps I enjoyed it because David Goldberg achieved what no other preacher did, he made me laugh out loud. Humour is one of the bedrocks of public speaking. The seeming inability of many preachers to use it is no laughing matter.'*

Bending God's Ear

IMOGEN DE LA BERE

Sermon preached at St Saviour's, St Albans, 12 October 1997.

Imogen de la Bere, 45, is a computer consultant, working for BUPA. Her husband, Jeremy Harding, is also a computer consultant. She obtained her doctorate in English Literature from Canterbury University in Christchurch, New Zealand. They have three children.

Although Imogen was born in Guildford, Surrey she grew up in New Zealand. She and Jeremy moved to St Albans in England in 1995. One of her grandfathers was an Anglican priest, the other a Methodist minister. Her father, a mathematician, is a pillar of the Anglican Church in New Zealand, and helped put together the new, modern prayer book there.

'We had got to the point in our lives where we were so busy, we just felt we needed to get away from New Zealand and do something completely different for a while', she says. If it had been possible when she was younger, she would probably have been ordained, but now considers her vocation to be a writer and preacher. Her first novel, The Last Deception of Palliser Wentwood, *about the possibility of forgiveness, is soon to be published by Jonathan Cape. 'In New Zealand, we have a different system of lay ministry', she says. 'People are not licensed as readers, but as pastoral visitors, or worship leaders, or preachers. I have a preacher's licence.' She preaches regularly at St Saviour's in Sandpit Lane, St Albans, a Victorian church built by Fr Harry Darwin Burton which is still in the Anglo-Catholic tradition.*

Her first preaching experience was a baptism of fire. New Zealand was celebrating the centenary of a famous detective writer, Ngaio Marsh, who had been a member of her parish. The Mass was being broadcast, and because Imogen was a well-known theatre critic, she was asked to preach. 'It went down well', she says. 'When I had finished there was a stunned silence, and then they started to clap. That just never happens in New Zealand. So I thought there must be something in this, and went on to do an academic course in homiletics. I now think of preaching as something I do for the glory of God. It is a vocation, and I take it very seriously.

'What I try to do is to convey the ideas that are in my head. These seem really important to me, but when they are on paper they can seem truly banal. I want to convey an image of glory, and of seeing the world in a different light. I talk about aspects of my own life, and problems of theology,

such as how we should regard the Bible stories, and what happens when we pray. People often get bland answers to these questions, but they really want to hear them thrashed out.'

She believes the Millennium is important in that it is a significant marker. 'It does not mean anything in itself, but we all like anniversaries', she says. 'They give us a fix on life.'

She is grateful she did not have to preach when the Princess of Wales died. 'I am very ambivalent about that whole subject. There is a tendency in this country to live through the lives of celebrities. I think the celebrity culture is very sad in many ways, because most people's lives are so different from the lives of the great, the rich and the glamorous. It makes people unhappy with their own lot. But at the same time it is important for people to have a mythic world, to have icons and heroes, people who are real and yet not real. People have to think whether they are living in the real world, or some mythic world that television and newspapers have created for them.'

Text: Luke 18:1–8.

T HE part of church life that I hate most is not cleaning the brass in the middle of winter or droning through the alto parts of old hymns at choir practice on a Friday night, when the rest of the world is down at the pub. The job around the church I hate most is writing the prayers. 'Let us pray for the world', I write. 'Let us pray for the people of . . .' and here follows a list of the current trouble spots, including generally about twenty or thirty million people. End of prayer.

How can that be an effective prayer? What is the value in pointing out to God that his people in Papua New Guinea are starving? Presumably God knows that better than we do. The starving people are praying to him for survival, the missionaries and teachers in Papua New Guinea are praying night and day for aid and strength. Their prayers are surely strong enough and relevant enough for God. What's the point in me standing up here and saying: 'Let us pray for the starving people of Papua New Guinea'?

A more honest prayer might be: 'Dear Lord, you know perfectly well, rather better than we do, where all the problems are, and you also know what you are going to do with them, so please get on and do it, and let us know when we can help.' There's precious little we can do to stop people in Rwanda tearing each other to bits. We don't know what God is going to do, we don't know how he's going to do it, and we don't even know, in fact, if he's going to do anything at all.

Sometimes it's tempting to feel that praying isn't going to do much good, isn't going to change God's mind or interfere with fate. Right now, many Christian parents in Papua New Guinea will be praying fervently that their children don't die, but some children, many children, will die. Did God fail to hear the prayers of their parents? People huddled in a church in Rwanda know their racial enemies are closing in to slaughter them – surely those people prayed passionately for deliverance? Was God deaf to those prayers? It would seem so.

And yet we are told the opposite in no uncertain terms in today's Gospel. We heard this: Jesus told the disciples a parable about the need to pray continually and never lose heart. Even the unjust judge is finally worn down by the widow's constant badgering. How much more therefore will the Father of justice and mercy be prepared to be swayed by constant petition? Jesus, the story continues, goes so far as to say, 'Will not God see justice done to his chosen who cry to him day and night? I promise you God will see justice done to them and done speedily' (Luke 18:1).

So here we have a clear statement in scripture from Jesus himself that God answers prayers. An unequivocal statement, not just that God hears prayers or takes note of them, but that he answers them and sees justice done, and that banging on about something has its effect on the Almighty. And yet at the same time, we have evidence around us all the time that praying does not save people from misery and death. It would be hard to believe in a God who answers prayers as your children die in your arms, one by one.

The answer to this terrible paradox lies in the way God answers prayer. God has given up on thunderbolts, even if he ever used them. God doesn't throw up miraculous walls of flame around the people huddled praying in the church to repel the murderers. God doesn't conveniently hand out a miracle every time someone prays for deliverance. We all think we'd like it if he did. But the implications are absurd and ridiculous. Under this scheme, if I get cancer and pray for deliverance, God promptly cures me. I break my back; I pray and God cures me. I get arthritis and God doesn't think that's quite bad enough, so he leaves me to put up with it. That's not fair, I cry, you fixed up the other things, why make me put up with this? When would God ever be able to stop saving us? If every time a band of bad men went out to rape and kill, God got in their way, what sort of bizarre Walt Disney sort of world would we be living in? We would be automata, coddled dummies. And we'd still find plenty of things to demand of God. 'I've got a bad cold today, Lord, and it's the flower festival so please get rid of it, thank you!'

But God does answer prayer. Terrible things are brought to an end. After centuries of praying and weeping and longing, the slaves in America went free. The Vietnamese army poured into Cambodia and put an end to the killing fields. The peacekeepers marched into Rwanda and the slaughter was stopped. Little boys born in poverty in England no longer climb up chimneys for a living.

God does answer prayer. But he uses human beings to do it. We have to do the work, and sometimes that takes a while. It took years to destroy Hitler and his minions. In the meantime millions died, but at the end the evil was wiped out. Can anyone believe that God watched millions die without wanting to act? The same God who in the person of his son Jesus experienced the extremity of suffering, who cried at the moment of death, 'My God, my God, why have you forsaken me?' This God, this God who was in Jesus, knows what it is to stand naked in the gas chamber. How much he must have longed to sweep the Allied soldiers through Europe unopposed and fling open the doors of the death camps. But human beings must do the work of God on earth. Ordinary soldiers fight battles, and politicians sit at tables and do deals. Business people organize relief; ordinary consumers refuse to buy shoes from sweatshops. You write a letter that Amnesty International has suggested and a prisoner is freed. This year, Mahlo came from South Africa and spoke to us here, and children and teachers in her school will be given the help they need. This is how God answers prayers. We do it.

So am I suggesting that petitioning God is simply a way of reminding ourselves what we need to do? Of pricking our own consciences? That we pray for Mahlo and that reminds us to put a pound in the jar? Someone prays for the victims of the famine in Papua New Guinea and someone else hears the prayer and decides to get on the phone to his cousin in Australia who grows rice? Just that simple? Cause and effect? A sort of self-regulating system, in which God does nothing at all except sit in the background and occasionally pat us on the head? I don't think so. Because if that were so, what would be the point of most of these prayers? No one here has a relative in Australia with a rice farm, so we can safely forget about praying for the famine. For its entire lifetime the people of God, assembled together, have prayed for things outside their direct control. 'We beseech thee to have mercy upon all prisoners and captives, all women labouring with child.' Have all those Christians for all those centuries been barking up the wrong tree? And what about those exceptional and wonderful people who spend their whole lives in prayer? Religious who pray as their job, not just contemplative prayer, but hours of intercessory prayer? No one is listening except God. Are they wasting their time?

And what about us – those stabs of prayer we send out when we hear or read of someone in trouble? I see a man lying bleeding in the street. His coat is soaked with blood, but the paramedics are there, the ambulance doors are open. I do not rush to his aid, but I cry out to God for his safety. Should I save my energy, since I can do nothing material to help?

The answer is this: these are the wrong questions. The questions should be: How can we *not* cry out to God for our sisters and brothers in need? How can we call ourselves human beings and children of God, if we do not bring the pain of the world into the presence of our father, who is Love himself? Sometimes we will be able to act; sometimes we will be able to influence others to act; sometimes we can do nothing. Not to pray because we are powerless to act is a form of cowardice.

For remember, it is to *God* that our prayers are addressed, not to each other. To pray for something – a person, a place, a country, peace talks, famine relief – is to see the person, the place, the situation held in the hands of God. Such an act of praying – to see the person or cause held in the hands of God – is the simplest and at the same time the most powerful thing we can do. In fact, it is the *only* thing we can do. We do not understand what God will do, nor how our prayers will be translated into human action. We do not understand God, but we may contemplate him.

And when we try to see those for whom we are praying wrapped in the love of God, intercessory prayer becomes, not a shopping list for God's attention, but an act of worship. Because that is the essential nature of prayer: communion with God. We used to be taught that prayer falls into two kinds – contemplative and intercessory. But the distinction is artificial. Contemplating God and bringing needs before him are part of the same act – you can't ask God for things without coming into his presence, without contemplating his nature and laying yourself open before him. So the people who mix the prayers of petition in with prayers of adoration are doing it right, and when I sit down to my chore of writing petitions, without any attempt at addressing the nature of God, I am doing it wrong. Prayers, no matter when or where, are one half of a conversation with God. We don't ring up a friend and say: 'Hello, it's me here. I need to borrow your lawnmower. I'll be round at two' and then put down the phone. Nor should we say: 'Dear God, help the people in Papua New Guinea and pretty soon too. Amen.' To pray for them we hold the suffering people in the hands of God, and know that he suffers too.

And we look on God and are silent.

Comments

Paul Walker: *'It must have been a great relief to her hearers to discover that she finds praying hard. Excellent sermon which tries less to provide answers and more to help us see things in a different way. She is bringing to her hearers that huge theological debate about if and how God answers prayers without getting bogged down in complicated language.'*

Kieran Conry: *'Striking introduction and well developed. The central theme of prayer and what we are trying to achieve by it is directly and honestly faced. The questions that I ask are all asked, and in the end an honest and inspiring answer is given.'*

Peter Graves: *'Sensitive, thought-provoking and balanced sermon on the use of prayer, helpfully illustrated and clearly developed. Perhaps too much emphasis on the problem of prayer rather than on its power and relevance.'*

Pictures that Last:
A Sermon for Advent

REV. JIM REA

Sermon preached 1 December 1996.

The Rev. Jim Rea, 53, is Superintendent of the East Belfast Mission. He and his wife Carol have two daughters and a son. This is the second time Mr Rea has made the shortlist of 30 in The Times *Preacher of the Year Award. He was one of the preachers invited to Jamaica as a result. His Belfast mission lies in the heartland of Ulster Loyalism.*

Mr Rea, Chairman of the Belfast District of the Methodist Church, was brought up in a working-class Presbyterian home in Belfast. He was ordained in 1970 and the Mission is his third posting. 'I became a Christian when I was a teenager, through attending a Pentecostal church', he says. 'My conversion came about when I attended a Watchnight service at the end of the old year. I was listening to the preacher and thought "There's another year ahead and what am I doing with my life?" I simply prayed a prayer of commitment to Christ, and became a Christian.' He left school at 15, joined the Methodist Church in his late teens after finding it friendly and inclusive, and went to night classes after his working day in a clothing factory had ended, to study for the ministry.

His Mission has a hostel for homeless people and a counselling service for alcoholics and others with various needs and difficulties. There is a restaurant, a job centre and a homework club for 'latchkey kids'. Meals are delivered daily to the local housebound.

But much of his work at the Mission, which is near the docklands in inner-city East Belfast and where the walls are covered with painted murals depicting Loyalist slogans, is concerned with working for peace. His church is 200 yards from the headquarters of the Progressive Unionist Party, the political confidant of the Ulster Volunteer Force. And just 100 yards away is the border of a strongly Republican area. Of the many funerals he has conducted, a distressingly large number have been for people killed in the troubles. Methodist ministers are usually expected to relocate regularly, but Mr Rea's work is considered so valuable that he has been given special permission to stay in East Belfast for at least 20 years.

'I am very interested in reconciliation in Northern Ireland', he says. He is involved in several initiatives to reach across the community divide, and has been active in dialogue with paramilitaries on both sides, helping with

liaison on the Loyalist side. 'Those of us who are committed to peace, and there is a group of Christians like myself who truly are, have really tried to talk to people, to build bridges between people who are divided', he says. 'I am talking constantly to the Orangemen. We do not do this on behalf of anybody except ourselves. If you do it on behalf of others, you are seen as an agent for them. I act as an individual, because that is the best thing to do. The peace process is fraught with difficulties but we hope and pray that it will work.'

His church has a congregation of about 240. 'I think there is something special about preaching', he says. 'Despite all the other means of communication, I think it still has a vital part to play in the communication of the Christian faith. As a preacher, I do not think I am a great theologian. What I try to do is to take the profound things of the Christian faith and simply put them into the language of the newspapers, the language that people understand.'

He adds: 'I am hoping when I preach that people will connect with Jesus Christ. There is unease about the Preacher of the Year competition and I can understand that. I do not preach in order to win a competition. I am simply trying to achieve some excellence, to present what I believe to a community or people who may not otherwise read or hear what I have to say.'

Mr Rea also works as a religious presenter for Downtown Radio, a leading commercial radio station in Northern Ireland.

He believes the Millennium is an important Christian festival. 'It is vital that Christians celebrate and affirm it', he says. 'It would be very easy for it to become like Christmas, where the Christian element is entirely lost. It is also a reminder to us that we live in the modern world, where things are changing fast. Christians need to keep up-to-date in terms of getting the message across.'

The Princess of Wales was, for him, 'a wonderful person'. He says: 'The way the British public reacted to her death, which seemed almost to have some religious significance, suggested an inherent, deep need for spirituality, a deep quest for something, as if there is a vacuum in society that the Church is failing to fill.'

Text: Philippians 2:7–10.

M Y EARLIEST memories of Christmas are of Christmas Eve and my father trying to creep into the house without me seeing the presents that were supposed to come from Santa Claus. I will never forget those Christmas Days of the 1950s, with Wilfred Pickles on the radio. Christmas morning didn't involve any church-going for me; instead we went to the Steel & Sons Cup Final at Cliftonville, a traditional football match in North Belfast. I am often fascinated by these, my memories and the vivid word-pictures that come into my mind as I look back. There's really something about the power of the mind to create images. A homeless man I know is an avid follower of Rangers.

When he was in our hostel he would often go to his room with a small radio, to tune in to the football. One day when I heard that the Rangers match was on television, I said to my friend: 'I suppose you'll be watching the Rangers today?' To which he retorted in a broad Glaswegian accent: 'Na, I'll listen to it. Rangers play better on the radio.'

The power of imagery is every bit as remarkable when it comes to Christianity, and for me the Christian faith is rooted in three great images. When I think of Jesus Christ I often think of three pictures and these supersede all the glitz and imagery of this season.

The manger

The manger is always part of the Christmas celebration. It is the place where Jesus Christ was born and speaks strongly of the God who is with us. Quoting Matthew, it says: 'The virgin will be with child and will give birth to a son, and they will call him Emmanuel', which means 'God with us'. The fact that God became human in Jesus Christ offers tremendous comfort that God is not removed from us. God in Jesus becomes one of us in a remarkable way. This is God's way of getting alongside us in our joys and also in our sorrows.

A young woman I know well whose husband was tragically murdered in the troubles here in Northern Ireland would often say to me: 'If I didn't feel that God was with me in all of this pain, I'd crack up.'

Taking human form is how Paul puts it: '. . . but made himself nothing, taking the very nature of a servant, being made in human likeness' (Phil 2:7).

It's all very miraculous, but it's vitally important that we have a God who is not removed but who is down where we are, truly nearer than hand or foot. That is why he was called Emmanuel. This thought is put poignantly by the poet and hymn-writer John Oxenham:

> For Christ is more than all the creeds
> And his full life of gentle deeds
> Shall all the creeds outlive.
> Not what I do believe but whom,
> Who walks beside me in the gloom;
> Who shares the burden wearisome;
> Who all the dim way doth illume
> And bids me look beyond the tomb
> The larger life to live.
> Not what I do believe but whom.

The cross

The story of Christmas does not end in the birth of a baby; there is the cross. While it may be out of season, you cannot separate the manger from the cross. The cross tells us that God is for us. It is the apostle Paul who says: 'Who, being in very nature God, did not consider equality with God something to be grasped, but made himself nothing, taking the very nature of a servant, being made in human likeness' (Phil 2:6–7). God's Valentine to us is in two shafts of wood, declaring 'I love you'. The cross has so many facets that it is impossible even to begin to comprehend.

It is essentially the most amazing way that God shows his love to humankind.

A story that originates in the United States is that of two young men growing up in a community together as firm friends. However, life went differently for them. One sadly became involved in crime, while the other became successful in the legal profession and ended up as a judge. One day they faced each other across a courtroom. The offender had committed a serious act of fraud. His friend the judge recognized a need to do right by the law, so he greatly shocked his childhood pal when he fined him the highest amount for the crime committed. Moments later the judge went to the centre of the court and paid the fine for his friend.

In such an act of generosity both justice and mercy were fully affirmed.

God's act on the cross is much more remarkable. Jesus is our representative. One aspect of the cross is that Jesus takes upon himself death as a way of sharing in our judgement. Therefore God forgives us. God is the judge who must punish our sins, but Jesus is the one who makes himself available, which in a remarkable way makes forgiveness possible.

The empty tomb
Then there is the empty tomb. This points us to a God who is before us and symbolizes resurrection. Jesus rose from the dead. When Christians celebrate Christmas they are not just commemorating some historical or mystical event, but they are worshipping the living Christ. It is not out of context that in a Christmas carol James Montgomery should emphasize the power of the risen Christ:

> Though an infant now we view him,
> He shall fill his father's throne,
> Gather all the nations round him;
> Every knee shall then bow down.

Despite modern medical science, with its advances giving some of us hope of longer life, death in the end cannot be avoided. That's what makes the risen Jesus relevant to everyone. The truth is that Jesus has gone before us. He is in the advance party and that means that death has been defeated by him. The consequences of this experience need no longer be feared. The outcome of his rising is for the benefit of all humankind. For Christians he has defeated death and makes eternal life possible. It is Jesus who says: 'I go to prepare a place for you.'

Just over three years ago on a beautiful Sunday afternoon my brother-in-law died suddenly over the wheel of his car on Belfast's Shore Road. I will never forget looking at his earthly remains lying in the ambulance. That afternoon stark reality faced me. Bobby was seven years younger than I was. I thought of my sister and my two little nieces. Life is tough. What sense is there in all of this, I thought. Such experiences do make Christmas a sad time. Old friends are missing around the table on Christmas Day.

Yet these images of hope enable us to press on. The manger, the cross and the empty tomb affirm to us again and again God's wonderful love. A love in every situation and in every age, making sense of life and giving hope for the future.

A few years ago a woman told me how sad she was when gifts she had sent to members of her family for Christmas were returned unopened. Sometimes that's what we do with God's greatest gift of love, we return it unopened instead of gratefully receiving what it all really means in that humble spirit of repentance; turning the dark days of December into the true cheer of Christmas and beyond. It is the familiar words of Benjamin R. Hanby that offer a timeless relevance to all that Jesus has done and is doing:

> Who is He, in yonder stall,
> At whose feet the shepherds fall?
> Who is He, in Calvary's throes
> Asks for blessings on his foes?
> Who is He, who from the grave
> Comes to heal and help, and save?
> Tis the Lord! O wondrous story!
> Tis the Lord! the King of glory!
> At His feet we humbly fall;
> Crown Him, crown Him Lord of all.

Comments

Kieran Conry: *'A very personal piece with conviction and sincerity running through it. A somewhat novel approach to Advent and Christmas that works well.'*

Peter Graves: *'An excellent Advent sermon that gets to the heart of the Gospel in a simple, clear and well-illustrated way.'*

Paul Walker: *'It is difficult not to sound stale when talking about Christmas, but this appears fresh and you realize that the preacher is still excited about the Christmas story.'*

Hope for Hereafter

NIGEL FREESTONE

Sermon preached on 9 November 1997 at Holbeach Baptist Church, Catford.

Nigel Freestone, aged 50, married to Veronica, a medical secretary, is a self-employed computer consultant and a member of Woolwich Central Baptist Church in south London. He is a member of the London Baptist Preachers' Association, which supplies preachers to churches without a minister of their own, and is invited to preach at different churches about once a month.

Mr Freestone was brought up in a Christian family, spending his childhood in the Congo, where his parents were missionaries. He had a conversion experience in about 1965, when a Christian friend at work challenged him on the fundamentals of his faith. 'Things that my parents had taught me and that I had known for quite a while suddenly came to life in a new way. I decided Christianity was for me and made a commitment.'

He did his first preaching in the late 1960s, when he was a member of a Christian music group. They would play in different youth clubs and Mr Freestone, the lead singer, would say a few words at the end. At the time, he was described as 'a rough version of Mick Jagger'. 'You don't get much rougher than that', he says. He would sometimes be asked to contribute in his own church, and his commitment to preaching grew from there. 'The minister formed a preaching and worship group, and those of us who were interested could have a go.'

He believes preaching still fulfils a need. 'Most people, even if they read the Bible, like to have some sort of explanation of what they have read', he says. 'The Bible is important in people's lives and it is certainly important in church life. The preacher's role is to bring out of the Bible what may be relevant for the life of the church at that particular time and to challenge people to live up to the demands it makes on them. Sometimes preaching can be a bit confrontational, it can be a hard challenge. Other times, preaching encourages and builds people up. But preachers have to make people think about what God's requirements are, and encourage them to live in the light of that.'

Mr Freestone, whose church is not far from Greenwich and the Millennium Dome, has strong views on the Millennium. 'The whole point about the Millennium is that it is a celebration of Jesus Christ', he says. 'Its only significance is that it is 2,000 years since the birth of Jesus, or since our best guess

of when the birth of Jesus was. So Jesus has to be central to the whole Mil-
lennium celebration, otherwise it just becomes another day in the week. I am
excited by the possibility that the church can take this and make something
of it, and show that Jesus is still relevant to the world, even after 2,000 years.'

He believes the death of Diana touched people because it brought home to
them their own mortality in a new way. 'Here was someone who was giving
a lot and who had plans for dealing with some of the important problems in
the world, such as landmines, and yet she was suddenly taken away from us.
Many people felt completely powerless. It was something the church could,
and in many cases, did take up, that there is hope, over and above this life. A
lot of people were searching for that sense of goodness personified that they
saw in Diana, and suddenly she was taken away from them. What I would
say is that goodness personified is to be found in Jesus Christ, and to point
people in that direction.'

Text: 1 Corinthians 15.

Y OU wait.
The darkness gathers about you. The blues of evening fade into
the black of night. The city is hushed and still. Those who ply their
business in these streets in daylight have gone. Home to wives, and
children, and beds. But you wait.

Above you the façade of the old railway station towers up into the
night sky. But the trains don't run anymore. No one arrives now. No
one departs. Yet, you wait.

You are not alone, others wait too. Huddled in twos and threes you
nervously whisper in subdued tones. A distant bell monotonously
chimes another hour. And still you wait.

Suddenly, the figure of a pale-faced, black-cloaked Victorian under-
taker complete with top hat materializes from the shadows. Abruptly,
all conversation ceases. You cannot doubt what you are seeing, everyone has noticed him. It's almost as though he is real. All eyes are on
him. He glides towards you. Instinctively, you step back, away.

What happens now? What does this ghostly apparition want? You
don't have long to wait. He speaks.

'OK everyone, it's £4.00 for adults, and £3.00 for students, children
and OAPs.'

You breathe again. Someone giggles. It is not what you feared. This
is your guide for the evening, but he is no spirit. You are about to start
the Ghost Walk, one of the guided tours through the back streets and
alleys of several of our major cities, visiting the sites of grisly and ghostly events of the distant, and not so distant, past. Ghosts, it seems, are
good business.

But how should we respond to stories like that of the Hooded Monk
who stalks through a London graveyard, or of a platoon of Roman

soldiers marching through a York stately mansion wall? What of those who claim to have been visited by a loved one or a friend only to discover later that their visitor was, at the moment of their appearing, dying in some accident miles away?

Perhaps many such stories have rational explanations. A surprising number, it seems, do not.

Whatever the answers, the story nevertheless raises a number of questions.

What really happens when we die? Where, if anywhere, are our friends and loved ones who have already died? Is there anything beyond this life? Or is death the end? Perhaps most importantly for each of us personally, what happens to me when I die? Can we ever know the answers to these kinds of questions?

A recent national opinion poll revealed that about half those questioned believe that death is simply the end. There is nothing else. There is no afterlife, no heaven, no hell, nothing. Death is the finish. Or, to use a colloquial expression, like a candle when you die you 'snuff' it. A smaller number of people, the national opinion poll reported, believe that there is some sort of life after death, but most of those questioned were not clear about the nature of this life. Like a blown-out candle from which smoke continues to rise, life after death is somehow vague, misty, ethereal and insubstantial. Without a real body or purpose the soul gently mixes with the universe until personality ceases to exist.

However, a growing number of people, young people particularly, the poll found, believe in reincarnation. Another real life to come, not unlike this one. Like the children's magic birthday candles, when the flame of this life is extinguished shortly afterwards a new flame, a new life, springs up in its place.

But is this the best that we can hope for? Another life like this one? Another opportunity to do better, or another chance to perhaps fail. Another chance to love and succeed, but also another round of weakness and pain and sorrow. Another turn on the treadmill, on and on, life after death, after life, after death, after life . . .

If I quote a well-known scripture to you, doubtless many of you will be able to complete it: 'Faith, hope and love abide, these three, but the . . . '? Yes, that's right '. . . but the greatest of these is love' (1 Cor 13:13).

David Pawson in one of his books deliberately misquotes the verse. 'Faith, Hope and Love abide, these three, but the *weakest* of these is Hope.' How strong is our hope in the face of life's calamities and disasters? Do we only have hope while we can sit in a warm church on a Sunday evening, have a good job to go to in the morning, enough money in the bank to meet the bills, and have good relationships with friends and family? Where is our hope when the job is gone, when we cannot make ends meet, when our relationships fail, or when we stand by a friend's graveside or lie in a hospice bed anticipating our own end? Christianity has never tried to hide the fact that death is real. We may put off thinking about it, we may choose to ignore it, but death comes to us all. As a wag once said, 'There are only two things certain in life: death and taxes!' Christianity has always been honest about death because at the very heart of the Christian faith there is death, a particular death. Paul reminds us in the scripture passage we read together (v. 1ff.) that at the very centre of the gospel there is the death of Jesus. He really did live and he really did die. He was crucified and buried. It is a fundamental part of the gospel, the Good News, we have believed and preach. Not only does he remind us that it happened, but he says that it is 'according to the Scriptures' (v. 3). Jesus' death was not a ghastly mistake, something unexpected, but actually part of God's plan that he had revealed long beforehand, foretold in the Scriptures.

But also central to the gospel is resurrection, rising from the dead. Not only did Jesus die, but he came alive again. Good Friday has the cross, but it means nothing without the events of Easter Day! He is risen from the dead. This too Paul reminds us is 'according to the Scriptures' (v. 4). Again, it was not an afterthought by God, designed to work around what men had done to his Son, but central to his purpose from the beginning. The evidence was there to be seen (v. 4ff.). There were those who witnessed the resurrection. Peter, James, the twelve together, even as many as 500 at one time, finally Paul himself. Some of these eye-witnesses had died, Paul admits, but most were still alive as he wrote. Implication – don't just take my word for it, go and ask them, check it out for yourself. For us today these eye-witnesses are now dead. But we still have the evidence of their accounts. There are those who have sorted through the evidence and presented it clearly for us, like Frank Morison in his book *Who Moved the Stone?* The challenge of Paul's implication remains. Check it out!

Given this wealth of evidence, Paul spells out the consequences (v. 12ff.). If Christ has not been raised we have no hope. If Christ has not been raised from the dead, we are still in our sins, our preaching is useless, our faith futile, we have lied about God, and our dead loved ones are lost and gone for ever.

But Jesus has been raised, he is alive, the sacrifice of the cross has been accepted, God has proved it by raising Jesus from the dead. The tomb is empty. He has been seen, and held, and worshipped and spoken with, by the disciples. They have been transformed from frightened, cowering nobodies into people who turned the world upside down with this Good News. Two thousand years later we still sing: 'Up from the grave he arose!' Sin and death are defeated. Therefore there is a life hereafter, there is resurrection available for us too. So naturally, we want to know what it will be like.

When Jesus was raised he was still the same. Still recognizable by and known to his disciples. But he was also different, he had a new glorious body. He was at once the same and radically changed. For us, some aspects of death remain. This body will certainly die (unless Jesus comes again first). The candle really will go out, but when it does a new, glorious, wonderful, magnificent life begins in its place. No more pain or weakness, tears wiped away, sickness and sin in all their forms banished for ever. But what kind of bodies will we have? The clues we are given are limited, so it's hard to say exactly, but an illustration may help.

When I am visiting smaller churches as I do from time to time, I have noticed that there may not always be flowers at the front of the church. They are an expensive luxury not every church can afford. So, today, just in case, I have taken the liberty of bringing along a few of my own. The wrapping clearly states that they are 'one-foot high Californian multicoloured poppies'. Now, let's see . . . well, frankly, I am disappointed. Anyone can see they are nothing like a foot high, and a simple inspection shows that they are all the same shade of brown.

'You stupid boy!' (as Mr Mainwaring of *Dad's Army* would say). Of course these are not the flowers, these are only the seeds. Put them in the ground, bury them, like a dead body, and they grow and bloom and the promise on the packet is proved to be true. Paul uses the same illustration in this chapter (v. 38). He points out what we all know, that when the seed dies a transformation takes place.

Notice two things.

The transformation is total and complete. To the unskilled eye there is no similarity between the seed and the flower. One is small, plain and insignificant, the other large and beautiful. So too with our bodies. This body is weak and helpless. Prone to disease and failure and sin. Paul calls it 'perishable, dishonoured, weak, natural' (v. 42). Then, we will have a new body, 'imperishable, glorious, powerful, spiritual'. We are told that when we see Jesus we shall be like him. Elsewhere, the scripture teaches that 'eye has not seen, nor ear heard, neither has it even entered into the mind of men what good things God has prepared for those who love him'. The egg is broken, but the bird soars on the wind; the chrysalis hangs dry and empty, while the butterfly flies free; the seed dies but the flower blooms, in cascades of rainbow shades; the candle flame flickers and dies only to burst into a thousand watts. What will it be like? The transformation will be total, complete, unimaginably different.

However, there is a direct link between the seed and the flower, between now and then. Plant these seeds and the promise is you'll get foot-high multi-coloured Californian poppies. But if what you really want are cabbages, or oak trees, these seeds are no good to you. Jesus told us: 'What a man sows, that is what he will reap.' You and I are immortal beings. Eternity awaits. God has created us with a dimension of our being that survives what we call death to take part in another transformed life beyond. A new life with all the possibility and promise God himself has invested in it. But the choice and preparation of the seed he has left for us. What you and I will be then, is determined by what we choose to be now.

Where are my loved ones? Is there hope as I stand by a friend's grave? Paul encourages us and then urges us to encourage each other. Jesus is raised from the dead, heaven is open, new life with new bodies awaits. Our loved ones who have died in the Lord are safe with Him. Heaven is not like walking into a new school on the first day of term. Heaven is becoming populated with those I know and love. Whether I will be there to join them one day depends on the seeds I develop now. Seed that bears fruit for God's kingdom, or not. How are yours? Let's pray . . .

Comments

Peter Graves: *'Well-developed ideas clearly related to the biblical material, contemporary belief and the need for an appropriate response.'*

Paul Walker: *'I admired this sermon for its daring. To talk about the resurrection is one thing but to deal with its nature is a brave act. Deals honestly from the point that most people find themselves on this issue, namely ghosts and reincarnation.'*

Jonathan Romain: *'Ends well, and culminates with a dramatic question that demands a response.'*

The Unfinished Symphony

REV. MERVYN ROBERTS

Sermon preached at St Mary's, Warwick on 22 February 1998.

The Rev. Mervyn Roberts, 43, is team vicar of the Collegiate Church of St Mary, St Nicholas Parish Church and Christ Church, Woodloes Park, in Warwick. He is also Religious Affairs Correspondent for BBC Radio Coventry in Warwickshire. He has responsibility for St Nicholas Church in Warwick. His wife, Sue, is a schoolteacher and they have two children.

Mr Roberts has been ordained for seven years. Previously, he taught music for ten years after doing his first degree at Birmingham and studying music as a postgraduate at Cambridge. He has a background in cathedral music, having sung as a chorister at Plympton St Mary's in Devon, and as a counter-tenor at Birmingham Cathedral.

He has been a Christian all his life. His family background is partly Plymouth Brethren, and although as a child he attended a traditional Anglican church, he was sent to a Brethren-run Sunday School.

'I did feel a vocation to teach and I enjoyed teaching very much', he says. 'That was the foundation for moving into a new area, the ministry. That was a long process that happened in my mid-thirties. I felt I was being led. But the experience of the actual vocation was quite sudden. I just woke up in the middle of the night and had this strange experience. I like to think of myself as a saner-than-rational person, and my Christian make-up would be described as liberal. But this was certainly a deep, spiritual experience that is very hard to explain. It was like a nervous energy. I just felt a calling.'

He agrees it could almost be compared, in some ways, to Samuel being called in the night by God. 'I just could not rest. The worst thing was plucking up the courage to tell my wife.'

Established now as a preacher, he finds his main critics are indeed his family. 'What is very important is to engage with the congregation and raise questions they can chew on, rather than being didactic. I see it as exploring, as going on a spiritual journey with them.

'Preaching has a very important part to play in the church, but it is more than proclaiming a message by word of mouth. Even though I put the sermon together, I always hope the congregation will participate. It is a two-way communication, in the same way that radio is. Hopefully, there is thinking going on at both ends.'

Perhaps because of his communications skills (he was involved with cable television on behalf of the Birmingham Diocese before moving to Warwick) he is unusually focused on the Millennium. For him it is not a future event, but something happening now. 'The important thing is to do the ground-work', he says. 'The Millennium is an important event, an important marker. It worries me a bit that people talk of doing something when the Millennium comes. We should be doing things now.' In keeping with this spirit, his parish church has this year for the third year running won the Warwick town carnival with its float, on which he, naturally, played God, and which had as its theme: 'He's got the whole world in his hands'. Mr Roberts says: 'St Nicholas is very much a church in the community and for the community.' In the last two years, the congregation at the morning services has almost doubled.

He was also actively involved in church events connected with the death of the Princess of Wales. Radio 1 broadcast the service at St Nicholas on the Sunday morning after her death. 'I heard about it early in the morning and went to the radio station', he says. 'I went back home and rewrote my sermon completely to fit what was required after such a shock. A chap from Radio 1 came wandering through the church and asked if he could record the service. There was this feeling of togetherness at that time, not just in Warwick but across the entire nation, a feeling of shared grief. I want to ask a lot of questions now about how a nation, a world, reacts to such a shocking event that no one is at all prepared for. The media want to go and go and go, to get every last drop of emotional energy out of it. But perhaps it is something that needs to be left, to be dropped for a while. People need time to reflect without the media doing the work for them.'

[Sermon opens with extract from first movement of the Elgar Third Symphony which then fades out.]

> . . . the symphony all bits and pieces . . . no one would understand
> . . . no one . . . no one.
>
> W. H. Reed, *Elgar As I Knew Him* (Victor Gollancz)

THESE were the anguished words of a great English composer as he realized that his last major composition, a large four-movement symphony, would be left unfinished. That man, Sir Edward Elgar, had just been diagnosed as having cancer, and within a few weeks he would be dead.

The news of his illness came as a bitter blow to Elgar because the particular large-scale composition he was working on was going to be something very special. Since the death of his wife, 13 years earlier, Elgar had written no major work of any consequence. But in his old age Elgar had at last turned again to his manuscript paper and pen, and slowly and painfully had begun to jot down his ideas: an opening melody fully scored for orchestra, some tunes here and there marked for particular instruments. Some rhythmic ideas, basic chord progressions as well as a few fully complete passages. Unlike writing a book, Elgar didn't compose starting at the beginning and working through each movement in turn, first, second, third and fourth. No, it was more like the construction of a jigsaw with different ideas put down in a higgledy-piggledy way, ideas that would eventually be formed and fused into a single great work.

At the time of his death however, Elgar's last great swan song was indeed unfinished . . . yes . . . 'all bits and pieces . . . no one would understand' . . . or would they?

Sixty years on from Elgar's death and a composer called Anthony Payne, a devotee of Elgar's music, was given permission to begin the task of restoring, or should I say resurrecting, the great man's final musical sketches into a symphony. Several years of hard work have now given us this music.

What would Elgar make of it? That's a question the answer of which we will never know. But one thing we can say: what were mere scratchings on manuscript paper have now come alive as music, beautiful music to enrich our ears and touch our hearts. Inspiring music that, dare I say, sounds and feels like Elgar. A new creation, with wonderful melodies and harmonies in the style of Elgar.

This all came alive before a studio and radio audience just a few days ago. What was lost is now found, what was dead is now alive. The wonderful achievement of bringing to life a piece of music, creating something beautiful out of sketches and ideas that seemed buried for ever is also something we Christians are called to do with our lives. Everyone of us is called to create, or should I say re-create.

But what are the materials, the rough and ready jottings, the ideas that motivate the creative passages on which we can build and construct a life that gives glory to God in a complete and consistent way – to fashion a life for God that is shaped and formed to his will rather than a life of 'bits and pieces'?

Paul's advice in Romans is for us to be a 'living sacrifice', not to 'conform to the pattern of the world but to be transformed by the renewing of your mind'.

Firstly, as with anyone reconstructing or restoring a work of art, whether it is a piece of music, painting or a play, one has to honestly admit that we will never know if we are fulfilling exactly the wishes of the original creator. Once we are humble enough to acknowledge this, the art of recreating can begin. For a work of art to really come alive, to be something more than an act of preservation, it requires a creator and a devotee, a disciple who will, through years of commitment, be in touch with his master's stylistic approach but, crucially, will bring something of themselves into the work. We can see it in stone, in this very building, where modern craftsmen will sculpture a face or a figure, using the style and technique of their medieval forebears, and yet the sculpture is new.

In order for Elgar's music to come alive it needed someone who was imbued with the spirit of Elgar, someone who could catch a glimpse of Elgar's vision for the work. Someone who not only had the skill to complete this work but could as a fellow-composer empathize with the struggles of his illustrious predecessor and, most importantly of all, share in creating something new by contributing something of himself to the work.

This kind of partnership can be seen in the writings that make up much of the Bible. A whole library of books, bound under a single cover, conveying a creative partnership between God and humanity. To give an example of this we need look no further than the Gospels, those books that were written to present us with the Good News of Jesus Christ. The Gospels of Jesus reflect something of the individual writers' minds at work, each one in their own particular way bringing to our attention a perspective on the life, death and resurrection of Jesus Christ to the reader.

From the sketches, rough notes and stories of eye-witnesses the picture that dominates and shapes the Gospel according to Mark is one of the Suffering Servant, who through pain and suffering, the way of the cross, will ultimately bring us to victory. With similar but more extended material Matthew gives to us the Messiah confirmed, promised, foretold by the prophets of the past. There is a sense of continuity that values the past but carries us forward into a future in which we will be in God's hands. Luke enables us to identify with a Jesus who cares for all. The Jesus who responds to the individual and presents us with a God who cares for us and loves us as a Father loves his son.

And finally from later sources the writer of John presents us with the Christ of faith, showing the influence of Greek ideas in shaping the picture of Jesus as the living eternal work of God enfleshed in Christ the Divine *logos*. More thoughtfully woven around a series of great themes, life and death, light and darkness, truth, love, peace and so on. John's Gospel truly reflects the coming together of the Divine spark of inspiration and the responding creative mind of a mortal.

Just as each Gospel gives us an individual and unique perspective on the person of Jesus Christ, so to with other biblical books, we are introduced to the actions and words of God in a multitude of ways. Stories, historical records, poetry and prose are ways in which the writers in each of their generations have tried to creatively interpret the raw materials of feelings, thoughts and ideas that are the foundations of our faith.

Jesus' call to follow his example and obey his command to 'Love one another as I have loved you' is just one of many melodic fragments the Gospel writers and others have set down for us. Are we able, or rather, are we willing to play our part in orchestrating 'something beautiful' that captures and conveys the spirit of our Lord? We are not all called to be in partnership with God through the using of our artistic talents, or through the reading of books, listening on a hi-fi system, or regular visits to an art gallery, but in the day-to-day living of our life, in which we allow ourselves to be transformed by God's Spirit so that we can create something beautiful for God, a life that is modelled and shaped on the ideas and raw materials of Jesus' life and ministry. In following his example we can truly be in tune with God.

[Close by playing final 30 bars of the Elgar symphony, last movement.]

Comments

Kieran Conry: *'An engaging piece, with a sense of the preacher's personal interest in music dominating the piece.'*

Jonathan Romain: *'I fear I learnt more about Elgar than I did about the Gospels. The exhortation at the end to "be in tune with God" gave the listeners a sound-bite to take away and mull over.'*

Peter Graves: *'A most interesting illustration is well developed into a full-scale sermon with good biblical insights.'*

A Palm Sunday Sermon
Rev. Trevor Hancock

Sermon preached at Cradley Heath Methodist Church, Grainger's Lane, Cradley Heath, on Palm Sunday, 5 April 1998.

The Rev. Trevor Hancock, 62, and his wife Anne, who has been active in voluntary work, have two daughters and two grandchildren. Mr Hancock was ordained in 1965 in Sarawak, Malaysia, in Iban Sarawak Provisional Conference, one of the Methodist Churches which has bishops. He had gone over two years earlier with the Methodist Missionary Society after doing his National Service and attending college in Birmingham. He stayed in Malaysia until 1972 working with the Ibans, the former headhunters. 'It was fascinating but also debilitating work because I met an amoeba out there which has since played havoc with my digestive system.' He suffers from a disease called sprue, which began as a form of amoebic dysentery and which means he cannot absorb fats as well as he should.

His term of service in Malaysia, a Muslim country, was restricted, so he returned to England when his children reached school age, working first in partnership with an Anglican congregation in Lincolnshire and then with a United Reformed Church in Wiltshire. After four years in Cumbria he moved to the Black Country, where he has three churches. The largest has 100 members. 'The Black Country is struggling as far as church life goes', he says. 'We are the second most deprived area in the country. We have vandalism, burglaries, delinquency, high unemployment. There is very little community and no heart to it.'

He says preaching is commended by God. 'But its shape is something that maybe has to change to something other than the traditional sermon. The message conveyed by sermons remains essential, but the old-fashioned 20-minute sermon is not popular. You can preach like an angel, but it doesn`t always put bums on seats. But I am convinced it is essential because, in one form or another, God works through the spoken word.'

For him, the Millennium is a 'golden opportunity' to express the Christian faith. 'Everyone should understand why we are doing it. The Millennium is connected to Christ, and we have to take this opportunity to speak about Christ.'

But he has mixed feelings about the Princess of Wales. 'It put it in context when Mother Teresa died shortly afterwards. Diana expressed a more modern approach to spirituality, while Mother Teresa had the traditional approach. But both had the same essence, the same charismatic gift. Both were concerned about people.'

HAVE you ever ridden on a seaside donkey? Have you ever wondered where they go in the winter? Many are boarded out with friendly farmers. The donkeys come in October when the season ends, and return for the Easter holidays. So if you want a procession on Palm Sunday, and you have a farmer in your congregation, you can just about borrow a donkey to lead.

We tried it once, and only once. Sunday School children were all decked out in costume, and waving pussy willows. With Bimbo in front, we set off for the church, everybody cheering and shouting 'Hosanna!' Bimbo went through the church door, then stopped, blocking up the aisle. He flatly refused to budge despite all our efforts, and to cap it all he left a deposit right where everybody had to walk. It was all rather nasty!

I can't remember much about the service; we couldn't finish fast enough. Yet why blame that donkey? It must have been about the only time in his life that Bimbo had the chance to make a personal statement about what he thought of his rather monotonous existence. Of one thing I am sure. The people who took part in the Palm Sunday procession will have that particular donkey ride fixed in their minds for evermore.

What of the original Palm Sunday ride, taken by Jesus Christ through Jerusalem? That didn't turn out quite the way it was planned either, and was even more memorable. The donkey, or the ass in this case, performed to order, but the people were stubborn and it was the crowd which made the contrary and unpleasant statement. All was well until the procession stopped and Jesus got off the donkey. Then the trouble started. The scene had similar ingredients to ours but in a more potent and volatile mix.

So long as Jesus rides the donkey, it's quite all right for the children to shout 'Hosanna' and to join in the holiday atmosphere, but when Jesus dismounts the events begin in earnest; then it is a different matter. Then it becomes an adult affair, and turns nasty. What followed was a travesty, a miscarriage of justice, a connivance by authority with everything that runs counter to decent civilized human behaviour. An innocent man was put to death, and the crowds came to watch him dying as though it was an entertainment. It was casual and off-hand, as though cruel and untimely death was the norm. It revolts and reviles. It leaves a very nasty mess on the carpet. And it still happens. A few days ago, in the friendly town of Jonesboro in the rural American state of Arkansas, two young boys set off on a killing spree. Not with catapults, which boys have traditionally and fruitlessly used to shoot at birds and rabbits, but with real rifles and bullets.

We all know what happened. Four schoolgirls and a teacher died, casually and off-handedly as though it were part of the school curriculum, yet just as cruelly and untimely as unforeseen death always is. Why did it happen? We don't know. The father of one of the boys said 'I don't have any explanation for this: nobody does. It's not something you would expect out of your child or anyone else's child.'

Out of the blue a holiday crowd turned sour, and Jesus Christ exchanged his donkey ride for a nightmare trip on a wooden cross, by courtesy of an obscure Roman colonial career official named Pontius Pilate – a good civil servant just doing his duty. To quote the boy's father again, 'I don't have any explanation for this; nobody does'.

Now that Cool Britannia has become European, the events currently taking place in a French law court in Bordeaux must be of some concern to us, even if only to show how low unredeemed humanity can sink. Eighty-seven-year-old Maurice Papon has been sentenced to ten years imprisonment for 'crimes against humanity'. He is the person judged responsible for the deaths of 1,600 Jews, including 233 children. This betrayal took place during the German occupation of France in the last war. The Jews were all deported to Germany where they were exterminated in death camps. Papon was the good civil servant who had the authority to sign the deportation papers. His defence, much like that of Pilate, was that he was simply following orders. Mentally he had washed his hands of all traces of guilt. After the sentence Papon's lawyer attacked the verdict as 'worthy of condemnation'. He declared: 'It's not over. The judges judge History. They should remember that History will judge the judges.' In the case of Jesus, that is indeed true, and it is why we are about to celebrate the Millennium.

So, what happened to Jesus had happened before, has happened since and it will happen again. A good civil servant gets cold feet and looks to his pension rather than to justice. We would probably have never heard of Pontius Pilate but for Jesus.

Looking back to our village donkey ride, I said I could excuse the donkey for making a mess on the carpet. There were extenuating circumstances. I suppose we can do no less for Pilate. It has been suggested that if you read the Gospel narratives carefully, you will discover that Pilate was a nervous wreck. Pilate may have been a better soldier than a diplomat. Certainly he made mistakes. He raised the Emperor's eagle standard in Jerusalem, which was anathema to the Jews. He built an aqueduct to supply the city with water, but paid for it out of the Temple treasury. Sacrilege and theft! There seemed no end to it. When the score of misdemeanours is added up, it's rather like President Clinton's daily skirmish with the special public prosecutor, who seems effortlessly to produce young women who claim to have succumbed with unfailing regularity to Bill's charms. But alas, no one seems to have loved Pontius Pilate. Listen to John's Gospel. His account gives us some indication of the Jewish scorn of Pilate:

From Caiaphas Jesus was led into the Governor's headquarters. It was now early morning, and the Jews themselves stayed outside the headquarters, to avoid defilement so that they could eat the Passover meal. So Pilate came out to them and asked, 'What charge do you bring against this man?'

John 18:28

Pilate was Caesar's representative. All subjects conceded their rights and privileges to Caesar. You come to him. He doesn't come to you. But the Jews were contemptuous and stayed outside, claiming a religious embargo. So, Pilate climbed down and came out to them, thus losing all credibility in the matter. From then on it was downhill all the way.

Pilate was just a weak man in the wrong place at the wrong time, a miscast bit-part player, occupying centre stage in the cosmic drama of world history only by the permissive will of God. It's all a travesty of justice; it's cruel and inhuman. It shouldn't have happened. And yet, somehow, God is in control. St Paul wrote to the Church at Rome: 'In everything . . . he co-operates with those who love God and are called according to his purpose' (Romans 8:28). Not every travesty is a complete tragedy.

Thomas Hardy's novel, *Tess of the D'Urbervilles*, has been on TV recently. At the end of the story, in which the desperately unhappy life of Tess is dramatized, Thomas Hardy makes a bitter verbal attack on God. He writes: '. . . the President of the Immortals had ended his sport with Tess'. Hardy believed in God, but a very different God from the Gracious Father of Jesus Christ. Hardy sees God as one above, who watches people suffer and even makes them suffer.

The difference in our belief is that God does not cause suffering, but he shares it with us. There are some situations which seem unjust and unkind, which roll on over us like an out-of-control juggernaut, but they also roll over God. Palm Sunday and the humble donkey is God's mark of quality control. It is like a personal statement that says: 'I'm in it too – and never mind the mess on the carpet. We'll clear that up together later.'

Comments

Paul Walker: *'An incredible number of modern parallels. In a world where people are no longer expected to know anything about the Bible, it is increasingly difficult to explain it.'*

Peter Graves: *'A novel approach that should help people see the Palm Sunday story in a different light. Clear and easy to follow, but lacking in biblical content.'*

Jonathan Romain: *'Story of the donkey creates a vivid picture in the mind of the listeners. The preacher skilfully refers back to it at the conclusion.'*

Rosh Hashana

RABBI STEVEN KATZ

Sermon preached on 29 September 1997.

Rabbi Katz, 49, is married to Sandra, a dental practice manager, and they have two children. He went to Queen Mary College, London to study history and then to Leo Baeck College in north London before being ordained in 1975. 'My father was a rabbi', he says. 'It is in the family.'

He believes preaching is essentially a teaching tool. 'Perhaps for many Jews it is the only time they have any exposure to Jewish teaching', he says. 'The rabbi's sermon is a chance to convey the relevance of this teaching to their lives. Preaching is therefore vital for the Jewish community. If we do not know how or why to maintain our Judaism, then it will quickly cease to have any sort of relevance or meaning to Jewish life. The sermon is a vehicle to show how and why Judaism can be a force for good. A sermon should show how Judaism can enhance their appreciation of aspects of daily life, whether it is at home with the family, at work or in the community at large. Of course, the first aim of any preacher is to wake them up. Every good sermon should contain humour, which is a great way of attracting attention. The point of a sermon is not to entertain, but there is no reason why a sermon should not be entertaining.'

From his point of view, the Millennium is not relevant at all. 'If it allows families and friends to come together to celebrate, then that is wonderful. Such opportunities should always be seized. But our synagogue will not be marking the Millennium in any shape or form. It so happens that the Millennium eve is a Friday night, and for us this should be celebrated in a Jewish context as normal. I really cannot imagine any synagogue having a special function or celebration.'

The Princess of Wales was, he believes, an example of how much one individual can achieve. 'Although she was in a privileged position, at one time married to the heir to the throne, she showed how much can be achieved. While it is possible to achieve more by working with and through a community, it must never be forgotten how much an individual can achieve on his or her own. I think everyone's hearts were warmed, just by the way she cared for members of society who are normally marginalized by our own lack of compassion.'

ROSH HASHANA, the Jewish New Year, is known as Yom Hazikaron, a time for remembering, remembering the hurt we have caused family, friends, community through word or deed or through withholding these precious gifts while someone close yearned from us an encouraging word, an appreciative gesture, a loving hug. And today is more than remembering, it is about restoring, reforming, refreshing those relationships which have become fragile or fractured through our neglect and our sins of omission or commission.

But tomorrow cannot be better unless we remember what we did yesterday. Who remembers last winter? It seemed unending, for weeks and weeks the sun hid behind a thick blanket of dense, dismal grey cloud. Spring seemed to be permanently postponed. Daffodils and cherry blossom, those gloriously colourful harbingers of spring, were reluctant to make their annual appearance and announcement. Then without warning, like a meteor tumbling from the sky, spring arrived. I remember the day well. The sun cast aside its heavy grey blanket, windows were flung open, there was a frantic search for lightweight jackets. I ventured into the garden and challenged Danielle, my elder daughter, to a game of swingball. Although the harsh morning frosts and occasional heavy snowfall had interfered with the early spring flowering process, the pole remained in a surprisingly pristine condition.

The game is one of speed of eye and hand, an excellent test of one's co-ordination. I had played the game regularly with my children, and the fact that I always won was, so I believed, reassuring confirmation of my youth. It was the first day of spring, we played the game. I lost. I offered a litany of imaginative and wholly implausible excuses and begged for a second game. Again, I lost. I thought of challenging Laura, my younger daughter, but a third defeat would be a humiliation too far.

Here were the unwelcome but distressingly obvious signs of ageing, a reminder that ageing is a slow but inexorable process. It creeps up on one. There is the first grey hair, the time our backs begin to go out more often than we do, when most names in our telephone directories carry the initials Dr, when whimsical nostalgia and talk of multi-vitamins seem to invade every conversation. Very quickly our children regard us as old and arid and so too does society. It has been said that there are two tell-tale signs of old age – one is that one forgets things and the other . . . I have forgotten!

In the same way that ageing creeps up slowly on us, so too does wrongdoing. As we reflect on fragile and fractured relationships within the intimate bond of our family or the treasured circle of our friends, and which words, which actions, loosened the bonds of love and kinship, of trust and loyalty, we think: if only we could retract, withdraw, play back the video.

Today, we are encouraged, urged, mandated to play back the video of our year's contact with family, friends and community and to express honest regret, sincere contrition for the times we failed to reach our own expectations of moral conduct and those of our tradition.

These next ten days of *teshuva*, repentance, from Rosh Hashana to Yom Kippur, the Day of Atonement, are intended through prayer, study and reflection to help us focus on what we have lost in relationships – in marriage, between parent and children, siblings, friends – lost in the way of nourishing love and engaging companionship. Most of these relationships have not been destroyed through a tempestuous row, an explosion of anger, but rather have been eroded through the drip, drip, drip effect of neglect and time.

There is an example from the world of nature.

If you place a frog in boiling water, it jumps out. Its instincts protect it from danger. But you can deceive its natural instincts by putting the frog in cold water, and slowly warming the water. If you do that, the frog will remain in the water and it boils to death. So too in our marriage the water heats up slowly and before we know it something dies.

Many experiences chip away at the relationship. Husband and wife take each other for granted, they become side-tracked through the stresses of work, the responsibilities of child-rearing and forget how to identify, let alone respond to, each other's needs and feelings. Little by little the water heats up, and before they know it they are in hot water.

The same with children. When they are babies and toddlers we look upon them as gifts from God, passports to posterity. They represent a huge privilege and an awesome responsibility. But as they grow, and face all-pervasive peer pressure, unending school exam stress, fraught relationship problems, they become troubled and they change. Our ambitions for them exceed their wishes and self-expectations, we speak to them but do not listen to them, we change also. Our relationship with them then changes, for the worse.

In our childhood our siblings were sometimes our favourite playmates, closest confidants, and most trusted allies against the common enemy – parents! At other times they were the source of continuous frustration and endless jealousy, but at all times we were united by the bond of family, ready to defend each other to the death. In adulthood, however, we have moved away from each other not only geographically but emotionally, causing lingering hurt to ageing parents and shameful loss to our impressionable children.

The same process takes place with friends to whom one was once bound in loyalty and trust, who were there for one in years past to nurse one through a broken relationship, a bereavement, an illness, a job loss. They slowly disappear without trace. Through the months and years we become too preoccupied with our own needs and problems to see and appreciate that others confront the same or worse.

The decay in the ethical quality of our lives and relationships begins slowly. In our Prayer Book for Yom Kippur, the Day of Atonement, we implore 'God to forgive us for pushing in queues, stealing telephone calls. For saying "It's not my business", "for pretending to be good".' These are the faults and failings that permit decay and deterioration to become destruction.

On Rosh Hashana we blow the shofar, the ram's horn, to blast away the niggling decaying habits before they become entrenched and breed more grievous wrongs. During the next ten days, Rosh Hashana to Yom Kippur, the New Year to the Day of Atonement, days of inner searching, may we discover the honesty to recognize the decay, the need to remove it, and the will to reconstruct our relationship with family, friends and community.

The season of *teshuva,* of repentance, is traditionally ushered in with visits to the graves of loved ones to remind us of the brevity, the preciousness of life. We do not have for ever to say 'I love you', 'I am sorry', 'Thank you'. Shortly before this season of repentance reaches its concluding climax we light memorial candles for loved ones, on the eve of Yom Kippur. The question, the supremely important, haunting and compelling question Rosh Hashana asks us and Yom Kippur reinforces is: 'Are we willing to search for the inner decay, to remove it, and to restore, refresh, renew our relationships with family, friends and community before more memorial candles are lit, either in our homes or in the houses of people close to us?' These Ten Days of Repentance, the *Aseret Yemey Teshuva,* are a gift from God. They are an opportunity for each of us to restore fractured relationships and strengthen fragile ones with our time and our interest and our care. It is time for repentance, to restore what is lost, to repair what is broken, in our relationships with family, friends and community. May God bless us with the courage, honesty and will to embark on this task, helping us, in the words of the American rabbi Harold Kushner, 'to transform the world into the kind of world God had in mind when he created it'.

Comments

Peter Graves: *'Clearly developed, pastorally sensitive and well related to contemporary life.'*

Paul Walker: *'What was particularly interesting was its practicality. He gives us very solid things to repent of – like the way we let friendships decay. Very valuable in a world where sin is viewed as either gross evil or fun, but rarely as slowly corrupting.'*

Jonathan Romain: *'A gentle but piercingly-accurate examination of the ageing process that affects us all. A powerful reminder to us to use what time we have to renew our lives. We feel the preacher is addressing our needs rather than his agenda.'*

Chosen People

RABBI DR HARRY RABINOWICZ

Sermon preached at Hendon Synagogue, Raleigh Close, on 18 April 1998.

Rabbi Dr Harry Rabinowicz and his wife Bella, a former lecturer in commerce, have three children – two lawyers and a doctor of medicine – and seven grandchildren. Dr Rabinowicz comes from a great Polish rabbinic family. His father, the Biala Rabbi, was a descendant of a famous dynasty of Cabbalists dating back to the eighteenth century.

Dr Rabinowicz began his career as an assistant minister at the St John's Wood Synagogue, north-west London, in 1947. He later occupied the pulpit at St Albans Synagogue in Hertfordshire, Ilford Synagogue in Essex, Dollis Hill Synagogue in Brent, and acted for many years as Regional Rabbi of Cricklewood, Willesden and Brondesbury Synagogues.

He has lectured extensively and has been an adviser to BBC radio and television, the Royal Shakespeare Company, and to various other film producers. He helped revise Singer's Authorised Prayer Book for the Orthodox Community, and has published many books, including an Encyclopedia of Hasidism *(Jason Aronson, 1996) and* A World Apart: The Story of the Chasidim in Britain *(Vallentine Mitchell, 1997).*

Dr Rabinowicz, whose last position before retirement was at the Willesden Synagogue, preaches regularly at a small synagogue at the Ella and Ridley Jacobs Home in Church Road, Hendon, north-west London, a Jewish care home for the aged.

Many of his family perished in the Holocaust, and his father died in London at the age of 47.

'Preaching is certainly in decline in Anglo-Jewry today', he said. 'There are not many Jewish preachers left, and few books on homiletics have been published. Rabbinical colleges no longer teach homiletics, though preaching still has an important place in the synagogue. In many instances it is the only part of the Orthodox Hebrew Service that congregants are able to follow.

'I try to keep the congregation attentive and awake by being topical and humorous', says Rabbi Rabinowicz. 'It is so easy to become boring. I believe that a sermon should end before the congregation has lost interest.'

He does not consider the Millennium to be of great importance to the Jewish community, because it is fundamentally a Christian landmark, although he acknowledges its secular significance.

On the Princess of Wales, he says: 'This affected everybody. Whenever a human being dies tragically, it affects other human beings.'

Text: Exodus 19:5.

You shall be mine own treasure.

The 'Election of Israel', the idea that the Jews are the chosen people, a concept with which the Bible, the Liturgy, and the Rabbinic writings are replete, has been extensively misunderstood both by Jews as well as by non-Jews.

How can we be the 'chosen people', God's 'peculiar treasure', when for nearly 2,000 years we were mercilessly persecuted, hated and despised, pillaged and lampooned? To mock us was the sport of children, to torture us was the amusement of kings. Chosen to be the objects of the worst passions in the human heart.

There are few countries whose soil has not been drenched with Jewish blood. Often we were forced to leave the places in which we were born, the places where we built synagogues and other cultural institutions, the places where the bones of our fathers and our forefathers were buried, and we had to search for new homes on the highways and byways of Europe. How then can we be God's chosen people? Chosen to be 'the suffering servants', chosen in the furnace of affliction, chosen to be the object of hatred and enmity.

All this is due to our misunderstanding of what the term 'chosen' means. Chosen has never meant to be the 'favourite'. Quite the reverse, the rabbis tell us. Why was the mountain on which the Torah was given called 'Sinai'? Because the Hebrew word 'Sinai' can also be interpreted as 'enmity'. Ever since the Revelation at Sinai, the rabbis tell us, hatred descended on the world. The pagans despised our Torah, feared our teachings, felt that the dream of the Jew spelled the breakdown of their own vision of brutality and hatred.

There is the story of the young Jewish poet who travelled through the ancient world. In Egypt, he admired the Pyramids – one of the seven wonders of the ancient world. In Rome, he saw the ruins of the Colosseum – the symbol of the might that was Rome. In Athens, he admired the Parthenon – the glory that was Greece; but in Jerusalem, all he could find were the remains of the Wailing Wall, the western wall of the old Temple. 'Is this all that my ancestors left behind? Are these stones a fit memorial for the teachings of the rabbis, the heroism of the Maccabees, and the martyrdom of Massada? Is this all that my ancestors left behind?' he asked.

But when the poet grew older, he grew wiser, and he realized that in the ancient world, the Hebrews made a tremendous contribution to mankind. They were the 'people of the Book', who gave the world the

Bible – the *Magna Carta* of mankind, the charter for the oppressed and the poor. The Jew turned to the Bible for comfort and hope and strength. It was, in Heinrich Heine's words, 'his portable fatherland'. The Bible has endured the test of time, the devotion of millions of readers, and remains a source of wisdom and inspiration. Its vision moulded states and societies.

We also gave to the world the peerless prophets who proclaimed the ideal of the 'fatherhood of God, and the brotherhood of mankind', proclaiming: 'Have we not all one Father?' 'Has not one God created us?'

'Why do we deal treacherously every man against his brother?' (Malachi 2:10). What can compare to the majesty of Isaiah, the mysticism of Ezekiel, or the humanity of Jeremiah?

We also gave to the world the Book of Psalms, which in the words of R. E. Prothero 'contains the whole music and the heart of man'. In it are gathered the lyrical burst of David's tenderness, the moan of his penitence, the pathos of his sorrow, the triumph of his victory and the despair of his defeat.

In the ancient world, the Jew could see through the rapacity of the Roman Empire, in whose way of life he refused to see a civilizing force. Coming out of the ancient Hebrew academies of Yavne and Bene Berak, where he heard teachers like R. Akiva proclaim the concept that all human beings were created in the image of God, and that 'Love your neighbour as yourself!' was the cardinal principle of Judaism, and going into the marketplaces of Rome, Alexandria and Antioch, what did he see? He saw masters whipping their slaves, mothers exposing their young feeble children to die. Small wonder, then, that the synagogues of Rome and Alexandria were filled with would-be converts, and the Friday night candles were lit in many a home.

In the Middle Ages, too, we Jews were true to our mission, as is reflected in the story of Don Immanuel, a minister of King Ferdinand and Queen Isabella. The Inquisition – the Gestapo of the Middle Ages – discovered that he was a marrano – a secret Jew. He was arrested, tortured and sentenced to be burned alive. On Good Friday morning the whole city of Barcelona was there to view the spectacle, the *auto-da-fé*. The king, the queen and the cabinet were all there. When the King saw his favourite minister about to be burned, he said to him:

'Immanuel, renounce your faith, all will be forgiven, and you will be restored to your former post.'

'But, Majesty', replied Don Immanuel, 'how can I do it? I am bound in chains.'

'What chains?' asked the King. 'I can see no chains.'

'But, Majesty', replied Immanuel, 'I am bound to the invisible chains of Abraham, Isaac and Jacob. I am bound to the chains of my faith, whose roots go back to the loins of Abraham. How can I renounce my faith?'

He died a martyr's death.

The Middle Ages were not the 'dark ages' for the Jews, nor were they a period of literary stagnation. The Jew was not a Shylock, that was the 'Jew that Shakespeare drew', nor was he a Barabbas, created by the fertile imagination of Christopher Marlowe. While clouds of Cimmerian darkness, ignorance, superstition and illiteracy were hovering over Europe, we produced commentators such as Rashi, codifiers such as Joseph Caro, grammarians such as Ibn Ezra, poets such as Yehuda Halevy and Solomon Ibn Gabriol, philosophers such as Maimonides.

In the nineteenth century, too, even under the cruel Romanovs' heartless bureaucracy, the Jews established schools and spiritual citadels, spiritual armouries that protected the Jew. There was the cradle song of a Jewish mother: 'Sleep soundly by night and learn Torah by day, for you shall be a rabbi when I am grown grey.'

Although few in numbers, the Jews have made a disproportionate contribution to the culture of the world. There are few branches in the arts or sciences that they have not enriched. Now that we are about to reach the new millennium, when science has changed the way people think, when technology has changed the way we live, when respect for authority has been replaced by egalitarianism, when the world is advancing, is the Jew remaining behind? Are we still true to our mission?

A nation that has survived the unprecedented anguish of the Holocaust and unspeakable crimes, when a third of world Jewry perished, when rabbis with holy Scrolls in their hands died, when the Nazis harnessed the machinery of a modern society to murder the people of God, yet Jews have not lost their faith in humanity or God, such a nation is not effete.

Nor is the miraculous rebirth, half a century ago, of the State of Israel, 'the beginning of the Redemption', with the ingathering of the exiles from the four corners of the earth, from North Africa, Russia and Ethiopia, increasing its numbers from 600,000 to almost six million, with Hebrew reborn as a living language, the people of the Book returning to the Land, creating a new civilization and 'taking up arms against the sea of troubles', the result of a decaying nation.

We never regarded ourselves as a 'chosen people', nor did we believe that God prefers one nation to the exclusion of any other, but rather felt to be 'a choosing people', the harbinger of world morality, proclaiming the great truth that the only way of worshipping God is by doing righteousness and justice. In the words proclaimed by the Prophet: 'What does the Lord require of you? Only to do justly, and to love mercy and walk humbly with your God' (Micah 6:8).

Comments

Paul Walker: *'The question of the election of Israel is an issue that challenges all the people of the book. Why did God choose the Jews? Harry Rabinowicz points to the enrichment of the whole world by the Jewish people in a truly non-offensive way that challenges Jew and non-Jew, religious and non-religious alike.'*

Peter Graves: *'A fascinating, well-illustrated reflection on the Jews as God's chosen people.'*

Jonathan Romain: *'The preacher calls on emotive but often negative material to illustrate his theme, but still manages to provide a positive message that offers hope and demands action.'*

Be Clean!

CHRISTINE SCOTT

Sermon preached on World Leprosy Day, Sunday 23 January 1998, at Lichfield Road Methodist Church, Birmingham.

Christine Scott, 57, a YT training consultant, is a Methodist local preacher. She attends Stockland Green Methodist Church in Birmingham and preaches about once a month on the local circuit. 'I would like to do more preaching', she says. 'It is not enough for me.'

As recently as last year, she began to worry she was not a good preacher. 'I began to think I should give it up, that God was not calling me to do this.' But she went instead to Cliff College in Derbyshire on a four-day preaching course shortly after Christmas. Her sense of vocation returned.

'One of the reasons I have found it difficult over the last couple of years is that preaching seems to have become devalued. We are expected instead to be "worship facilitators", to be children's entertainers. I have not been called to be either of these. I have been called to be a preacher.'

She recognizes that, as someone who preaches in church, she is preaching to the converted. 'It is important therefore to build up people's faith, especially at a time when they might look around at everything going on in the world, and wonder whether it is worth having a faith at all. Preaching can help people believe God does matter, that we are all going somewhere. A good sermon should inform, it should certainly encourage, and it should sometimes move. And it should also contain the name of Jesus, because after all that is why we are here.'

She is not concerned with the Millennium. 'I don't think it makes any difference. It is the here and now that counts.' But she believes the reaction to the death of the Princess of Wales shows people have become more emotional. 'They can be moved as much by what people are as by what they say. I think perhaps we should be using that more in the Church. Sometimes we do not appear to stand for a great deal. We just, sort of, are. But in this day and age, people want something or someone they can identify with, and Diana gave them that.'

Text: Mark 1:41.

Jesus was filled with pity and stretched out his hand and touched him. 'I do want to, ' he answered. 'Be clean!'

H E HAD never thought that he would become a leper.
He found the first spot one morning when he was washing.
It was so small, he felt that it really couldn't be anything at all.
Certainly nothing to worry about!
But, over the next few months, before his horrified eyes, it grew and grew.
There wasn't any good reason why he should tell anyone. It wouldn't make any difference.
He would simply be making a fuss over nothing
There was no way it was anything special.
But one morning, as he kissed his wife, and cuddled his small daughter, he suddenly realized their danger, the danger that, through touching him, they, too, might become lepers.
Could he condemn them to that? He, who loved them both so much!
Quietly, he began to put his affairs in order, to sort out his possessions, to sort out his finances. He had to make sure that everything would be all right.
Finally, came the day he had dreaded, the day he had to tell his wife.
'My dear, I have to go away.'
As he looked at her, the person he loved best in all the world, he didn't know how he would live without her. 'It's very hard for me to tell you this, but darling, I'm a leper.'
As he left, he broke his heart.
In the years following, his heart broke many times.
For the life of a leper was hard. There was little food, little comfort, and, what was worst of all, little hope. For leprosy was incurable.
Sometimes he thought he would go mad. Was this why he had been born?
To wait, day by day, for death to release him?
Was this all that he could expect? Would he never again see a friendly face?
Would he never again feel that someone cared?

Many years ago, a woman who lived in the docklands of the East End of London went, on impulse, to the women's meeting at the local church. She had been living with a Chinese sailor and had a small baby. She brought the baby with her to the meeting. She found that she enjoyed the meeting and so she went back again and again. And then the vicar arrived on her doorstep.
'I'm afraid', he said, 'I must ask you not to come to the women's meeting again.'

The woman was surprised.

'Why not?' she said.

'The other women say that they'll stop coming if you come', said the vicar. Wistfully, she looked at him.

'Sir', she said, 'I know I'm a sinner. But isn't there anywhere a sinner can go?'

There wasn't anywhere that a leper could go. As the disease took hold of him, so his skin thickened, and his face changed so that he didn't look like a man at all. Even his own mother wouldn't recognize him. He spent his days wandering aimlessly. He took to visiting the villages late at night and in the early hours of the morning, just on the off-chance that he might hear another human voice. It was on one of these visits that he heard a conversation. They were talking about a man called Jesus – Jesus of Nazareth – a teacher and a healer.

As he listened, for the first time in many years, the leper felt a small flame of hope light up in his heart.

Could it be true? Had Jesus really healed all those people? And, if this Jesus had healed others, couldn't he heal him? But it was against the law for a leper to approach any ordinary person. He could be stoned if he tried. Was it worth it? How much did he want to be healed?

Two friends were going swimming, when they began discussing religion.

Just as they were going into the sea, one said to the other: 'What wouldn't I give to find a faith?'

'How much do you want it?' asked his friend.

'Oh, very much indeed', he replied.

To his amazement, his friend suddenly seized him and pressed his head under water. In spite of his struggles, he held him there until he was nearly suffocated. When, at last, he released his grip, and the man could stand up and breathe again, he demanded to know what he meant by it.

'What did you want most in the world just now?' asked his friend.

'Why, air of course.'

'Well, when you want a faith as much as you wanted air just then, you'll find it!'

The leper found that he wanted to be healed more than he'd ever wanted anything. For that, he would risk stoning. For that, he would risk rejection. But would Jesus want to heal him?

It took him some days to find Jesus.

When, at last, he saw him, he could have cried with relief.

He ran forward and fell at Jesus' feet.

'Sir', he said, 'if you want to, you can make me clean.'

Jesus looked down at the kneeling figure. The leper was covered in dirty old rags. He was shapeless, smelly and repulsive, hardly a man at all. Gently Jesus took away the cloth that hid the leper's face, touched all the deformities that the leprosy had made, and looked deep into the man's eyes.

'Of course I want to', he said. 'Be clean!'

Then he took the leper's hands in his own and raised him to his feet.

When Jesus enters a situation everything changes. He touches the untouchable. To Jesus the deformities didn't matter, he simply saw a man in desperate need. And, where there is need, then Jesus always does something about it.

In the first week in January, some friends and I attended a preaching course at Cliff College, the Methodist College in Derbyshire, just outside Matlock. One of the lecturers on the course was the Rev. Dr Donald English, an ex-President of the Methodist Conference. Dr English's wife died not long ago after a serious illness. When the doctors said they could do no more for her, and that she had only a short time to live, a Christian friend, who was a healer, asked Dr English if he could pray with her.

There were three people in the room for the healing but, as they prayed, so Dr English said that he could see four. Jesus was there with them.

Some time later, the friend came again. Again, there were three people in the room, and, again, Dr English saw four. Jesus was with them again.

Dr English said that it was as if Jesus had come to see what they were doing, to say: 'That's fine. That's OK. But I'll be back.'

Mrs English lived on for three more months after the date that the doctors had given. But Jesus came back as he said he would. Dr English said that he came back to take her home.

The leper was certain that Jesus could help him. But only if he wanted to. Jesus left him in no doubt, that he did want to, just as he wants to help us. The help we get may not always be the one we hope for. Dr English cried as he told his story. But the love and power that healed a leper is at work today. It brought the East End woman from the coldness of the Anglican Church to the warmth of the Salvation Army. It gave Donald English the courage to stand up and tell us about his experiences of bereavement.

When bad things happen to us, we are tempted to forget, to forget how much Jesus loves us and how much he wants what is best for us, and that his love and power can transform the most hopeless situations. We may be knocked down but we are never knocked out.

'Sir', said the leper, 'if you want to, you can make me clean.'

'I do want to', said Jesus. 'Be clean!'

The love that was crucified on Calvary for us is always with us.
May we never forget it!

Prayer to follow the sermon:
Lord, we are humbled as we wonder at your greatness and power, your
gentleness and love:

Help us to worship you truly in our words, in our thoughts and in
our lives.

Amen.

Comments

Peter Graves: '*A well-developed use of imagination makes a well-known
Bible story come alive. The sensitive use of contemporary illustration helps us
apply the story in a very helpful way.*'

Paul Walker: '*I seem to be hearing more of this style of sermon at the
moment, especially from women preachers. There is effective use of a kind of
internal psychological profile. The juxtaposition of different experiences of
rejection and isolation resonated powerfully. I was not sure I was comfortable
with the idea that Jesus always does something about difficult situations,
however.*'

Strength in Separation

JOHN A. OLDHAM

Sermon preached at Outlane Methodist Church, Huddersfield.

John Oldham, 51, and his wife Elaine, an infants schoolteacher, have two children. Mr Oldham, a Methodist local preacher who preaches regularly throughout the Pennine Circuit in Huddersfield, is a partner and joint managing director in a Huddersfield printing company, Regent Print, specializing mainly in promotional leaflets and literature. He bought the firm he used to work for after spending some time on the dole when he was made redundant 20 years ago.

John left school at 15 with a handful of O levels and a burning passion to be a printer. After going to Leeds Printing College, he was unable to get into printing itself, so went into print management instead. 'I studied very hard at evening class for ten years for a Diploma in Management Studies.' He trained at the games and packaging group Waddington's, and then became production director of a publishing group. After a brief period with Yorkshire Television he joined Regent Print in the depths the recession. He tried unsuccessfully to turn it round, but ended up having to make 150 people redundant. 'I took my own P45 as the last person out of the door', he says.

He used his redundancy money to buy the firm back, but his only regret is that he has not yet been able to recreate all 150 jobs.

'I have the best of both worlds, because I have a ministry as a lay preacher, and can also get on with the job of printing which I love so much.' He is an avid collector of books. 'I am fascinated by reading, by books and by people who write books.' He has become an adviser to the Prince's Trust, to support young people who set up their own business, and has been commissioned to write an article about the history of Huddersfield. He joined a writing group, which he says has helped him with his sermons. 'It has made me think very hard about the end listener', he says.

'I sort of drifted into faith, and it has been very sorely challenged over the years. It has seemed at times that I have one foot in the Christian Church and one foot in the world. I feel for people outside the church, because I myself have had a lot of problems with prayer and faith.' His family were against his becoming a preacher because he has a slight stammer. Ironically, when he is preaching it disappears.

He is concerned about the 'fringe elements' which are threatening to take centre stage in the Millennium celebrations, but has not given it a great deal of thought. 'My ministry here is more about supporting and servicing the needs of the local congregation. And for me personally, the Millennium has been a nightmare because of the Millennium bugs and the computers in the company.'

He was moved by the response of the local church to the death of Diana. 'I had to take a service the Sunday after her funeral. We decided to make it a service of celebration for her life. I did something I had never tried before with the congregation, which was to leave a blank sheet of paper for intercessory prayers they wanted to offer during the service. I was warned that I wouldn't get a single prayer, but I was inundated. There was a real outpouring. In that way, the people made it their service.'

(Dedicated to Andrew and Amelia, for without them there would not have been a sermon.)

LET me share two experiences with you.

One fateful day last summer I found myself at Manchester Airport in their 'check-in' area. Unfortunately I wasn't checking in my own luggage, I was saying 'Good-bye' to Andrew, our son, who had decided to give up a college course and go to work in the bars in Tenerife. He had no job, no lodgings – nothing.

As I crossed the airport concourse and gave him a final wave I felt the sharp stab of pain which separation from a loved one brings to you. I felt what it must have been like to be the father of the Prodigal Son. The only words that could come to my mind form the text for this sermon: '... the younger son gathered all he had and took his journey into a far country' (Luke 15:13).

The second experience I want to share with you is an incident which happened when we were returning from a family holiday in France. Amelia, our daughter, wanted to see the ferry leave port. Now I don't know about you, but my idea of the perfect channel crossing is to get my head down at Roscoff and wake up in Plymouth!

Yet I could not let Amelia down, so we set off to find the highest deck on board the ferry. It was the one just under the bridge; you know, the one where they land the helicopter in an emergency, just to make you feel safe! We were very high above the quay because the ship on which we were sailing was an enormous channel ferry called the *Bretagne*, which carries hundreds of cars, lorries, caravans, coaches and passengers.

It was midnight when we finally arrived on deck, and we gazed down on the illuminated port. The night was clear and we could see lights twinkling around the north Breton countryside. Two lighthouses kept winking at us on this tortuous yet beautifully rugged coastline. The little town of Roscoff, with its cafes and restaurants, was still lit up. The crew were going through their final preparations for embarkation. The massive bow doors were being raised, the huge ropes which tethered us to the quay were being hauled aboard and just for a moment the ship seemed to be motionless, neither tethered nor free. Almost imperceptibly the ship began to move, ever so slowly, away from the quay and the giant engines roared into life. Without any ceremony, without any warning we were waving '*Au revoir*' to France.

It is an event that has stayed with me. For some unknown reason it was something about which I felt very emotional. It was just as though I was being torn away from a part of France which I have come to know so well and love so much. Just like the time at Manchester Airport, I felt that sharp pain of separation we have all experienced at some time in our life. I'm pleased it was reasonably dark, because Dads aren't supposed to cry, and I hoped that Amelia could not see my moist eyes. I remember saying to myself 'Just pull yourself together, you silly old fool, why are you getting so emotional about this?'

Yet when I thought about it, I realized that I was experiencing one of those moments in life which we all have to face, the pain of separation, the pain of being torn apart from someone or something we love so much. There can be scarcely one of us, even of the greatest good fortune, that has not experienced this sudden intrusion of pain into our lives through separation from someone we love. Yet I want to share some thoughts with you about coping with a very special sort of separation, it's that separation which takes us away from our faith.

We can, of course, bring someone else to mind who experienced the pain of separation. It was caused admittedly through his own stupidity, yet nevertheless the pain of separation was clearly there for all to see in the Prodigal Son, not forgetting of course his father and mother if she was still living.

Oh, I nearly forgot to tell you, Andrew's back home safe and sound. Just occasionally I wish he was back in Tenerife, when I can't find a pair of clean underpants!

The story of the Prodigal Son is one of the best-loved parables of our Lord. It's been called a parable for the outcast. For there is a strong underlying theme or sub-plot here that offers a gospel message for everyone, at whatever stage of the journey on which we find ourselves.

This parable teaches us a lot about ourselves. It's a parable, which says we will fail, and don't think we will not. It's a parable that says something about the freedom that I believe God has given to us in our faith. It is the freedom to 'wander away' as it were from our faith, and to return to it. It also tells us what sort of people we shall be when we return. We shall be different, something has happened to us and we have changed. It brings to mind that wonderful picture of Jacob, having been given his new name Israel, limping to meet Esau in the morning sun after his rough and tumble with God at Peniel.

It's a parable which tells us something about this special kind of separation, a separation from our faith. It acknowledges that this separation, with God's connivance no less, will be painful, for both us and for God. It shows us what it is like to grow up in the faith, just as the Prodigal Son did a whole lot of growing up through his experience.

It is *not* a parable that offers any false or empty promises. It doesn't offer us cheap and effective relief from the pain of separation. Neither is it a parable that tells us about a God who doesn't want to know us when we don't toe the line.

It tells us something very positive about our God who not only judges, but who has also given us the freedom to make our mistakes, and through these mistakes to learn how to grow up in the faith. *Our God never turns his back on us.*

It is a very powerful parable, with many different lessons for each of us. Someone once said that there are at least 130 sermons in this parable! Surprise yourself and read it some time!

What I want to share with you takes me back to the departure lounge at Manchester Airport and the quay in Brittany.

We have all experienced separation; it may have been sought or it may have been forced upon us. For some of us it would have been leaving home to go to college, to do National Service, or, heaven forbid, to go and fight a war. Some of us left home with a mixture of happiness and sadness to set up our new homes when we were married, or wanted to achieve our independence.

There are the tragic cases of separation through bereavement, and sad cases of separation through divorce and families splitting up. Families who can no longer cope with the behaviour of their children, and young people who have had to depend upon care homes have separation forced upon them.

Yet what I want to share with you is not so much a physical or even emotional separation, but a very special kind of separation. It's the separation of ourselves from our faith. We leave home, not physically but in a religious sense. We choose to separate ourselves from God. Sometimes it's because of something which has or hasn't happened to us. We rebel against God when he appears to let us down, and our lives, with all its stress and strains, do not match up to our expectations. It may be that we leave God when we feel we can simply do without him, just as adolescents feel the loosening of dependence on their parents. Or we may just simply drift away from God, because that's what happens sometimes.

The one thing that has kept me in the faith and in the pulpit is that I believe Jesus understood our need to be separate from our faith. He knew what it was like to want to 'blame' God when things go wrong and our need to 'test' our faith or simply do without it sometimes. He knew about growing up in the faith and giving people the freedom to make their own mistakes. When I read the gospel record I see someone who is committed to giving to each man and woman he met the chance to take just one further step in the direction of the Kingdom. I believe he offers that to each of us today.

Yet this is the heart of what I really want to share with you. It's this picture of God that Jesus is desperately trying to share with us:

The God whom we worship and in whom we believe is big enough, compassionate, strong enough, forgiving enough to say to us 'Take your freedom, the separation will hurt you and me, but take it, grow up in the faith and come back to me when you are ready.'

It's a constant challenge and threat. I know, because I struggle so much with my faith. I continue to separate myself from my faith, just as the Prodigal Son and my own son separated themselves from their families. I continue to test my faith in God, sometimes to near destruction, yet drat it, God is still there, loving, caring, creating and helping me to grow up in the faith and stand on my own two feet.

A Prayer

Lord, you knew the pain of separation when you lost your Son in death on the Cross. We pray for all those who suffer the pain of separation because of their bereavement.

We pray for those who have separated themselves, or who have drifted into separation and who are still journeying.

We pray for all those who have separated themselves, and do not have the courage to return, or sadly do not know how to return.

Be with each of us, whether in separation or union with the Father, that we may never be given up for lost.

Amen.

Comments

Peter Graves: *'An unusual approach to a well-known story that helps us to see things in a new light.'*

Paul Walker: *'I can see this sermon would be a great comfort to many who struggle with their faith and it says what people long to hear, that it is all right to be angry with God.'*

Jonathan Romain: *'The preacher shares his own experiences with a quiet sincerity that is very moving, although it should be noted that anecdotes from one's own life can sometimes seem trite to others and so they need to be handled with care.'*

Instant Gratification or Patient Expectation

Canon Michael Botting

Canon Michael Botting, 73, and his wife Mary have two children and six grandchildren. Canon Botting, a canon emeritus of Ripon Cathedral, studied science at London University and taught at a boys' school for two years before going to Ridley Hall, Cambridge, to train for the priesthood when he was 29. Although brought up in a Christian home, it was not until he was a student at Imperial College that his faith, through the Christian Union, came truly alive for him. His call to the priesthood came some three years later when he was travelling on the London Underground during the run-up to Christmas and saw a whisky advertisement, surrounded by holly, with the words 'Unchanged in a changing world'. 'My mind immediately went to the text in Hebrews which refers to Jesus Christ as the same yesterday, today and for ever. Here we were at Christmas, about to celebrate the birth of Christ, and whisky was being promoted as the unchanging thing. It hit me for six – I just felt I was called to put the record straight. It just so happened that John Stott was leading a mission near where I lived. I went to see him, and he immediately accepted everything I had said as a call to the ministry.'

He became curate at St Paul's, Onslow Square for five years and went from there to St Matthew's, Fulham. He was elected a member of General Synod when it first started, and in 1972 went to St George's, Leeds, famous for the Christian social work in its crypt. In 1984 he was called by the former Bishop of Chester to help set up a diocesan lay training course, which had attracted some 2,500 members by the time of his retirement at the age of 70. However, his preaching skills are such that he still finds himself in a pulpit most Sundays and sometimes morning and evening. He is currently honorary assistant minister at his local church, St Michael's, Newton.

'I think preaching is essential', he says. 'It is a fundamental way in which people become Christians. When I am in the pulpit I always bear in mind that there may be some people who are there for the first time, and some people who are there for the last time. I always aim to preach so that even if a person has never responded to the Gospel, he or she is at least challenged to consider it. And I aim to teach. I believe people always need to know more of what the Scriptures say.'

He had one unsettling experience during his curacy, when a member of his congregation stood up, shook her fist at him and walked out. 'But it was a long time ago', he says.

'One of the things that has dominated my ministry stems from my time at Fulham, when I noticed we were getting lots of children in the Sunday School but we rarely saw their parents. So I started a 45-minute Morning Service based on Morning Prayer, without any Psalms, and which I called a Family Service. It took off and drew in parents. Now very many churches in the country have a Family or All-Age Service. However, I believe ours was the first.' He has since written eight books on the subject of the Family Service.

He believes strongly that people should be reminded that the Millennium commemorates the birth of Christ above all else. He has written a 24-page book on astrology, expected to be published in 1999, where he mentions that astrologers see the Millennium as the end of the 'Age of Pisces' and the start of the 'Age of Aquarius'. 'I make it quite clear that it is all absolute nonsense', he says, although he does point out the odd coincidence that the symbol of both Pisces and Christianity is the fish.

'G. K. Chesterton said that when people give up believing in God they will believe in anything. I point out that astrology is condemned by Scripture in a number of places. Many of the things astrology seeks to do, Christianity has the answers for. And Christianity happens to be true.'

Canon Botting was on holiday when the Princess of Wales was killed. 'I have heard a number of people reflecting on her', he says. 'I am apprehensive to think of what would have happened if she was still alive, and I know I am not alone in that.'

B Y THE changing of the clocks we are briefly reminded that we are creatures of time. But how do we, as late twentieth-century Westerners, relate to time and eternity? As Christians do we behave any differently to the world around, in our attitude to time?

About thirty years ago I attended a conference where a sociologist-speaker divided up the three main classes of English society into upper class, or aristocrats, living in the past; working class, living in the present; and the middle class, living in the future, and believing in 'deferred gratification'. I wonder whether these distinctions still apply today, with our seemingly national demand by everyone for instant gratification of our desires – I hesitate to use the word 'needs' – instant coffee, credit cards that 'take the waiting out of wanting' and numerous firms offering to lend some of us inordinate amounts of money, obviously at some cost eventually, when the less frugal will be hard pressed to pay the premiums.

Recently there was a run on some item on the menu at one of the branches of a popular fast-food chain. A teenager was told there would be a delay for his order of 40 seconds – could he wait? One of the most alarming books I read some years ago was *The Seventh Enemy* by Ronald Higgins, because it exposes the reality behind the façade of those who work in the corridors of power. Life apparently consists of lurching from one crisis to another and hoping that the real crisis point is accurately recognized at the time.

But the life of many people is little different as they commute up and down the motorways or across the Atlantic, washing down a sharp deal with a few drinks – not even time for the extended business lunches these days! There is the perpetual struggling to maintain last year's standard of living, the rushing into co-habitation, occasionally marriage, and unhappily out again. There may be the anxiety of kids' exam results, because they must get their offspring launched as fast as possible into a similar rat race. And if some time off is managed, the pattern can be much the same. The weekend can be filled with DIY home improvement, which could be achieved far better by competent tradesmen, who could easily be afforded and would be grateful for the work. Or there could be flying off somewhere or another for an exhausting round of pleasures, night and day, with no time to stop and stare.

Archbishop Dr George Carey said in *The Times Magazine* at Christmas 1995: 'There is no longer space in the daily routine and life of the nation to allow enough sacred moments.'

But as a nation we have not always been dominated by time. Prior to the coming of the railways, for centuries it mattered not a whit that anyone knew what the right time was. Every town and village had its own rules for time – each village varied from the next. One consequence was that there was an increasing difference in time the further places were from London. But the railways needed to standardize the country's time in order to write timetables. From Britain, as railways spread worldwide, so inevitably did standardized time. It certainly reached Germany, where my wife and I have been impressed with the punctuality of its railways. I am told it is a different story in India!

In Psalm 90:3–4 we read '. . . from everlasting to everlasting you are God . . . a thousand years in your sight are like a day that has just gone by, or like a watch in the night . . .' This draws our attention to the relationship of God to time. Isaiah describes God as 'he who lives for ever' (57:15 NIV) or who 'inhabits eternity' (RSV). All the biblical words for eternity point to it as being everlasting, rather than timeless. The doctrine of divine timelessness, which has been held by some, really creates more problems than it solves. Professor John Polkinghorne suggests 'there must be an experience of time within God, in addition to his eternal nature'.

For the moment, however, though God 'has set eternity in the hearts of men' (Eccl 3:11), yet he has clearly set humanity in time, and limited time, according to the same Psalm: 'The length of our days is seventy years – or eighty, if we have the strength, yet their span is but trouble and sorrow, for they quickly pass, and we fly away' (90:10).

'Time is a great teacher', remarked the composer, Hector Berlioz, 'but unfortunately it kills all its pupils.' It is no doubt partly because human life on our planet is comparatively short that we are so concerned to pack so much in. However, the Psalmist's prayer is: 'Teach us to number our days aright, that we may gain a heart of wisdom' (90:12). And the apostle Paul's exhortation to the Ephesians and other churches was: 'Be very careful how you live – not as unwise but as wise, making the most of every opportunity, because the days are evil' (Eph 5:15–16).

We have an important spiritual lesson to learn: that our God is not in a hurry and our lives as Christians should not be dominated by a demand for instant gratification, but of patience. 'If we hope for what we do not yet have, we wait for it patiently' (Rom 8:25).

'But the fruit of the Spirit is . . . patience . . .' (Gal 5:22).

Way back in the Garden of Eden story God declared his plan to redeem mankind in Christ. It took many centuries to be fulfilled, when 'the time had fully come' that 'God sent his Son, born of a woman, born under the law, to redeem those under the law, that we might receive the full rights of sons' (Gal 4:4–5). Many commentators see significance in this time that had 'fully come' – that God had chosen that moment in history as the very best moment for the spread of the good news of sins forgiven, that his Son was going to achieve, and the command to proclaim the message worldwide.

The significance of the moment is also apparent in Jesus' ministry, when he said his time had not yet come, till we reach the visit of the Greeks to see him, when he declares: 'The hour has come for the Son of Man to be glorified' (John 12:23), by which he meant laying down his life for the sins of the world.

Christians worship a patient Creator and have to learn that patience is good for us; it is part of the image we have to reflect in our witness to the God we serve in the power of the Spirit.

For Christians the response to the world's demand for instant gratification is patient expectation as it is so splendidly spelt out by the Apostle Paul in Romans 8:18–25. Here he faces up to the world's temporal conditions, but also provides the Christian anticipation:

1. Pain and suffering: 'Our present sufferings' balanced by 'glory' (v. 18).
2. Futility: 'the creation . . . subjected to frustration'. The whole of the Book of Ecclesiastes so pertinently spells this out, as if it had been written specially for the late twentieth century. It is balanced by 'hope' (v. 20).
3. Creation mortal and corruptible . . . 'its bondage to decay . . .'. Ecclesiastes 12 specifically describes vividly creeping old age. But it is not just in ourselves. In our homes, moth and rust, woodworm and many other pests bring withering and decay. This is balanced by the 'glorious freedom of the children of God' (v. 21).

109

4. Creation and Christians groan: 'We know that the whole creation has been groaning as in the pains of childbirth right up to the present time. Not only so, but we ourselves, who have the first fruits of the Spirit, groan inwardly as we wait eagerly for our adoption as sons' (vv. 22–23).

We do not know when Jesus Christ will return to earth to bring about this transformation. During his own time here, he did not know either (Matt 24:36). However, when this glorious mystery does occur, then believers will not just be spectators, but participants, magnificently changed to conform to the image of God's son.

Martin Luther said he only had two days on his calendar, namely 'today' and 'that day'.

Meanwhile Christ has put his Spirit 'in our hearts as a deposit (or foretaste) guaranteeing what is to come' (2 Cor 1:22).

A small child goes into the kitchen on a Saturday, where mother is preparing some special pudding for Sunday dinner. The child is given a sample. This is not only a foretaste, but a guarantee of much more to come.

Our Christian patient expectation, therefore, is no wishful thinking, pie-in-the-sky when we die, but based on the promise of Jesus Christ and confirmed by the Holy Spirit. Surely such a prospect should show in our lives and be a witness to our friends and neighbours – caught up in the rat race and tyrannical demand for instant gratification.

May it keep us singing songs of patient expectation:

> One the object of our journey,
> One the faith that never tires,
> One the earnest looking forward,
> One the hope our God inspires.
> Soon shall come the great awakening,
> Soon the rending of the tomb:
> Then the scattering of all shadows,
> And the end of trial and gloom.

Comments

Jonathan Romain: *'Paints a picture of the problems of time and pressure which many listeners can identify with. The sermon did lead us from thinking about time in this world to considering time in the future. The mark of a good sermon is taking the listeners on a journey, starting from where they are and ending where the preacher wants them to be.'*

Paul Walker: *'Like Michael Botting I am fascinated by time, but unfortunately don't have time to think about it. Ironically I read this sermon while trying to fit in a thousand other different things. The sermon made me think again, it reminded me of the prison walls I have built for myself by deadlines.'*

Peter Graves: *'Thought-provoking sermon on an important theme, clearly related to contemporary needs. Perhaps fewer scripture references developed more fully would be more memorable.'*

Football:
The New Religion

RABBI HOWARD COOPER

Sermon preached in September 1997 on the Jewish New Year at Finchley Reform Synagogue, north London.

Rabbi Cooper, 45, is a psychotherapist in private practice. He trained at the Leo Baeck College, and works with Rabbi Jeff Newman, principal rabbi at Finchley Reform Synagogue. He preaches and leads services there at New Year and on the Day of Atonement, around September and October each year.

He became a rabbi first, and then a psychotherapist.

'Psychotherapy was what I wanted to do', he says. 'It is a way of working with people which is more intensive than working within a rabbinic framework.'

He adds: 'I became a rabbi because I was very inspired as a teenager by certain charismatic rabbis and teachers, people such as Rabbi Lionel Blue. I felt this was what I would like to do.'

He was brought up in a traditional, Orthodox household that switched to the Reform movement. He attended Sussex University and the Leo Baeck College before training as a psychotherapist with the Association for Group and Individual Psychotherapy.

'Most sermons I hear are either feel-good sermons or be-good sermons', he says. 'I try to avoid both these types. My stance is to help people deal with the fact that there is uncertainty in life. We have to learn to deal with the fact that we don`t know very much. We always think we know more than we do. I want to help people tolerate uncertainty, and maybe be inspired by the unknown in themselves and in the world. I don't think many preachers do this. Instead they prefer to talk about what is known, to give people a sense of certainty and security.

'I do not think that approach is particularly helpful, but that is because I am a psychotherapist.'

He believes everyone is searching for certainties in life. 'We all grasp whatever little scrap comes our way', he says. 'This is what religion should resist, not offer. When we grasp certainties, we are deluded into accepting a substitute for what is true. A pseudo-solution is always easy to grasp hold of, but it is ephemeral.'

The response to the death of Diana was, he believes, a mark of the sentimentalization of culture. 'I am a dyed-in-the-wool sceptic in relation to the many things attributed to this woman. I see almost no redeeming features in the phenomena associated with her death.'

On the Millennium, he admits: 'I have been thinking a lot about this, and I do not yet know what to think about it. I know it is something which could have value and significance, but I am waiting to see what it is. I think we can inevitably expect a lot of low-level hysteria.'

His books include Soul Searching – Studies in Judaism and Psychotherapy *(SCM Press, 1988) and* A Sense of Belonging – Dilemmas of British Jewish Identity *(with Paul Morrison; Weidenfeld and Nicolson/ Channel 4, 1991).*

W HEN we look back at 1997, can there be any other topic about which we could say that it touched the lives of countless people throughout the country, was the cause of shock, disbelief, spontaneous tears, heartfelt tributes to someone whose personal vision, whose contribution to our lives, will never be forgotten?

Truly a unique personality.

For many of us the retirement of Eric Cantona was indeed a traumatic moment.

Who did you think I meant? (I will say more about 'her' later on.)

1997 was also the year that I finally succumbed to temptation and took out a subscription to Sky Sports. And so it was that from July onwards, during every commercial break, one began to hear this stirring invocation:

Life. It can be difficult. We all know that. We all need someone to rely on.

Someone that's going to be there. Someone that makes you feel that you belong.

Someone constant . . .

Meanwhile on the screen, in black-and-white images that Leni Riefenstahl might have been proud of, there were ecstatic crowds, and bodies-in-motion, and footballers, and faces conveying ecstasy and anguish and joy and despair. And then, with quickened voice and throbbing, urgent beat:

It's part of our history, part of our country, and it will be part of our future. It's theatre, art, war and love . . . It's a feeling that can't be explained but we spend our lives explaining it. It's our religion.

Even without Sky you couldn't have avoided the huge billboard campaign plastered across the country, accompanying and quoting from this elegantly filmed, expensively cast, pre-season advert, which climaxed with this visceral appeal to the emotions:

They're our team, our family, our life. Football: we know how you feel about it, because we feel the same.

And with that final cliché – a sign of the new culture of emotionality that we are living in – perhaps we are not so far from that other event that shook so many people: the death of the Princess of Wales.

Decades ago, when the American philosopher George Santayana was asked what he meant by the word 'religion', he replied 'Another world to live in.' But when he said that, he could not have anticipated how, for hundreds of millions of men and women throughout the world, what he meant by 'religion' would one day be displaced in the most immediate, emotional sense by organized spectator sports.

Yet this religion, this 'other world to live in', contains not God but numerous gods – reigning athletes of extraordinary (if sometimes ill-fated) gifts. This religion is not a transcendental spiritual bond with a purposeful universe extracting from its believers rigours of conscience and behaviour, but an immanent dramatic bond sometimes sharply defined in terms of nationality, class or locality, at other times transcending race, religion, class, colour, nationality – there are pictures of Manchester United stars and teams in bars and bedrooms around the world.

The decline of religion as a source of significant meaning in modern societies has been extravagantly compensated for by the rise of popular culture in general. Sportsmania is just the most visible manifestation of this. Sport now is not just a pastime or hobby. Nor is it overwhelmingly male, as it used to be. It's no longer lowbrow but has become the stuff of serious literature (even sermons!). Because sport has invaded areas of life where previously it had no presence. We now have sport as fashion, as business, as showbusiness; sport for health, as the body beautiful, as a new source of values. And by sport I don't just mean the old sports and competitive team-games that we all used to do at school, but the new sports like aerobics, and jogging, and bungee-jumping, and martial arts, and skateboarding . . . the list is endless. The emphasis now is on choice, self-expression, creativity, fitness, health – the body as a source of value in itself.

One *could* say that all of this is narcissistic self-indulgence. There's even that whiff of the fascistic in aspects of this devotion to the body. But Judaism never split the body from the soul in the way that some versions of Christianity did. The body always remained a vehicle for the exploration and celebration of the spiritual. And in a secular world, the spiritual can be found in the most unlikely of places, places left open by the decline in religious belief, and the failure in the West for religion to keep itself open to the always elusive but always present spirit of God, which can manifest itself wherever and whenever we are open to it: even on a football field, even in a synagogue.

And as more people do sports, so too more of us watch sports. For the sports fan the team, or idolized individual player, provides a kind of externalized soul: there to be celebrated, but – as the God of the ages apparently was not – there in full public view. You can still buy Manchester United replica shirts which instead of the Frenchman's name on the back, have just one word: *Dieu*.

And early last year Manchester Gallery of Art exhibited Michael Browne's twelve-foot high oil painting, based on two Old Masters, in which the original figures of the risen Christ, and Caesar surrounded by Roman soldiers, were replaced by the figure of Cantona, with the United manager and some of the younger players from the team standing in for the original onlookers.

Adulation and adoration on this scale is telling us something about the deep human need which we all have, a spiritual need, for heroic figures who can represent for us certain ideals and values, and who can give us access to moments of joy, of rapture, to visionary moments of the sublime, to a sense that the old religious categories of mystery and wonder and awe are momentarily present within our de-sacralized world. (The near-sanctification of Diana the Compassionate – or was it Diana the Victim-Martyr? – is linked to this.)

It's theatre, art, war and love . . . Is it? How is football 'theatre'? It's true that there is an element of drama within all well-contested matches, and there are actors and audience (so to speak), and sometimes there is the experience of catharsis by the end of a particularly important game – when we are finally released from the inner tension generated between our excitement and hope for victory, and the fear of imminent defeat. And of course defeat is by far the most common experience for players and fans alike (particularly for those of us who follow a team like Barnet!). Defeat is built into the structure of the game in a particular way: only one team can win the Cup, only one team can win the League – all others have to face the poignancy of loss, the pain of mourning, of waking up the next morning knowing what might have been, but isn't. Like a death, like the failed dreams in our lives, defeat scars the soul over and over again with the awareness that failure and loss are unavoidable aspects of our shared human condition. Just as religion consoles us with a belief that something of us does survive even the ending we call death, so too, in the religion that is football, the pain of defeat and loss is lived through, and survived: there is, after all, next year – and hope can be renewed.

But unlike theatre – where plays have scripts, and one knows that Lear always dies at the end – a game of football has no prepared script. However rehearsed the players are in skills and tactics, what generates passion in the viewer is the unmediated experience of spontaneity, of the unpredictable, of living moment by moment not knowing what will happen next. This is where the experience of watching football

can be seen to intersect with the religious insight that there is no knowing, no controlling, what life will reveal next. The Jewish understanding of God is that God is process, God is present, God is present not in
space but in time. *Adonai,* we recall, means Being, That-which-is. 'I am
what I am' God says to Moses, which means that God can never be
pinned down, is never predictable. The unexpectedness of what can
occur, moment by moment, on the football field gives its watchers a
kind of secular spiritual experience: we can experience in a concen-
trated form the extraordinary mystery – which we might glimpse only
rarely during the rest of our lives – of life unfolding, unrepeatably,
before our wondering eyes.

Two years ago, in the final of the European Cup Winners' Cup, one
could sit through a tense unfolding drama of a match, more than two
hours long, up to its final 30 seconds, when in one moment of unimag-
inable spontaneity, of consternation and wonder, a moment which
caused overwhelming joy or heart-wrenching despair depending on
which team you supported, the Spaniard Nayim lobbed the ball from
the half-way line in a long, looping arc, which soared and rose and
then, breathtakingly, plummeted beyond the desperately retreating
Arsenal goalkeeper into the net to win the match for Zaragoza. For supporters of these two teams, moments like these become etched in the
mind far more powerfully and long-lastingly than anything conventional religion can offer: they teach of sorrow, or thankfulness, of how
in one moment one's life can turn from hope to despair, or despair to
gratitude; of how one action, or one moment of vision, can transform
one's destiny. The spiritual significance of football becomes revealed
within these unrepeatable moments.

I say unrepeatable, but here we have a difference between watching a match in person and watching on television. The experience in
the flesh can open us to feelings which we may be sorely missing in
our own lives: the experience of community, of unity, of shared purpose. Some of this is experienced by the viewer too, but what television does in addition is allow us to revisit these moments of
inspiration. The experience of watching football on TV can make us
realize how painful it is sometimes that we cannot replay or freeze-
frame our own lives. Our moments of inspiration, of awe, of pleasure,
can never be revisited, never re-captured. Photos, videos, may provide us with memories, but in that distance between the past and the
present there is the unspeakable knowledge of loss, the pain of time's
arrow, which flies in one direction only: to the grave. There is no
going back. The past is unrecoverable, unrevisitable. There are no
action replays of the lives we lead. This is part of the harshness of
human existence.

It's theatre, art, war and love . . . What about football as art? Well here
just a short quotation must suffice. In case the drift of what I've been

saying about the spiritual component of football hasn't been clear, let me quote that cultural icon *de nos jours*, Eric Cantona himself:

> An artist, in my eyes, is someone who can lighten up a dark room. I have never and will never find any difference between the pass from Pelé to Carlos Alberto in the final of the World Cup in 1970 and the poetry of the young Rimbaud, who stretches 'cords from steeple to steeple and garlands from window to window'. There is in each of these human manifestations an expression of beauty which touches us and gives us a feeling of eternity.

That we poor human beings, in all our frailty, are capable of creating moments that touch the soul of others, moments of eternity – whether the medium is music or poetry or art or literature or sport – this creative spirit is a mystery, beyond analysis. At these moments we may glimpse our connection to that Creative Spirit which animates all of existence, that energy with a thousand names, that we the Jewish people have named *Adonai*.

It's theatre, art, war and love . . . clichés maybe, but every cliché contains at least half a truth. Of course not all sport, not every football match, exists in this dimension. More often than not, it is tedious, frustrating, just plain disappointing. But 'war and love' reminds us that sport generates in us elemental passions, that it offers us opportunities for the control of aggression in the service of something grander; in fact success in competitive sports necessitates the transformation of aggression into creative rather than destructive channels. If war is the undisciplined outpouring of uncontained aggression, sport is its benign, creative counterpart. It provides a model of the capacity in human beings to control and discipline and re-direct their innate aggressive feelings into moments of inspiration, and creativity.

And what of love? Well, the individuals and teams who become the finest, the most skilful, exponents of their chosen disciplines do evoke in those who follow them emotional bonds as passionate as any in human experience – not excluding marriage and family. And as in any relationship, love also includes a measure of idealization of the beloved. Which leads me to Diana.

Amidst all the brouhaha surrounding her death, one theme stands out. There is a yearning in our society – a spiritual yearning – for something which religion used to give, but now hardly ever does: the experience of being cared for by a compassionate loving Being, of being supported by a presence that comforted and strengthened one in one's sorrow, of knowing that inside we might feel vulnerable or inadequate or ashamed but we were, nevertheless, essentially good, and lovable.

In the past this yearning was met by feeling part of a community, a community of faith in which we could celebrate joyful moments, or receive solace for our pain, a community which thought in shared ways about the things that mattered, which existed as one link in a chain of tradition that reassured us that we still lived in an ordered, meaningful and benign universe.

If much of this has now withered, that does not mean that the yearning has disappeared. It is still alive and seeking to express itself within that vacuum of loneliness and insecurity that so many people nowadays inhabit. And this modern alienated condition has come about through the failure not just of our religious institutions, but of our political and educational and social institutions to help people feel part of a collective and caring environment. The British revolution that we are living through is a revolution born of the need for intimacy.

Religion used to enable people to feel close – to one another, and to God. After Diana's death people created shrines of flowers, and gathered prayerfully on the streets with the religious impulse for quiet reflection, because they felt, rightly or wrongly, that they had lost someone who cared, and someone whom they felt they had an intimate connection with. Just as on 1 May they deserted in their millions the party who were seen, rightly or wrongly, to be indelibly tarnished by the callous, dismissive, cold-heartedness epitomized in that notorious phrase 'There is no such thing as society'. Tony Blair, with his overt Christianity, was seen, rightly or wrongly, as caring about society; as standing for the wish, religious in its impulse but taking on secular forms, to rebuild the social order with care and compassion. That he speaks with real emotion – and not just after Diana's death – is seen as a mark of his sincerity. And this is one of the hallmarks of this quiet British revolution: the stiff upper lip is being replaced by the quivering lip.

It seems that some of Diana's favourite images of herself were those where she was captured tearfully, Madonna-like, holding a sick or injured child. In that extraordinary combination of selflessness and self-regard she presented herself to the psyches of millions of people as a perfect vehicle for a whole spectrum of projections. Caring, loving, compassionate, healing – she was the fantasy of our potential, how we would like to think of ourselves. But at the same time as being our potential, she was also a reflection of our everyday fallible and mundane selves: troubles in her marriage, a victim of circumstances, doubts about her looks, an eating disorder, a prey to vanity and the urge for revenge, having therapy, perpetually searching for happiness. And all her flaws becoming virtues by dint of that confessional style, compulsively self-revelatory, which now passes for honesty.

Suddenly we find that we are living in an Oprah Winfrey culture where emotion equals honesty; tears mean sincerity. And image is everything. We are living through a transformation in our society, but during it we should be alert to this deep confusion between show and substance. That religious yearning, that spiritual impulse in us, which seeks out meaning, and community, and the values of caring and compassion, must be able to discriminate between true and false emotion, between image and reality, between fads and idols which come and go – and that other timeless Presence which remains with us, beyond images.

As we watch this new culture of emotionality unfold we need to recall our historical experience as Jews, where we so often learnt of the deadly consequences of living in societies where group emotion went unchecked by the counterbalance of reason, rationality, analytical intelligence. To develop our own emotional intelligence, to become emotionally literate, is quite different from the emotional bulimia which disgorges undigested feelings into the public domain.

And in a culture increasingly dominated by the image we Jews can also remind ourselves that, historically and religiously, we were iconoclasts: image-breakers, distrusting the illusory security provided by false gods, manufactured images. We chose the more austere path of following a divine presence who refused to be made into an image, fixed and static, and thus under our control. Our challenge was to discern the spiritual within the material world, to attune ourselves to that unseen Presence that lies beyond the image. That challenge still remains.

Comments

Paul Walker: *'A stunning sermon. Howard Cooper treads on dangerous territory. He gives us a wonderful critique of our failed society. He does not say things are better or worse, but that they are different.'*

Peter Graves: *'Good example of how to use contemporary secular experiences as a window into the spiritual quest. An arresting style which communicates deceptively simple concepts with insight and power.'*

Jonathan Romain: *'Uses good, homely images, weaves in and out of football imagery and religious insights. The result is both entertaining and educational.'*

The Search for Unity

CANON JOHN YOUNG

Sermon preached in Southlands Methodist Church, York, for *The Morning Service* on BBC Radio 4, Sunday 25 January 1998, during the Week of Prayer for Christian Unity.

Canon Young, 61, is the only preacher to make the final 30 in three of the four Preacher of the Year awards to date. He has a roving brief in York Diocese, given him by previous Archbishop, now Lord, Habgood, with an official title as Diocesan Evangelist and based at St Paul's Church, although he attends St Edward the Confessor. He and his wife Isabel have two children and two grandchildren. Isabel worked until recently with children with special needs at a comprehensive school, but now works at an after-school club. Canon Young's father was a Welsh miner who went to London looking for work, and who met his mother, the barmaid at the Lion and Lamb in Hounslow, Middlesex, when he popped in for a drink.

Before his ordination in 1964, Canon Young did two years' National Service and also worked as a physical education teacher. He became a committed Christian as a student at Loughborough, when he was 21.

'Two things brought this about. One was the friendship of a Christian man. The second was when he invited me to a Christian weekend where the speaker was Dr Donald English, who went on to become twice the President of the Methodist Conference. Before that, although I went to Sunday School like most children of my generation, I was not an active Christian.' Soon after this, he began to think about ordination.

Canon Young preaches every week in a different church, not always Anglican, in the diocese. He also chairs an ecumenical organization, One Voice, which links some 250 churches from many denominations including the Salvation Army, the Methodist Church and the Roman Catholic Church.

He has had some varied preaching experiences.

'Only once have I preached in St Paul's Cathedral, and on that occasion I stood in the great pulpit, opened my mouth and 30 people walked out. I like to think they were tourists who didn't understand English! Once, as a reward for preaching at a Lifeboat service, I was taken for a ride in the boat. One mile out from shore I was told they needed some hands-on practice, and I was thrown overboard! Luckily after ten minutes they came to reclaim me. I'm not sure if this was them commenting on my sermon or not.

'Preaching is not a lecture, although obviously they have something in common', he says. 'Like a lecture, there needs to be a structure and a clarity. Good sermons can change people, they can really help with the stuff of life by giving people encouragement about their faith. I hope we have all had the experience of sitting through a sermon and feeling a cloud of difficulties lift as we see our problems in the perspective of the love of God. Or we have sat there and thought, yes, tomorrow I must write that letter of reconciliation, or send off that cheque. Preaching sets our lives within the context of the love of God, which is encouraging, but it has to be shared, which is challenging. When I am in the pulpit, I hope to get through to people, to encourage and to challenge – to inspire even. It is not me and them, it is us.'

He wants to harness the Millennium for Christ. 'I don't think it is going to be the end of the world or anything like that. But through the value that Christians place on the Church year, we acknowledge the rhythm of time. It will be a pretty hard-hearted person who, the moment the clock moves to 2000, is not moved to do some re-evaluation of their life. It ought to be like a grand Shrove Tuesday, where we think that this time we are going to do something about those resolutions. Also for the churches, it is an opportunity to forge a link between 2000 and the name of Jesus Christ. There is a lot of evidence suggesting that link will have to be made by us, because it is not coming naturally to people's minds. It is a great challenge and a highly significant opportunity.'

Canon Young was presenting the BBC Radio York Sunday religious programme the morning after Diana died. He spent the day travelling around, interviewing the Archbishop of York, Dr David Hope and other senior clergy. 'I was very involved', he says. 'Diana's death links with the Millennium, in the sense that whatever one feels personally about it, as a nation we wanted to share our emotions. I think it showed that there is a desire for togetherness. The Millennium will be the same sort of thing, but a time of penitence and celebration rather than a time of grief.'

ON 25 May 1971, a terrorist dumped a bomb in the entrance hall of a police station in Belfast. Sergeant Michael Willetts of the Parachute Regiment was in the station and discovered what had happened. He entered the hall and held the door open to allow people to escape as quickly as possible. He then stood in the doorway, shielding those taking cover. The immense blast killed him. Michael was awarded the George Cross for his bravery. The official register states: 'By this considered act of bravery Sergeant Willetts risked – and lost – his life for those of the adults and children.'

That incident illustrates one of the answers which the New Testament gives to the question: Why is the death of Christ so important? It illustrates the love of God. Michael Willetts proved his concern for his neighbours by giving up his life. God proved his care for us by giving up his Son. Jesus proved his love for us by consenting to the cross.

Rather than using his powers to dominate and control, Jesus chose to submit to the worst that human beings could do. So the power of God is seen in symbols of weakness – in a borrowed manger and on a wooden cross. Here is power kept in check; power handed over; power utterly controlled by love.

And here we see the miracle of love. For Jesus took the ugly things which sent him to the cross – jealousy, greed, cruelty and fear – and he used them as the raw materials from which to quarry our salvation.

No, the preacher has not forgotten the date. He is not confusing the Week of Prayer for Christian Unity with Good Friday or Passion Sunday. I began like that as a reminder that Christian unity starts at the foot of the cross. We believe that Jesus died for the whole world. But he died for the Church too. 'Christ loved the Church and gave himself up for it' was how St Paul put it.

Having prayed for his disciples that they might be one as he and his Father are one, Jesus gave himself up for them, to bring this about. The implications of this are immense. We gather this morning in this Methodist church in York, from a range of churches. We come together, not as individuals interested in religion; nor as people sharing a common interest. No. We meet as the company of the redeemed. Calvary was the place of our redemption. Crucifixion was the cost of our redemption. Deep and joyful gratitude must be the mark of our redemption.

'We love', wrote St John, 'because he first loved us.' Christian ethics, Christian lifestyle, and Christian unity are responses to that love – the love revealed so clearly in those symbols of weakness – the hired cradle, the wooden cross, and the borrowed tomb.

So – at the deepest and most significant level – we *are* united. Our task is to seek to become what we are: one body, one living temple, one family of God. We have been bought with a price – each and every one of us. We have a common inspiration, we share a common faith, we rejoice in a common baptism and a common covenant. We owe allegiance to the same Risen Lord, under the inspiration of the same Spirit.

We may not yet kneel at a common table. But we do kneel together – in heart and in imagination – at the one true cross of our crucified Saviour and Risen Lord. Over the past few years the churches have made encouraging progress in working and worshipping together, and many deep friendships have been made across the denominational divides. But we are not at liberty to leave it there.

The search for an ever deeper unity is not something for a minority of Christians 'who like that kind of thing'. It is a divine imperative, passed to the whole Church by Jesus Christ.

Of course, unity does not mean uniformity. Let a thousand flowers bloom. The modern Church is living proof that we can worship in spirit and in truth, in a wide range of styles and moods. But if there is no true fellowship among us, no deep and costly love one for another, no deep desire to meet and share our different perspectives, no willingness to listen and to count others better than ourselves, then we belong to a religious club, rather than to the Church of Jesus Christ. And we have nothing to say about reconciliation and forgiveness to our broken and divided world.

And this is one major aim of the exercise. Christian unity, togetherness and harmony are good in themselves, of course. But they serve a wider purpose too. Jesus prayed that his disciples might be one, in order that the world might believe. This is one of the key points of the great prayer of Jesus, recorded in the seventeenth chapter of St John's Gospel. A united Church is a serving Church and a witnessing Church.

I end with a true story. A friend of mine has an antique stall in Covent Garden. One day she bought a piece of modern coloured glass for £1. Later that day she sold it for £10. She was very pleased until she discovered that it had been sold for £6,000. Later – at auction – it went for £14,000. My friend admits that she simply didn't recognize its true value. As Christians we have been entrusted with the Gospel – the pearl of great price. It is only when we recognize its true worth that we shall determine to allow nothing – certainly not our unhappy divisions – to prevent it being displayed, in all its healing beauty, to our troubled and divided world. We turn all this into prayer, as we sing our next hymn, which begins 'Lord of the Church, we pray for our renewing'.

Comments

Peter Graves: *'A clarion call to Christian unity. Profound insights are clearly and simply developed and very well illustrated.'*

Paul Walker: *'An interesting link between the message of unity and the doctrine of salvation.'*

Jonathan Romain: *'A good use of story at both the beginning and end of the sermon, the former to introduce his main theme and the latter to crystallize the message in an anecdote that will be remembered long afterwards.'*

Building Bridges from God to God

Rabbi Frank Hellner

Delivered on 24 January 1998, at Finchley Progressive Synagogue.

Rabbi Frank Hellner, 63, and his wife, Valerie Boyd-Hellner, are both married for the second time. Between them they have six children and four grandchildren. Rabbi Hellner was born in Philadelphia, although his mother was British born and her family emigrated when she was a child. His father emigrated to New York from Russia at the turn of the century, fleeing the Russian pogroms. Rabbi Hellner was brought up in a secular household, but became ultra-Orthodox in 1946 after joining a Zionist organization. 'My first encounter with religious Judaism was through Zionism', he says.

He attended the Orthodox Yeshiva University in New York, but gradually became disillusioned with Orthodoxy. 'Intellectually and emotionally, I could not accept it', he says. After his first degree he went on to the Hebrew Union College, a training institute for the Progressive rabbinate. He was a rabbi in New York for two years before coming to the Finchley congregation, a Liberal synagogue, after Rabbi Sidney Brichto, a leading rabbi in Liberal Judaism, suggested they would make a good match. He is currently collecting material for an anthology on Jerusalem.

His congregation, of about 500 members, at the Finchley Progressive Synagogue, is growing. One reason is a policy of welcoming the non-Jewish spouses of members as far as possible. 'If someone marries a non-Jewish partner and wishes to convert, we organize a programme which lasts a minimum of a year, in which they study the basics of Judaism', he says. 'If they don't wish to convert we respect their wish to remain in the faith of their birth, but they are still welcome to participate in virtually all aspects of the synagogue and be as supportive as they wish.' He has just set up the Friends of Finchley Progressive Synagogue for such people to join.

He is sometimes surprised by the impact his sermons make. 'I often get people who quote to me things I have said in the distant past, which I have completely forgotten. I am amazed at how much actually does go in. People will often challenge me if they think I am contradicting myself in different sermons. I tell them that even a rabbi grows in perception, and changes his mind.'

He points out that a rabbi, although ordained, is not a priest. 'A rabbi is really just an educated layman. So the task of a rabbi is to teach. That is what

I hope to achieve. I also try to give people an awareness of Jewish sources, of what tradition says, and where we might agree or disagree with something said in the past. I hope to impart Jewish knowledge, and also to console and offer hope, particularly in an age where people have lost hope.' A good sermon should be 'sculpted', he says, like a work of art. 'It should have a beginning, a middle and an end, and somewhere in there have three illustrations. They must be good transitions between points. I often hear rabbis who do not carry people along with them, and then they lose them.'

He was trained in homiletics by a Shakespearean actor. 'He told me that you can have the best sermon in the world, but if the delivery is poor, forget it. It is just the same as Shakespeare in the mouth of some poor actor; without delivery it is nothing.'

The Millennium has special meaning for him because 1 January 2000 is his 65th birthday. 'It was very farsighted of my mother to arrange that', he says. 'I officially retire then. So for me it is a momentous date.'

He says that, obviously, from a Jewish perspective it has no religious significance. 'But it has a secular significance in the way that the beginning of every new decade is significant.'

And he compares the death of Diana to the shooting of President Kennedy. 'It is one of those occasions when you always remember where you were when you heard. I was sitting on a friend's yacht in Turkey when someone rang and told us what had happened. It was such a sad and terrible loss for her family and children. It was heart-rending.'

WHEN our new gender-inclusive prayer book, *Siddur Lev Chadash*, first appeared three years ago, there were those who voiced reservations about the change in God's name from 'Lord' to 'Eternal One' and from 'King' to 'Sovereign'.

With the passage of time, many of us have become more comfortable with these new designations. But even for those who were initially cynical about such changes, it was never a question of ideology or about the validity for such changes in gender, but merely one of preference of one name over another.

It was and is absolutely clear to all of us, I believe, that the old masculine names for God were not only in contrast to the traditional *spiritual* nature of God – in which by definition God has no gender – but tended to marginalize modern Jewish women who were finding it increasingly more difficult to relate to a God in exclusively masculine language.

The problem of God's 'name' – how we address God – is as difficult a problem as the belief in God itself; and in a very real sense, it is the other side of the theological coin. How we define God tells us a great deal about our comprehension of God and, perhaps, even more about ourselves and how mature or immature our theological perspective is. Like everything else in life, 'change' is endemic and so each age must seek to redefine the name of God within the ideological framework of that age. This, of course, does not mean that God changes. Merely, that our *concept* of God changes as our understanding of ourselves and the universe about us undergoes reassessments as time goes by.

All this is not at all foreign to the spirit of Judaism. I am sure that most of you are familiar with the rabbinic understanding of the repetition in the *Tefilah* of the words 'God of' before each of the patriarchs. It would have been sufficient simply to pray 'God of Abraham, Isaac, and Jacob . . .' instead of 'God *of* Abraham', 'God *of* Isaac', 'God *of* Jacob'.

The reason for the insertion of 'God of' before each patriarch, our sages tell us, is to remind us that the God of Abraham was not the same as the God of Isaac and that the God of Isaac was not the same as the God of Jacob. Again, not that God changed, but that the perception of God changed with each patriarch as each underwent his own unique experiences which coloured his own world-view.

This attempt to find God and *define* God is ancient. And so it is, that in our Torah reading of last week, at the burning bush, when God charges Moses to go to the Israelites and take them out of bondage, Moses asks God: 'But when I come to the Israelites and say to them, the God of your ancestors has sent me to you, they will ask me "What is God's name", what shall I say to them?'

And God responds to Moses: '*Ehyeh-asher Ehyeh.*'

'This shall you say to the Isaraelites: "Tell them, Ehyeh has sent me to you!"'

And God concludes:

'This shall be my name for ever; this shall be my appellation for all eternity' (Exodus 3:13–15).

God's reply, it seems, rather than clarify, appears to obscure. Just what does this esoteric *Ehyeh* mean? Anyone conversant in Hebrew knows that it is a form of the verb 'to be'. Dr Joseph Hertz in his famous Torah translation renders it: 'I am that I am.' Rashi, the eleventh-century biblical exegete, translates it: 'I will be what I will be.' And the contemporary American Jewish Publication Society despaired of translating it and simply transliterated the Hebrew as *Ehyeh-Asher-Ehyeh*, with a little footnote that says: 'Meaning of Hebrew uncertain; variously translated "I am that I am" or "I will be what I will be"' (*The Torah* (JPSA, 1962), p. 102).

Once again, in this morning's Sidra, we find God confronting Moses with this introduction: 'I am *Yahweh* (invariably translated "Lord"). Until now I appeared to Abraham, Isaac and Jacob as El Shaddai, but I did not make myself known to them by my name *Yahweh*' (Exodus 6:2–3). Whatever else *Yahweh* means, it is clear that like *Ehyeh*, it too derives from the verb 'to be'.

It is *here* that we must search for our definition and perhaps, it is in the very elusiveness of the verb that we find our answer. God *is* what

God *is* to every generation. God is defined by the insights of the world in which we live even as God *will be* what God *will be* to future generations. Total comprehension of the infinite is not possible to the finite human mind. We can only apprehend God, not totally comprehend God. We can only know God within the limitations of the human mind and within the context of the spirit of the age in which we live.

To the patriarchs, God's distinctiveness from other gods as *El Shaddai* or *Elohim* was essentially one of degree, not of essence. Moses, however, now begins to see God in a new light: a God whose very essence is unique. A God who is faithful, compassionate and meaningful and who will ultimately redeem humankind. This new insight into the nature of God will deepen within Moses throughout the course of his career and, towards the end of his life, will emerge as ethical monotheism – the belief in one God who demands justice, righteous living and moral behaviour from all.

Ever since then, human beings have sought to understand God's essence by redefining God by name. And so it was that even in patriarchal days, the name of God underwent changes; so it has continued throughout history. Whenever an older concept of God was inadequate to unify all the people's experience, the definition of God grew to embrace new experiences, and with a change in name came a change in what people felt God wanted for them. Thus Philo, the Alexandrian-Jewish philosopher of the first century, expressed his concept of God in purely Platonic terms as the *Logos*, the 'word' or 'idea', which influenced the early conceptualization of God as found in the Gospel of John.

But, with the destruction of the Temple, the Torah's grasp of God's essence, with a lust for animal sacrifices, brought through the mediation of a priestly cult, fell short of the realities of that age. Neither the biblical Yahweh, nor Elohim, nor El Shaddai were sufficient to satisfy Judaism when the Greco-Roman civilization disrupted and radically transformed the Middle East.

With Hellenism's stress on the pre-eminence of the individual, the entire conceptualization of the human being's role in society changed. Men and women saw themselves no longer as *passive* recipients of divinely revealed laws, but as active participants in lawmaking.

Was God to be only what the Torah described God as being? Was its idea of God's unity no larger than the confines of Middle Eastern mentality?

To address these new realities, an entirely new and revolutionary Jewish scholar class arose – sages, to parallel the philosophers of the Greco-Roman world. These Pharisees, as they were known, and their spiritual heirs, the 'Rabbis', launched Judaism into a new orbit. They did not extract the conventional 'Old Testament' concept of the deity, nor did they seek to perpetuate old names for God. Instead they audaciously posited a new concept of God who reflected the highest ideals and values of their age. *Elohim-Yahweh* of the Pentateuch became known again by new names:

Avinu-Shebashamayim, Our Father in Heaven;
Hakadosh Baruch Hu, The Holy One, Blessed be He;
Shechina, The Divine Presence;
Makom, the Omnipresent.

These are names not hitherto found in any of the Jewish writings. This was a new idiom for a new age in which the individual could approach God directly, through prayer and *mitzvot* without the intervention of priests and sacrificial offerings. Thus in a troubled society dominated by foreign occupation, the rabbis posited a God who would guarantee the faithful a good life if not in this world, then certainly in the world to come.

The Pharisees and Rabbis thus established a one-to-one relationship between the individual and God; the one striving after a standard, the other, the standard itself. The one finite and transient, the other infinite and abiding for ever.

Thus, on the brink of a new society, the rabbis spanned the turbulent waters which threatened to douse the divine spark, by building a bridge from the God of Moses to the God of the rabbis.

The bridge that they built was indeed a sturdy one. It spanned centuries and continents. For more than 1,800 years, this bridge carried the survivors of pogroms, crusades and inquisitions, during which time still new names for God were found: The *Ein Sof*, The Infinite One, *Hasibah Harishonah*, the First Cause, *Makor*, The Source, thus stripping the God concept of all anthropomorphic attributes. It lasted until the modern age when, with the advent of the Enlightenment, Emancipation and its stress on science and reason, the bridge began to sag under the weight of analytical discoveries and pure logic. Humankind was coming of age!

Yes, modern men and women could visualize a messianic age. But it was not the one that would be ushered in by angels or even a man riding on a white ass. Moderns saw that 'day of days' emerging out of the cogs and iron wheels of industry – out of the pains of class struggles, out of man's striving to perfect himself and the world. They saw messianism around the corner and felt its pain but this was no mere metaphysical happening. This was mankind evolving within the complexities of civilization.

Again, the old bridge was inadequate to bridge the tremendous chasm. Neither the God of Torah nor the God of the rabbis nor the God of the medieval philosophers could adequately encompass all the complexities of the nineteenth-century idealism and morality. Revelation may have begun at Sinai, but it did not end there. Revelation they saw as a continuous process. For them, God is revealed not only in the annals of antiquity, but whenever the oppressed find liberation and whenever righteous indignation burns within the human soul against injustices. It is there and then that God is revealed, and through human beings God would affect the ultimate plan.

Once again a bridge was built from God to God and, armed with nineteenth-century idealism, God was able to overcome scepticism and withstand science's thrusts. God, in co-partnership with human beings, was on the move towards the dawn of a new day.

But those living then had no idea that their march towards world unity and brotherhood would have so short a journey. Auschwitz and Hiroshima exploded the dream and shrank the foundations of the bridge. Many despaired of the God of process and progress. In their desperation and gloom, they reverted back to the old God and Sinai – the God of the Burning Bush. The world made no sense . . . unless one could make that huge leap of faith across the abyss – unless the 'I' could experience the eternal 'Thou' and somehow find meaning in existence. Another bridge was built and a new name for God coined.

All that was yesterday. And here we stand on the banks of another abyss. We, too, like Moses before us – like every generation since, ask: What is God's name to be now? How will we relate to the God of the Millennium? Will the name we find be adequate to encompass all the exigencies and difficulties of the modern age? Will we yield to despair and give up belief and faith altogether – or will we – as did our ancestors before us – be courageous enough to continue the task of building bridges from God to God?

History itself has provided us with the solution in God's esoteric reply to Moses: *'Ehyeh asher Ehyeh* – I am that I am and I will be what I will be.' I am that I am: as for me, my nature and essence remains eternally the same, but as for you, I will be what I will be: I will be understood anew and differently in each generation to come.

As for the present, referring to God as the 'Eternal One' in our Liberal prayer book may seem a self-conscious attempt to describe God in the modern idiom, but it is theologically correct for our time and articulates a concept of God which is in tune with the ethos of our age.

God remains the same, but our definition will continue to alter as our conception of life, our values, our goals undergo change and evolve. And as we comprehend reality and come to know truth just that much clearer, so will we better comprehend the source of all reality and the ground of all being. For the present, while our knowledge of God continues to expand, it will continue to be partial and God will be known by many names. Like Moses, we shall be blessed with only a glimpse of God's presence.

And for the future? When humanity is forged together in a real and lasting unity; when the millennial dream of real peace is achieved; when war and hunger will be forgotten and disease and plague will be conquered, when our relationship to God and each other has become ultimately clear and stable – then God will have only one name, for then we shall be one, and on that day, *bayom hahu*, as our prayer has it, *bayom hahu, yihiheh Adonai echad u'sh'mo echad* – God, too, will be one and God's name will be one.'

Comments

Jonathan Romain: *'A sermon that is all about us and gives a powerful message that not only rings in our ears long after the sermon is finished but demands that we take some action in our own lives. It is a sermon that tackles real issues and helps us face them, too.'*

Paul Walker: *'A brilliant sermon. I read it again and again and again. Frank Hellner points out that while God is changeless, the way he is perceived does change, and that the Bible gives a precedent for this.'*

Peter Graves: *'A well-developed argument, clearly taught in a relevant way for people of today.'*

The Problem of Pain

Sir Alan Goodison

Sermon preached at Eucharist at St John's, Hampstead on 15 March 1998, the third Sunday in Lent.

Sir Alan Goodison, 71, who with his late wife, Rosemary, has three children and four grandchildren, joined the Foreign Office in 1949, where he learned Arabic. Half of his career was spent in, or dealing with, the Middle East, and half in or on Western Europe. 'My career went backwards and forwards between working in the Foreign Office in London advising ministers, and working in embassies abroad', he says. He was deputy ambassador in Rome from 1976 to 1980. In 1983 he went to Dublin as ambassador, where he was engaged in negotiating the Anglo–Irish agreement of 1985. He retired in 1986 and became director of the Wates Foundation for five years. His responsibility was to help distribute up to £1.5 million a year in grants to young people who were disabled, homeless, who missed out on an education or who were disadvantaged in other ways. After stepping down from that he began to study theology seriously, and gained an MA in systematic theology from King's, London, last autumn.

However, he has been a reader in the Anglican Church for 39 years. The son of a bank official, he was brought up a Methodist and went to Colfe's Grammar School in Lewisham. He became an Anglican when he got married.

When he was an undergraduate at Trinity, Cambridge, studying German, he did not attend church regularly. 'It was getting married that had an important effect on me, and having a family. But I have never been what used to be called "an enthusiast". My church in Hampstead is mainstream. The priest wears vestments and we have occasional incense.'

He began as an Anglican reader in Lisbon, Portugal when the vicar fell ill and there was no one else to take the service. 'They appointed me reader because I had done a lot of preaching in the Methodist Church', he says. 'I took the services every Sunday for six months.' Since then he has been a reader in Anglican parishes and chaplaincies worldwide, including Jerusalem. He recalls once preaching in Dublin on baptism. 'The main point of the sermon was to reassure people that God looked after babies, whether they were baptized or not. As I was coming out of the church, a woman thanked me for emphasizing how essential it was to have babies baptized as early as possible. She had heard the opposite of what I had said! When I preached at St Patrick's Cathedral in Dublin, the Dean said to me: "Whatever you do, don't preach to the people. Preach to the microphone."'

He believes the sermon is the most direct way that God can speak to people. 'I only say "can speak". I don't say "does always speak". But when preaching, I hope to be a channel, to help God to get the message across.

'I think people are less and less prepared today to spend time and energy listening to a sermon. As a result it is very important to keep the sermon short, to keep it pithy and to attract people's attention right at the beginning. Because once you have lost it, you will never get it back.' He continues: 'A sermon should be Bible-based. But I do my best to try to give people an angle that they might not have thought of themselves. I do not necessarily give them the obvious message.' He normally preaches fortnightly, before Sunday morning Eucharist congregations of 150 or more, or evening congregations of about 60.

When speaking of the Millennium, he is not shy of speaking his mind. 'I really think it is rather a boring subject. It seems to me an entirely artificial date. All the evidence suggests it does not really represent 2,000 years since the birth of Christ at all.'

Likewise on the death of Diana, Princess of Wales. 'I met her on a number of occasions, having been director of a charity. The last time I met her was in a very small group at the opening of a house for people with AIDS, to which my charity had contributed some money. It belonged to St Mungo's in Hammersmith. I think she was a well-meaning person but that she did not deserve the adulation which was poured out on the occasion of her death. I was preaching the Sunday after she died and it was necessary to say something. I certainly considered it important to give the people in church an opportunity to feel their grief had been expressed, whatever I thought.'

Text: Luke 13:2.

> Do you think that because these Galileans suffered in this way they were worse sinners than all other Galileans? No, I tell you; but unless you repent, you will all perish as they did.

TODAY'S Gospel drives us to consider the problem of undeserved suffering and the problem of pain. The anecdote has an authentic ring; it is clear that Jesus was asked to comment on news of the day, news which no other record has retained, though we know that Pilate was eventually sacked because he was responsible for a massacre of Samaritans on their holy mountain. His interlocutors may have hoped that Jesus would say something treasonable about Pilate. Instead, he firmly dissociates suffering and death from sin.

Suffering has nothing to do with what you deserve; it is not a punishment. That was a sensational statement in the light of prevalent beliefs at the time; indeed, such beliefs have not yet entirely disappeared, as popular prejudices about AIDS demonstrate. It is a great pity that no more of what Jesus said on this subject has been preserved. Here, as so often, we have been left obliged to work out our ethical problem ourselves.

In a very moving presentation of *Shadowlands* at the Pentameters

Theatre last month, Bill and Sylvia Fry, among other things, showed us how C. S. Lewis's view of the problem of pain became less dogmatic and more uncertain with his experience of it. It seems to me that, in considering this problem, we must begin with the fact that Jesus suffered, and, in doing so, demonstrated that there is suffering at the heart of the Godhead. It seems to me that everything we know about Jesus Christ is simultaneously a window through which we can see a part of the life of God. Suffering, then, is not the consequence of sin, since Jesus was sinless; it is the consequence of being alive and sharing in the image of God. I do not suggest that pain doesn't hurt, or that the pain of the body is somehow not really real; a Christian Scientist would take that view, but it is neither scientific nor Christian. Of course the body, and bodily pain, are important; God made them, and Jesus feared the pain. So I believe that God understands and feels it with us.

Sometimes, people talk as if human beings make God suffer pain. I find it a rather difficult idea, that we should control God's reactions. It seems better to think of God feeling with us the pain which we feel. This pain comes from nature, from accidents like the collapse of a tower, or disease, or from wrong relationships, whether political, like Pilate's, or personal. We know that God feels such pain, because Jesus suffered, and we know that he feels it in sympathy with us, because Jesus did so. This consciousness of God's feeling for us and with us is in itself a consolation, because it means that we never suffer alone; each one of us is part of what God is concerned about. (I hope, by the way, that it is clear that I am talking about *all* human beings here; I am sure that God feels the sufferings of wicked people just as much as those of good people, if he distinguishes between the two.)

But of course, even if you accept what I have said so far, there are further questions I have not answered. First of all, why have pain in the created order at all? The fact that God shares it does not explain its existence. If we had made the world, we wouldn't have made it like this. I can only say that I am coming round to the conclusion that God regards pain as less important than we do. Even in our Gospel reading, it is noteworthy that Jesus expresses no regret at the untimely deaths recorded. In the parable, he allows that more time may bring forth the fruits of the Spirit, but he is not bothered by the idea of cutting the tree down. We must not be led astray by Victorian images of Jesus from observing that in some ways God is quite ruthless and tough. We must suppose that if life is unfair and painful that is what God intended, and we must suppose that he knows best.

You may argue that the unfairness and toughness is not due to God, but to some secondary power, like the Devil, or just wicked human beings. At first sight, such theories appear to answer some of our questions, but it seems to me that they invariably lead to scenarios in which God is helpless in the face of evil. I am entirely against any such ideas.

Before you know where you are, you are facing a dualism in which you think evil is at least as strong as good. Such a view may have some popular support, but it has no place in a Christian pulpit. I would much rather believe that our Father in heaven sees benefits in suffering which I cannot understand; I cannot suppose that he is not in charge. If I did, I wouldn't bother to come to church.

The other question is of course: Why should the wicked flourish like the green bay tree when innocent people suffer? I think our Gospel reading suggests the answer. Everybody suffers, one way or another. The fact is that we notice it when a sweet old lady dies of cancer and we don't remark on it when a hard-drinking old rogue dies in a car crash. Death comes to all of us, not because we deserve this way of dying or that way, but simply because towers, and strokes, fall on people, and cancers, and thugs, murder them. Let us at least, on the basis of this Gospel reading, stop complaining about what happens to people. There is no one to complain to. God is not going to be bargained with about it. Jesus clearly took the view that things are simply like that.

I realize that this is not a very common line to take from the pulpit, and that the orthodox view is that God is just and deals justly; I rather think this is a view left over from Judaism, and that it Is not borne out by experience. The fact is that what God is overwhelmingly concerned with is love, and love never bothers about just deserts; it gives people not what they deserve, but all it can give. Love does not think in the categories of what is earned or what is due; it is concerned, not with pain or well-being, but with relationships.

It reminds me of the way my children behaved when they were small; they were continually complaining that things, or, more often, their parents, were not fair. What they usually meant was that each wished us, or fate, or someone, to give them a better deal than their siblings. We loved them all and wanted to give each every good thing that we could; that did not mean we could protect them from broken collar-bones or early boarding-school. I do not suggest that the complaint of grown-ups against pain or suffering is not concerned with real problems; but I do suggest that it is measured against an ideal of happiness which is illusory. We think that we do not deserve to suffer, ignoring one or two unfortunate episodes in our past, and consider that therefore it should not have to be endured, and we forget that Jesus made it clear, so long ago, that questions of deserving were irrelevant and that endurance is a divine virtue.

Comments

Peter Graves: *'Brief and to the point. Helpful insights clearly shared.'*

Paul Walker: *'Sir Alan Goodison faces that most thorny of all questions faced by the theist, how can a God of love allow suffering. The comforting answer is that the nature of suffering is of the nature of God, something which many people need to hear.'*

The Word Became Flesh

Neil Booth

Sermon preached at Bolton St James Church, Bradford, West Yorkshire, at Midnight Communion, Christmas Eve, 1997.

Neil Booth, 56, is a lay reader in the Church of England. His wife Yvonne, who has multiple sclerosis, teaches music at home. He has two children by a previous marriage. They have been married for 20 years. Mr Booth, a former partner with the accountants KPMG in their Leeds office, retired four years ago after a heart attack. A chartered accountant, he was for many years recognized as the country's leading expert on National Insurance.

Mr Booth became a Christian when he was 11 years old. 'I was taken by my religious education teacher at my grammar school to a Scripture Union children's rally in Manchester. The preacher was quite famous in his day, R. Hudson Pope. He gave a straightforward presentation of the Gospel and asked for a response. I started writing to him, and we corresponded regularly for two or three years until I was established in the Church.

'My parents were not churchgoers, although I had been baptized in the Church of England. I started going to the local Methodist church and I trained as a Methodist local preacher at 16. In 1969, I became a reader in the Anglican Church. I decided to be ordained and went to St John's College, Durham. But after two years there, my first marriage broke up, which was why I left theological college and went back to accountancy. At the time, it seemed a huge disaster, but it has all worked out right.

'I had this heart attack and a quadruple heart bypass in 1993 but my blood pressure was uncontrollable and I was told I had to retire. I still preach every other week at my local church, Bolton St James in Bradford.'

He recalls an early preaching experience when he was 16. 'I went to a village near Bradford. A woman in the front row proceeded to breastfeed her child right through my sermon. It was very disconcerting. I tried to look anywhere but at her.'

Preaching is vital in today's society, he believes. 'I would not put myself through what I go through each fortnight if I didn't think it had a value. I feel very, very called to preaching. It is not just a hobby with me. I believe it is one of God's chosen ways of speaking to people. People are used to listening in a different way because of the influence of television. But that simply means we have to change our approach to the sermon. But we must still grab people's attention and keep it to get God's word through to them. For me, it starts before I even get into the pulpit. When I know I am preaching on a particular Sunday I look up the readings and try to find out what God's message is from them. Everything is then crafted to that end, and getting the message across. Whatever God is saying, the important thing is that I help to get that into people's hearts and minds.'

The experiences of illness in his family have strengthened his faith. 'I very much believe that God can and does heal directly, as well as through the medical profession. One of my formative experiences in recent years was a conference on healing in Harrogate, where John Wimber was one of the speakers. At that point I was a 60-a-day smoker. I had been a smoker since my teenage years. I had tried everything known to mankind to stop smoking, and I could not. At the conference, in 1995, one of the speakers asked if anyone there wanted deliverance of anything. I put my hand into the air and went into the aisle. The speaker commanded in the name of Jesus that the addiction would be broken. I fell down on the floor. I lay there for about half an hour. One of the helpers told me that the Lord had taken away all the withdrawal symptoms, and had given me back the years of my life I had lost by smoking. I have not wanted to smoke since. I regard that as a healing, particularly when every doctor I saw told me I was killing myself with cigarettes.

'It was a wonderful experience. I believe very much in healing. My local church is thinking of introducing healing sessions into some of our communion services, and I am looking forward to that very much. I equally believe that God has healed my heart, through the skills of the surgeons who worked on me.'

Text: John 1:1–14.

May the words of my mouth and the thoughts of all our hearts be now and always acceptable in your sight, O Lord our strength and our Redeemer. Amen.

'May the words of my mouth . . .' Oh, I love words! I always have done.

On the morning I began to attend Keighley Boys Grammar School in 1953, I very nearly alienated myself from the rest of my intake because of words. The English master asked: 'Who likes reading dictionaries?' and I put my hand in the air, expecting most of the other boys to do the same, only to find that I was the only one . . .

But it didn't put me off. I still like reading dictionaries; and I still like to find out where words come from. Only last week, the word 'wassailing' cropped up in an old carol. 'Now what does that mean?' I wondered. 'And what are its roots?' Ten minutes later, I had the answer. Wassailing is from two Anglo-Saxon words: *wes*, meaning 'be' and *hal* meaning 'healthy'. '*Wes hal*' was an Anglo-Saxon toast. They would raise their glasses and say: 'Be healthy!' That is: 'Good health!' as we would put it today. But I got a bonus. I read on in my reference book and found that, in those Anglo-Saxon days, you didn't raise a *glass*, you raised a kind of jug called a 'piggin'. So put the jug and the toast together to make a name for your inn and what do you get? 'The Piggin Wes Hale', or, as we now spell it and know it: 'The Pig and Whistle'. Fascinating, eh?

But words, of course, are not just there for our amusement. Indeed, that's the least of their functions. Words are first and foremost the means of getting things done. Words are for making things happen. People say: 'Actions speak louder than words' and maybe they do. But it's usually words that bring about the actions. 'Stop!', 'Go!', 'Shoot!', 'Hide!', 'Charge!', 'Help!' Think of the changes that the utterances of just those few words have brought about in the history of the world and in the histories of countless individuals in it. And they'll go on doing so until the end of time. Words change things. Words make things happen.

So maybe it's not surprising that St John, when he thinks back to the beginning of everything – the creation of this world and the entire universe – speaks about a word that brought it all into being, that made it all happen. It was not a new idea. The Greeks had come up with it 500 years before Christ. A philosopher called Heraclitus argued that only a word, a *logos,* of great power could call everything there is into existence and keep it all held together and running smoothly. But the Jews had had the idea for even longer. They, too, believed that the heavens and the earth and everything in them came into being because of the word – the *dabar* – of God.

> By the word of the Lord were the heavens made, their starry host by the breath of his mouth.
>
> Psalm 33:6

> And God said, Let there be light and there was light.
>
> Genesis 1:3

And so now, to Jew and Greek, who together make up the world as John knows it, John begins by saying something that they already know and with which they can readily agree:

> In the beginning was the Word [*logos* to the Greek, *dabar* to the Jew] and the Word was with God and the Word was God.
>
> John 1:1

So far, so good. Heads are nodding in approval.

He was with God in the beginning. Through him all things were made; without him nothing was made that has been made. In him was life, and that life was the light of men.

John 1:2–4

Heads are still nodding, but not quite so vigorously. Both Jew and Greek can still go along with John . . . except for his puzzling use of the words 'he' and 'him'. Surely he means 'it' – '*It* was with God in the beginning. Through *it* all things were made. In *it* was life'? Surely you can't talk about a word as a person?

But yes, John can. Indeed, this is the heart of the astounding message with which he is about to assail the ears of horrified Jew and incredulous Greek.

The Word became flesh and dwelt among us.

John 1:14

He who called the very universe into existence and sustains it through every moment of time has himself entered that universe as a human being.

Can you begin to grasp the enormity of that message? Let me put it to you another way. Millions of years ago, God spoke, and the universe began. If anyone had been around to hear the sound of God speaking (which of course they weren't), they would, so the physicists and cosmologists assure us, have heard a 'big bang' – the sound of a gigantic explosion as raw energy became primal matter and began to accelerate away from the point at which the word was spoken. Awesome!

But then, just 2,000 years ago, God spoke again. And this time there *were* people around to hear him – but just two at first, a young girl, Mary, and her husband Joseph – and what they heard was this.

[Sound of baby crying played through audio system.]

The voice of God. The cry of a baby. The Word has become flesh and moved into Bethlehem. Many of our Christmas carols take up the theme:

Lo, within a manger lies He who built the starry skies.
'See Amid the Winter's Snow', Edward Caswell (1814–78)

Ah, Lord, who hast created all, How hast Thou made Thee weak and small?
'Give Heed My Heart', Martin Luther (1483–1546)

And that line of Charles Wesley's that I love the best of all:

Our God contracted to a span, incomprehensibly made man.
'Let Earth and Heaven Combine', Charles Wesley (1707–88)

And the big question, of course, is why? Why does God clothe himself in flesh? Why does the All-mighty become the All-lowly – soiling the straw of a cattle trough, depending for his very life on milk from a peasant girl's breast? What on earth is the Eternal God thinking of when he does such a thing?

Well, in a word – he is thinking of 'you' . . . and 'me'. As the carol says:

> Mild He lays His glory by,
> Born that man no more may die;
> Born to raise the sons of earth,
> Born to give them second birth.
>
> 'Hark, the Herald Angels Sing',
> Charles Wesley (1707–88)

We've all been born once and we'll all die. But God did this astounding thing that we all might be born again, born into his family, receive his life, inherit his kingdom.

> He came to that which was his own, but his own did not receive him.
>
> John 1:11

No, they took him outside the city walls and nailed him to a cross.

> Yet to all who received him, to those who believed in his name, he gave the right to become children of God: children born not of natural descent, nor of human decision or a husband's will, but born of God.
>
> John 1:12–13

This whole amazing event – this stupendous self-emptying by God – was a rescue operation motivated by unspeakable love. Love so great that it broke the barriers of space and time. Love so great that it broke the barriers of life and death. Love so great that it broke the barriers of flesh and spirit. The Word became flesh and dwelt among us. Indeed, he did. And now *the* Word awaits *our* word. Awaits a word spoken in sincerity in your heart and mine as, once again, we contemplate Jesus, Immanuel, God with us, lying in a manger. He awaits a simple 'Amen' to all that he has done; a simple 'Yes' of acceptance.

Yea, Lord we greet Thee
Born this happy morning;
Jesus, to Thee be glory given!
Word of the Father,
Now in flesh appearing:
O come let us adore Him,
Christ the Lord.

'O Come, All Ye Faithful',
Anonymous, trans. Frederick Oakeley (1802–80)

A joyful and peaceful and blessed Christmas to you all!

Comments

Jonathan Romain: *'A good opening that gains both our attention and our curiosity, leaving us wondering where the preacher is going to lead the sermon after taking us to the Pig and Whistle pub. The touches of informality – heads are nodding – helps keep us on the preacher's side.'*

Paul Walker: *'If our words have power then God's words must also have power. There is a real attempt to connect with the God of the big bang. The result is that the incarnation becomes even more awe-inspiring.'*

Peter Graves: *'Interesting development of a classic text which moves forward to a clear challenge to respond to the amazing grace of the Christmas message.'*

D . . . . ing Thomas

MICHAEL TOPLISS

Sermon preached 19 April 1998 at Methodist churches in Walsall, in the morning at Moxley and in the evening at Aldridge.

Michael Topliss, 63, a local preacher of Bloxwich, Walsall, and his wife Hilary have two children and three grandchildren. They are both retired teachers, he of religious education and Hilary of domestic science. Mr Topliss, whose father was a minister, has been an accredited Methodist local preacher since 1960. He went to a Methodist school where chapel was compulsory. 'I did have at the time rather an obtuse attitude towards the formality of the religious set-up there, but then and since I have remained committed.'

His preaching grew out of his college training and teaching. 'I felt a moral responsibility to use on Sundays as well some of the theological understandings I was seeking to grasp.' He preaches regularly in the eight churches of the Bloxwich and Willenhall Circuit, to congregations varying between 10 and 200, and sometimes, as on this day, outside the circuit as well.

He has had some interesting experiences in the vestry, where it is customary for the steward to take a prayer with the preacher before the service. 'On one occasion, the steward prayed that we should all become like the Ethiopian eunuch. At the time, I did not feel I could say Amen to that. But I realized later that he wanted us all to go on our way rejoicing! That's fine.

'Preaching is certainly alive today, though for most of our preaching, we are not faced with many outsiders. I have a high doctrine of the sermon. The sermon has to be wrought: there needs to be a wrestling with the text. It may comfort, challenge, or confirm in the faith. In the pulpit, I sometimes try to encourage people to see things in a new light, and maybe challenge them to think or to do things differently. It helps to have an occasional surprise in a sermon, and something memorable for people to take away. Mind you, you cannot accurately anticipate which idea they will latch on to, and sometimes they remember words you never said!'

He believes the Millennium must be taken as an opportunity to proclaim Jesus Christ, but he 'would also wish God's whole world to be able to celebrate (that which the pious tend sometimes to hug to themselves as an individual religious experience) the cancellation of unpayable debt.'

Text: John 20:19–31.

T HOMAS DIDYMUS, also known as 'Doubting' Thomas, does get a bad press. Most of us seem to prefer people whose stance is definite. Those newspapers which declaim their judgements in the boldest headlines are the popular ones. The Christian denomination which accepts the infallibility of the Bishop of Rome when he speaks *ex cathedra* is the largest one. The preachers attracting the greatest crowds are those declaring what, on the face of it, the Bible says.

But, you know, there is an unacceptable face of religion. There is an intolerance, amongst some branches of Christianity, which assumes that 'our' way is undoubtedly God's way. Adamant certainty can be the bane of the Church. And because certainty so often is intolerance, and because doubt is frequently a reasonable stance, I have tended to think of Doubting Thomas as a man after my own heart.

Many of the great discoveries have resulted from an individual's courage to question the received wisdom of his time. Many scientists have been justified after bravely doubting the certainties they were taught. And when it came to religion, Tennyson had it that 'There lives more faith in honest doubt, believe me, than in half the creeds' (*In Memoriam*, xcv).

So you will understand that when I first saw what was the Gospel reading appointed for today, I was all for approaching 'Doubting Thomas' with tolerance and sympathy. And, like many of you perhaps, I have always imagined Thomas's words to have been spoken hesitantly:

> Except I shall see in his hands the print of the nails and put my finger into the print of the nails, and put my hand into his side, I will not believe.
>
> John 20:25

The expression of doubt and the questioning of God are important aspects of the Bible. Read the Psalms, not in the bowdlerized versions we find in the hymn books where the awkward bits have been edited out, but read them in the Bible itself. There's plenty of doubting and questioning in the Psalms: 'How long, O Lord?' (Psalm 13:1). There's a great deal in Jeremiah: 'Why did I come from the womb to see only sorrow and toil to end my days in shame?' (Jeremiah 20:18). Or try the Book of Job: 'God's onslaughts wear me down!' (Job 6:4).

And the Church needs to let doubts and confusions and uncertainties surface. Let the questioning be aired – that's the way to faith. The minister at Dunblane after the massacre had it right. 'No explanations.' No glib answers are in order when life hurts. But you can press your questions. The appropriate hymns of complaint have yet to be composed. But it is OK, it is biblical and it may be courageous to doubt.

'My God, my God, why . . . ?' 'Why have you forsaken me?' (Matt 27:46). You see, it's Christian. Doubting Thomas, you're all right. And there are times when we're with you.

But do you know, I think we might have been led astray. Now I read afresh what Thomas said, it doesn't sound at all like doubt.

EXCEPT I SHALL SEE IN HIS HANDS THE PRINT OF THE NAILS AND PUT MY FINGER INTO THE PRINT OF THE NAILS, AND PUT MY HAND INTO HIS SIDE, I WILL NOT BELIEVE.

That is not doubt. That is plain disbelief!

'Doubting Thomas'? Who coined the phrase anyway?

Well, it was a Victorian parson: a man called Sparrow, as recently as 1877. And then it was used in *Harper's Magazine* in 1883. We've all been led astray for over a century!

But before that, Mrs Gaskell, in her novel *Mary Barton* in the 1840s, knew what she was talking about when she has one of her characters refer to herself as 'an unbelieving Thomas'.

Yes, if Thomas had only doubted, I would have defended him. Through the challenge of doubt, your faith can be strengthened.

But now I look at Thomas again, I find he is suffering from the very type of prejudice I most condemn. Whether or not I agree with its conclusions, I don't approve of a closed mind. And Thomas, in his denial of what his fellow-disciples are telling him, is intolerant and aggressive.

Doubting Thomas? No, distrusting Thomas, disbelieving Thomas, dismissive Thomas. Let's look at what he says:

'Unless I see . . .' Unless I *see*.

We've got that daft phrase: 'Seeing is believing.' But you will have had many an experience to make you modify that idea. Seeing is just not sufficiently reliable as a basis for believing. I vividly remember the first time I was given gas at the dentist's: as I came round, voices were telling me to spit out. And there was this glorious, shimmering, swirling, psychedelic basin on my right, and I felt privileged to be allowed to expectorate into it. And so a copious mouthful of bits and blood landed down the nurse's skirt, for the sanitary white spittoon was actually on my left! On another occasion, I recall racing to a Yeoman's bus-stop outside Hereford to catch one of their green buses that I'd seen coming: only to find that the bus left me standing there because it was a Midland Red. And when my mother-in-law was in Walsall's geriatric hospital, one night she described convincingly a visit they'd all been on that day . . . to Bradford Cathedral! She'd seen it all!

Listen to two rival supporters after a football match: one has seen a famous victory by a team of heroes; the other, a daylight robbery and an incompetent referee. And then of course, so much of what we are allowed to see in the press and on television has already been edited. Our seeing is conditioned sometimes in order to influence belief.

And having said all that, there are of course plenty of things which we are prepared to believe although we do not see them: things which are not apprehended by our physical senses – qualities like love, courage, faithfulness, honesty – which nevertheless we trust and accept and admire and know are real.

Unless I *see* – won't do.

'Unless I see . . .' Unless *I* see.

But this is just not true to the way we live, is it? We do not require first-hand experience of everything. We are prepared to trust other people in many spheres of life.

We don't sit in front of the television set saying: 'Unless somebody explains to me how this works, I will not switch it on!' We don't refuse to register our vote just because the candidate hasn't come and knocked at our own front door. You don't make a personal examination of all the details of its structure before you sit on a chair or climb a stile. You don't take your coffee black just because *you* didn't milk the cow. We trust. We take people's word for it. And yes, sometimes we are let down. But our standard frame of mind is not suspicion but confidence, not distrust but a preparedness to rely upon other people. And think how angrily you react when somebody chooses to test the veracity of your word: 'There aren't any biscuits left', you tell your son . . . and still he tries the tin! Don't you seethe?

Unless *I* see (for myself). We don't like that in other people.

'Unless I see . . .' *Unless* I see.

This is even more unpleasant and sinister, isn't it? We're into the world of argument and threat.

Remember at school: 'Unless you take your elbow off my half of the desk, I'll . . .' and he didn't, and you did, and he hit you back, and playtime became a fight-time, and when you got home you had to explain your bloody knuckles and your black eye. And later on in life, some parents and some teachers never learn to be careful about making threats. Your bluff is called and you lose face. Or perhaps you carry out the threat, and things go from bad to worse. Unless . . . If you don't . . . Such bargaining and threatening is so destructive of our personal relationships.

Unless I see – is no go.

Unless I *see* – says Thomas, in defiance of our common experience.

Unless *I* see – says Thomas, hurting all his friends.

Unless I see – says Thomas, threatening to break with them completely.

O God, how I hate this Thomas!

'Denying' Thomas with his unreasonable demand to see before he'll believe anything. 'Dissenting' Thomas, with that self-importance which demands that everything requires his personal sanction. 'Defying' Thomas, with the argumentative stance which distances, making unbridgeable the gulf he sets between himself and others.

Doubting Thomas, I could have sympathized with. Distrusting, disbelieving, defiant, disputative Thomas, I cannot stand. And you know why? Because I am that Thomas!

Unless I see.

'I'll believe that when I see it!' How many times have we been dismissive of the possibility of somebody's change of heart?

'They wouldn't have got away with that if I'd been there!' You remember when something unexpected turned up at that church council you missed because they had the inconsiderate presumption to convene it on your birthday!

'Unless I get an apology from her . . .' Do you too wield threatening weapons like 'Except . . .' 'If you don't . . .' 'Without . . .' 'Until . . .'?

I cheated earlier on when I suggested that we'd all been too ready to believe that Didymus was 'Doubting' Thomas. There are in fact some wise commentators who saw all along that the man's real problem was his cussedness. They speak of his vigorous disbelief, his extreme incredulity, his belligerent pessimism. And yet, seeing Thomas in this light makes the account of the conclusion to this incident the Gospel for today. It is good news indeed. Great news for Thomas. And wonderful news for us.

When on the Sunday after Easter Day the Risen Jesus comes again, perhaps Thomas has already mellowed a bit. After all, he is back with his fellow-disciples.

Here you are! says Jesus to Thomas, offering his wounded hands. But there is no need.

For it's the climax now of St John's account.

This is the Gospel's defining moment.

For *believing* Thomas mouths the ultimate pronouncement of Christology. He makes, not just *a,* not merely *his,* but *the* Christian profession of faith:

'My Lord and my God!' (John 20:28).

That's definite. It is definitive. This is 'Defining' Thomas!

And then there is declared the concluding blessing for all the Christians down the centuries who without seeing have believed that Jesus is Lord, whose faith in the divinity of Jesus is based upon the apostles' testimony and whose experience of Christ's presence today is as real as theirs then.

No ifs and buts: it is their faith, it is Thomas's belief, it is your experience and mine that Christ is alive.

'Peace be with you!' he says.

And we respond:

'My Lord and my God. Alleluia!'

Comments

Paul Walker: *'This wonderful sermon made me look all over again at the story of Thomas; I don't think I will ever call him doubting Thomas again. The real value of this sermon is the way Michael Topliss's psychological profile of Thomas works with his profile of himself and then, at least in this case, with the hearer. Definitely one of the best.'*

Peter Graves: *'A helpful and perceptive reflection, not only on doubt and faith but also on many of the attitudes with which we approach God. Much solid content clearly applied.'*

Jonathan Romain: *'A good example of a preacher taking us into his confidence, so that we give him ours and then suddenly he opens our eyes to something new and we emerge with a fresh understanding.'*

Skin-deep Christianity

PASTOR IAN SWEENEY

Delivered at the City Hall, Sheffield on 27 October 1996 at a celebration organized by the Sheffield Black/Majority churches called 'Together in Unity Now: A Celebration of Christianity in the City'.

Pastor Ian Sweeney, aged 33, and his wife Jennifer, a nurse who also teaches sewing part-time, have three children. Mr Sweeney's father was an engineer, and both parents, who came to Britain from Antigua in the 1950s, were Seventh-day Adventists in Leicester. 'Being a minister was always what I wanted to do. I was brought up in a Christian home but, all credit to my parents, I was never forced to go to church. At the age of about ten I felt a deep conviction that my life should be spent sharing the word of God.

'From that age, I never had any inclination to do anything else.' He has three congregations, with about 150 worshippers in Carterknowle, Sheffield, 110 in Burngreave, Sheffield and about 25 in Chesterfield, Derbyshire. The largest two are predominantly Afro-Caribbean, with the smallest being mainly indigenous English.

Mr Sweeney was ordained in 1994 after studying for Bachelor's and MA degrees in theology at Newbold College, Berks.

'The value of preaching as I see it is that I am trying to help people come to a closer encounter with God, or a clearer understanding of the reality of who God is and what God desires for their life. I try to make God a reality for people by being as relevant as possible to where they are in their life. I do that by trying to make my sermons as applicable to their experiences as possible. So I will try to make a spiritual point by using illustrations people can relate to because they have been there in their lives.'

He says that a good sermon must have an aim, a purpose or an object. 'I have to be going somewhere with a sermon. There might be one point, two points or three points I want to convey. They have to be points that are relevant and applicable to people's lives right now. The sermon needs to be illustrated as much as possible, because people remember the illustration more than anything else. Humour helps because it engages people. People have to engage with the message. We live in a time when entertainment is so fast, immediate and colourful that if you stand up in front of people for 20, 30 or 35 minutes and are not creative, they will go to sleep on you. That is a fact.'

As a child, he recalls listening to a fiery sermon when the preacher's false teeth flew out halfway through. 'He was going hammer and tongs in the pulpit. He was an old West Indian and was really giving it something. But he clearly must have played cricket. Because as his dentures flew through the air, he caught them with one hand and whipped them back in as fast as they came out. It happened so fast most people missed it, but us youngsters at the back nearly died. The preacher was as cool as anything.'

He has not seen The Full Monty. *'But I find Sheffield tremendously warm. The people are characteristically Yorkshire, in that they call a spade a spade. Even though Sheffield is a large town, there is still a strong sense of community here.'*

His response to any racism he encounters is one of Christian understanding. 'My parents instilled in me a sense of my own worth, a sense of dignity. While I would be lying to say that words do not hurt me, my parents taught me that ignorance will always seek to attack that which it does not understand. I accept that the world does have a number of ignorant people in it. That is a reality of life. I don't allow things to hurt too much.'

He believes strongly that the Millennium is primarily a Christian festival. 'It is set around a time period. My hope is that it will bring people to a sense of the reality of Jesus Christ. Like Christmas, there is a danger it will be too easily hijacked and understood in terms of everything other than its original purpose.'

The death of Diana moved him, and he preached the following morning on the importance of living life without regret in each day. 'I preached the weekend immediately following the death of Diana, on the Sunday morning. I made aware to the congregation the fact that death does not announce its arrival. We have to be sober – not morbid – but to be aware that death can approach at any time, and under unexpected circumstances. We have to live our lives in the present moment with a sense of completion. If we have things to say, we should say them now, because we cannot be sure we will have an opportunity to say them tomorrow. Either we, or our loved ones, might be met by death before then. This is not morbid, it is comforting, because if we live like this, we need never have regrets. We have to try and make our lives complete for every day.'

Text: Galatians 3:26–28.

I CANNOT speak for anyone else, but I was hooked by the year-long trial of O. J. Simpson. The various twists and turns of the case were constantly being analysed and evaluated in my mind. Often times I role-played the events in courtoom no. 103 in Los Angeles. Never mind that Judge Ito was presiding over the case, I became a judge too. Never mind that Marcia Clark was the chief prosecutor, I was prosecuting too. Never mind that Johnny Cochrane was part of the defence dream team, I also was there preaching, in my summing up, and crying out:

'If the hat doesn't fit, you gotta acquit.' I don't know about you, but I was gripped.

On Tuesday 10.00 Pacific Time, the United States practically came to a standstill to await the verdict. Even at the White House, all presidential briefings were postponed as the President followed the proceedings. The tension was unbearable as Judge Ito went through the various preliminaries prior to the reading of the jury's verdict. My heart was in my mouth.

While watching the programme *Court TV* last night, it was said that on hearing the verdict 'Not guilty' black Americans, on the whole, rejoiced whilst white Americans were dismayed. Robert Shapiro said that Johnny Cochrane had dealt the race card from the bottom of the pack. One juror is alleged to have told her daughter that although she believed O. J. was guilty of the crime, the lying testimony of the clearly racist ex-policeman, Mark Fuhrmann, undermined the prosecution's case. The Los Angeles police department had braced themselves for a violent whiplash from black and ethnic minority communities in Los Angeles in case the jury returned a 'Guilty' verdict. In following this case, it seems to me that for many Americans, the innocence or guilt of O. J. Simpson had no deeper basis than the colour of his skin. For many, the issue of his innocence or guilt was only 'skin deep'.

Skin-deep Christianity in church

Experience has shown me that for many Christians, evaluations are made of one another, not on the commonality and unity of being washed in the blood of Jesus Christ but rather on the colour of our skin. In July 1995, in Sheffield, the churches ran a tent crusade. I was the evangelist and my name and number was advertised as the person to contact for further information. Very early one morning I received a call from a lady who gave her name and said that she was the leader of a small group of house Christians who met in the north of the city of Sheffield. She expressed a desire to come but there were a few doubts in her mind and so she enquired if her group would be welcomed. I said: 'Of course!' She asked about a few of our beliefs and she was happy with the responses. Then she asked the question: 'If we come, will we be swamped by a lot of black people?' When the telephone suddenly wakes me up from my sleep, I do not generally think at my best, and I can say things which I later regret. But the Lord Jesus issued a command to my tongue: 'Peace be still.' I said nothing. The silence was embarrassing. I think she understood the silent rebuke, because after a few minutes, she began to stammer and stumble with her words and she concluded the conversation by saying: 'We'll need to pray about it.' I said: 'Please do.' She never turned up, but if she had, Lord knows that I, who rarely greets with a hug and a holy kiss, would have given her one. What hindered her from Christian fellowship with Seventh-day Adventists had nothing to do with bad publicity concerning Waco, or theological difference. Her hindrance was the evaluation of fellow-Christians that only went skin deep.

Racism and prejudice have, unfortunately, been a part of the very fabric of the Christian Church from its inception. The racism of the early Christian Church was not the result of God's design but of man's sinfulness. Of the apostle Peter, we through the Gospel are made well aware that he was impulsive and violent (John 18:10) and possessed a filthy tongue with which he could curse with the worst of men (Matt 26:74). And then, Acts 10 reveals another flaw in Peter's character. To put it bluntly, he was a racist. Many of us are familiar with the story of God's response to Peter's prejudice and racism. A vision was given showing a sheet with all manner of unclean animals of which Peter, a God-fearing Jew, was told to eat. He was puzzled as to why God should command him to eat of those unclean animals. Acts 10:19, 20 reads:

> While Peter was still thinking about the vision, the Spirit said to him, 'Simon, three men are looking for you. So get up and go downstairs. Do not hesitate to go with them, for I have sent them.'

The three men who were looking for Peter came from Cornelius' house, a Gentile centurion living in Caesarea. Now Peter seems to have understood why God gave him a vision: on reaching Cornelius' home he tells his host:

> You are well aware that it is against our law for a Jew to associate with a Gentile or visit him. But God has shown me that I should not call any man impure or unclean. So when I was sent for, I came without raising any objection. (vv. 28, 29)

The Christian author Ellen White makes the comment: 'How carefully the Lord worked to overcome the prejudice against the Gentiles that had been so firmly fixed in Peter's mind by his Jewish training!' (*Acts of the Apostles*, p. 136).

Peter seemed to have struggled to overcome his racism and prejudice to the point that some time later, Paul publicly condemned him for his attitude. You can read of this in Galatians 2:11–14.

There is a saying: 'What goes around, comes around.' The Christian Church is still wrestling with issues of prejudice and racism. In the six years that I spent as a student it was often proudly announced that Newbold College is a mini 'United Nations'. We had up to 41 nationalities living in peace and harmony. Be that as it may, my friends, the

Seventh-day Adventist Church faces an ongoing challenge of countering what I term 'Skin-deep Christianity'. The Church is not afraid to challenge theological differences and diversities; but of racism, prejudice, tribalism, nationalism, caste systems, apartheid and the like we can be deafly silent.

Learn the lesson

One of the greatest lessons that I learned during my time as a student was not in the classroom. I'm still trying to get my head around some of those deep theological concepts taught by Doctor Metzing in the class. One of the great lessons I learned was that God's family was not to be divided by race, language, tribe or culture, but rather God's family embraces every race, language, tribe and culture and that I can experience a unity with my brothers and sisters through the blood of Jesus Christ. My evaluation of others ought not to be skin deep, so that I can love others from my heart. I am still learning that the things which separate us are not as important as the Spirit of God that unites us. I can't change my colour, I was born black and will die black. What God has made me, I am happy and proud of. I cannot change my culture. I am very much bound by it and live through it. My culture largely determines how I worship, how I preach, and how I praise God. It is not the differences of race or culture in the family of God that are supremely important. What is supremely important in the family of God, is the oneness, which implies that my skin colour is not better, it is just different. My culture is not better, it is just different. And though we are different, because of Jesus we are one family. We must learn to live and appreciate our differences in Christ.

Conclusion

In closing, permit me to paraphrase the words of the apostle Paul to the Galatians in chapter 3, verses 26–28, changing the second person plural 'you' to the first person plural 'we'.

We are all sons and daughters of God through faith in Jesus Christ, for all of us who were baptized into Christ have clothed ourselves with Christ. There is neither Jew nor Greek, slave nor free, male nor female, Hutu nor Tutsi, Croatian nor Serbian nor Bosnian, Conservative nor Labour, North nor South, East nor West, small island nor big island, Brahmin nor untouchable, postgraduate nor undergraduate, lecturer nor student, rich nor poor, Loyalist nor Republican, black nor white, for we are all one in Jesus Christ.

Comments

Kieran Conry: *'A good and gripping introduction leads easily on to a challenging and very honest examination of a controversial issue, race and colour prejudice. Well illustrated with appropriate reference to the scriptures and personal testimony, this is both personally challenging and informative.'*

Peter Graves: *'A clearly developed and challenging sermon that obviously starts where people are and moves forward to a very moving and scriptural conclusion.'*

Out of Great Tribulation

CANON MICHAEL BOURDEAUX

Sermon preached at King's College Chapel, Cambridge, at 10.30am on 24 May (the University Sermon).

Canon Michael Bourdeaux, aged 64, has two children from his first marriage, to Gillian, who died in 1978. He married again, to Lorna, and they have two children. Their daughter, Lara-Clare, has recently won a choral scholarship to Exeter Cathedral. Canon Bourdeaux specialized in languages from school upwards, and learned Russian at Cambridge during his military service. He went to study theology at Oxford and was an inaugural member of the British Council's exchange programme with Moscow University, spending a year there before his ordination in 1960. His calling came to him during his second year at university. Previously, he had never envisaged himself becoming a priest. 'It suddenly struck me that what I wanted to do was put my languages to the service of the Church', he says.

After four years as a curate in Enfield, London, he moved into academia and then into study of the area that was to become the focus of his expertise: religion and communism. In 1969 he founded the Centre for the Study of Religion and Communism in Kent, now the world-famous Keston Institute. He has done many lecture tours and is a recognized and established author on Russian affairs and religion in Eastern Europe. In 1984 he won the Templeton Prize for Progress in Religion, the world's largest monetary award and the religious equivalent of the Nobel Prize. In 1996 he was awarded a Lambeth doctorate of divinity by the Archbishop of Canterbury, Dr George Carey. In addition, he is an established choral singer, has directed the Iffley Festival associated with his parish church in Iffley, Oxford, and is an international tennis umpire, having officiated at Wimbledon, New York and Melbourne. His eight books include the seminal work, Gorbachev, Glasnost and the Gospel, *published in 1990, and he edited in 1995* The Politics of Religion in Russia and the New States of Eurasia.

But it is arguably for his work at Keston that he will go down in history. For 20 years, Keston untiringly analysed and disseminated information on how religious belief was sustained under communism. Keston is continuing, post-communism, to monitor government policies and social developments and how they affect the practice of faith throughout Eastern Europe, along with continuing its work of monitoring countries still under communist rule, such

as China, Tibet, Cuba and Vietnam, where anti-religious government policies remain unchanged. Canon Bourdeaux remains as passionately devoted
to this cause as ever, and is particularly exercised at present by the fact that
there have been more martyrs for Christian belief in this century than any
other, chiefly as a result of communism. He is also concerned that the ideological gap left by the collapse of communism in the former Soviet Union is
being filled by consumerism on one hand, and by an alarming rise in extreme
nationalism and anti-Semitism on the other. Keston, which employs seven
full-time and several part-time members, is constantly in need of funds to
help continue its invaluable work.

Canon Bourdeaux admits: 'I have not done a lot of preaching, but I have
lectured extensively. I think my preaching tends to be more like lectures than
sermons. In preaching, the aim is to bring people closer to God, to enable
them to follow in the footsteps of Jesus Christ. I do that by holding up Eastern Europeans, particularly Russians, some of whom I have known personally, as examples. These come from the Church and the world of the second half
of the twentieth century. I have never had my own pulpit, so when I am invited to preach it is always in connection with my work on Eastern Europe. I
think preaching has very great value, but I would class myself as a listener to
sermons rather than a preacher.'

In the run-up to the Millennium, he has been working through the relevant
organizations to promote a stronger Christian content to the Dome. As this
sermon indicates, he is lobbying for an exhibition to give recognition to twentieth-century martyrs. He also expects to be involved in the Millennium celebrations in his own parish, where the church of St Mary the Virgin is one of
the country's few surviving purely Norman churches.

He believes the funeral of the Princess of Wales brought the nation together in a way that has not been seen since the last World War. 'The way
Westminster Abbey organized the event was quite outstanding', he says.

Text:

If the King of Souls has sown us in the field of sorrows – let us
bloom in sorrow. If he has sown us in solitude, let it be solitude,
for the Creator sows even the most beautiful of flowers on inaccessible tracks between mountain paths, and they have their
value, even though nobody sees them.

This century has produced more Christian martyrs than the nineteen
which preceded it and the words I have just quoted were smuggled out
of a Soviet prison in 1976. The Lithuanian who wrote them survived,
but tens of thousands of his countrymen sacrificed their lives for their
faith and their nation between 1945 and 1991.

St John the Divine's vision of a new heaven and a new earth contains many startling images. Few are more unforgettable than that of the Christian martyrs read in our second lesson this morning: 'What are these which are arrayed in white robes? And whence came they? . . . These are they which came out of great tribulation, and have washed their robes, and made them white in the blood of the Lamb.'

As we approach the end of the century, we note the existence of a growing number of memorials in this country to those who have made their robes white in the blood of the Lamb. Salisbury Cathedral has a complex window by a French artist, Gabriel Loire, celebrating them. Canterbury Cathedral has a whole chapel commemorating ten by name, with an annual memorial service on St Thomas's Day. Notable, too, is an event to take place on 9 July when Her Majesty the Queen will unveil a rank of ten statues on the West front of Westminster Abbey. Each one represents a martyr of the twentieth century: two victims of Nazism, two of communism (Soviet and Chinese), two African, two Asian, one Melanesian, another Latin American.

However, the number of such memorials is pathetically small compared with those to the victims of the Holocaust, even though communism caused an even worse destruction of human life: perhaps three times as many victims. Not only are there fewer memorials, but there is less documentation. Concerning Christian martyrs specifically, systematic documentation does not exist. When Westminster Abbey held a conference on modern martyrdom before the unveiling of the statues, there was a session devoted to Dietrich Bonhoeffer, another to Latin America, but strangely none to any victim of communism.

The era of the persecuted Church in Eastern Europe has, we trust, now passed for ever. However, the voice it found while being called 'the Church of silence' must continue to be heard. Dietrich Bonhoeffer's great book, *Letters and Papers from Prison*, has encouraged millions, while a very different book, *The Diary of Anne Frank*, has been a world best-seller for decades. There are many texts which survive from communist oppression which are just as inspirational, and yet are barely known.

By contrast, who has heard the name of Petras Plumpa, the author of the smuggled letter I quoted at the beginning?

So in Russia. In the 1930s an Orthodox priest from Leningrad shared the fate of tens of thousands of his fellow-pastors. Only in his Siberian labour camp did Father Pavel discover inner resources which he did not know he possessed. A young criminal whom he brought to faith in Christ wrote the story of this secret ministry. The manuscript was smuggled out of the Soviet Union about 25 years ago and published here in 1978 under the title *The Unknown Homeland*. It received scarcely a press notice, sold only a few hundred copies and has been out of print for many years. Yet it is one of the spiritual classics of the twentieth century and a great work of literature also. I quote the final paragraph, which is among the best descriptions of the survival of the faith under persecution:

> So the story of the exiled pastor came to an end ... But though the storm blows over the new and old grave mounds, covering them with snow, though time goes by and the years disappear, though no one comes there any more and the small cross with its worn inscription falls off its base and collapses on to the ground ... still the cherry tree will go on arraying itself anew in its wedding colours every spring, and the path of remembrance, prayer and veneration which leads to such graves will never be overgrown.

Here we face a paradox: the Russian Orthodox Church has been sanctified by martyrdom; yet its public face still exhibits the defects of fallen humanity. It is now a 'church triumphant' in a Russia where President Yeltsin loves to invite the Patriarch to share his platform on state occasions, where no new public enterprise is complete unless a bishop blesses it. However, far from being purified by suffering, the Russian Church is beset by pride, excessive nationalism, an exclusivity sometimes bordering on xenophobia. There is no other explanation of the new law on religion, passed in September 1997 and inspired by the Moscow Patriarchate, which gives every incentive to treat Protestants and Catholics as second-class citizens.

At the same time, scarcely any of the 'heroes of the faith' to whom we used to pay the highest tributes and support with our prayers have become influential – in the secular sense – in the new Russia. None plays a leading role in the shaping of a new society.

One could quote the example of the 'Christian Seminar', a cell of young intellectuals who 20 years ago wanted to introduce Christian values into an atheist society. The authorities expelled its leader, Alexander Ogorodnikov, from his Institute. For a time, the group continued to meet in a tiny nightwatchman's hut. They were betrayed and brought to trial. Ogorodnikov's sentence was ten years. He now works thanklessly, still harassed by the authorities, among Moscow's down-and-outs. The words of the Lithuanian prisoner who wrote 'the Creator sows even the most beautiful of flowers on inaccessible tracks' are relevant for today also.

Some other churches of the former Soviet Union do honour those who suffered, and two men come to mind whom I have met this year. One of the very last Christian prisoners to be released under Mikhail Gorbachev's amnesty was the Lithuanian Catholic priest Fr Sigitas Tamkevicius. This mild and modest man was considered an especially dangerous criminal because he recorded the outrageous treatment of his church by the communists. During years of imprisonment he refused to recant. He is now archbishop of the important diocese of Kaunas in a country which, almost miraculously, has become free. He told me that the work of Keston Institute was instrumental in keeping hope alive during those dark years. 'And the church in the East needs your support just as much today', he said.

In the Protestant Church I think of Iosif Bondarenko, who paid his first visit to Keston Institute in March. He trained to be a naval officer 40 years ago. Converted to the Baptist faith, he was summoned to renounce his beliefs. Instead, he fell on his knees before the whole company of 1,900 students and staff and re-affirmed his commitment to Christ. He spent more than half of his next 30 years in jail. Only recently the judge who pronounced the last sentence on him came forward from the crowd at the end of a Christian rally in Russia. He said: 'I am the man who sentenced you to twelve years' imprisonment, and yet you offered to pray for me in the courtroom. I could not understand such love and lack of bitterness.'

This ex-judge and his family are today all Christians and his son is one of Russia's leading evangelists.

This first meeting with Iosif Bondarenko, whom I first wrote about over 30 years ago, has caused me much reflection. My mind first went back to the commission I received in 1964 from a group of Ukrainian Orthodox women, whom I met on the site of a church which had just been torn down. 'Be our voice and speak for us', they said. Circumstances are very different today. Yet problems in the lives of the churches of Eastern Europe are so complex that there must still be voices which interpret sympathetically and speak for them.

My second reflection is on the significance of martyrdom today – for us, as well as for the churches in the countries where it happened.

Think of the Millennium Dome. As martyrdom is one of the principal marks of the Church in the twentieth century, here is an unmissable opportunity to record the names in a public place, as are the names of so many victims of the Holocaust. The historical record needs to be more complete; this should be a time for compiling more case histories, a time for recording fading voices. The resources of Keston Institute, which has built up its archive over almost 40 years, should contribute to such a project.

It is not only those who sacrificed their lives who merit greater recognition: the survivors of persecution, too, have a message for the world, one which is barely heard. It is not that the media always turn away from Christian voices: Archbishop Tutu, for example, is still widely reported even after the collapse of the old system in South Africa. What Archbishop Tamkevicius of Kaunas, Lithuania or Iosif Bondarenko, the Baptist preacher from Riga, say may be just as important, but their visits are unreported and their names remain unknown to the world at large.

It is not only the sufferings of Russian Christians which should be better known: there are positive aspects to the life of the Orthodox Church today which are also largely unreported. Visitors to the parishes find a smiling welcome and a readiness to share hospitality, even when there is such poverty in the countryside. The physical rebuilding of churches after decades of destruction and neglect provides people in thousands of towns and villages with a sense of purpose, as well as beautifying the scene in a tangible way. Parishes are alive again after a hiatus of three-quarters of a century. Last October Radio 3 marked the 80th anniversary of the Revolution by devoting almost eight hours of unbroken programming to the new St Petersburg. The restored churches there, as in many other cities, are a symbol of a new spiritual life in the former captial: how inadequate, then, that this renewal went unreported by the dozens of people who spoke on the programme.

Universities and theological colleges have not done well, either, in putting anything of significance on church life in Eastern Europe onto their curricula. The few initiatives deserve more support. Oxford has its Theological Exchange Programme which, over the past seven years, has funded 30 young people to study subjects not available at home. Leeds University now teaches 'Religion under Communism' as an undergraduate subject. In this university, Cambridge, King's College has inaugurated a valuable research programme on religion and national identity in Russia today. Westminster College has recently put out a call for theological books in English to fill what is still an almost complete void from 1917 to the present in the library of the St Petersburg Theological Academy. This gap of almost a century goes some way towards explaining the current obscurantism in some sections of the Orthodox Church. Perhaps with a better library this institution would not recently have expelled Fr Veniamin Novik, one of its most enlightened theologians. He is well known and much loved from his visits to England and Scotland. He is an active ecumenist, a man who has studied the social involvement of the Church in the UK and Italy and attempted to take back this experience to Russia.

If we widen our field of vision, there is much to encourage us. Last year the Ecumenical Assembly at Graz, Austria, in which Roman Catholics fully participated, involved lay people in an unprecedented way. The unwillingness of Catholic and Orthodox Church leaders to meet each other was offset by an invasion from the East – unreported in our press. Young people predominated in the thousand or more from Romania and there was a trainload from Ukraine.

Nor do I believe that the spirituality so nobly evolved under communist oppression has simply melted away. It seeped into the hidden corners and the cracks of the desecrated buildings. There is a well of concealed experience from which life-giving water will be drawn by future generations. Overall in Eastern Europe, the Christian faith has made an astonishing comeback. If there is ever to be a new Europe constructed on the basis of anything other than self-interest, this renewed faith will have a major role to play.

The vision of St John the Divine belongs to our common heritage, or as T. S. Eliot put it:

> A Christian martyrdom is never an accident, for saints are not made by accident. Still less is a Christian martyrdom the effect of a man's will to become a saint, as a man by willing and contriving may become a ruler of men. A martyrdom is always the design of God, for his love of men, to warn them and to lead them, to bring them back to his ways.

> *Murder in the Cathedral*

Comments

Peter Graves: *'Important material powerfully and graphically communicated in a very challenging way. More of an address than a sermon however.'*

Jonathan Romain: *'Informative talk about a topic.'*

Paul Walker: *'Among all the sermons, this is unique. Here is a very particular yet powerful message. There were more Christian martyrs and other martyrs in the communist East than in other repressive regimes, yet this has rarely been reported. There seems to be a scandal here. The sermon lays open some very disturbing facts, particularly for someone like myself, on the left of the political spectrum. This sermon deserves the wider audience this book will give it.'*

What Happens
After We Die?

JOHN ALDRIDGE

Sermon preached at the morning service at Great Glen Methodist Church on Sunday 19 April 1998.

John Aldridge, 60, with his wife June, a former schoolteacher, has two children and one grandchild. He attends Oadby Trinity Methodist Church and preaches every three weeks on the Leicester Trinity Circuit, where the superintendent is the Rev. Martin Smithson.

Mr Aldridge has worked in the newspaper industry all his life, with the Northcliffe Newspaper Group, the regional division of the Daily Mail. *After 15 years as chairman and managing director of the Leicester Mercury Group, he has just retired. His first job at 16 was clearing out printing blocks that were surplus to requirements and taking them for scrap. He progressed to being tea boy in the advertisement department of the* Grimsby Evening Telegraph. *'That was my big break because it got me into mainstream publishing where I have had a very enjoyable, and some might say successful, career.'*

He was converted to Christianity when he was nearly 17. 'I had not even been baptized. There was an evangelical campaign very much like a Billy Graham crusade in a wonderful town called Cleethorpes, run by the Methodist Church. It was a life-changing moment. My parents were surprised and initially I think a little disappointed. But as they saw it was the real thing, they came to be great supporters of me.' While at school he worked for his father, the local wholesaler for The News of the World. *After working early Sunday mornings, he would go home, put a suit on and go to church. 'That was quite a major step to take. Sunday had been a working day, and it became a working-and-worship day.*

'I began to give epilogues to a Methodist youth club. I progressed from that to a mission band. From that, I felt a calling to be a preacher. I submitted to the training of being a Methodist local preacher. I was asked if I felt the call to be ordained, but I strongly did not. I felt, and have felt so all my life, that God had called me to be a Christian in the secular world. Given that for 23 years I was the managing director of two different regional newspapers, I was able to practise my Christian beliefs in these newspapers. I felt this was no accident.'

He is currently chairman of The Methodist Recorder *and has been on the board for many years. He is also chairman of Leicester Sound, part of the*

GWR group of commercial radio stations. He is past president of the Rotary Club of Leicester and has also been president of the Newspaper Society. 'I remember when I started work as a local preacher I went to preach in a little village called Cottager's Plot near Grimsby. It was the first time I had preached on my own, without another preacher being with me. It was a rainy night, and I had cycled about five miles. I put my bike outside this little church and began the service soaking wet. I was in the middle of the opening prayers when, all of a sudden, a loud voice said: 'Stop this prayer!' I looked up in astonishment and so did the congregation of about eight people. The man said that much more important than the prayer was that it was going to rain again. Everything stopped while he went to bring my bike inside the church! This made me recognize that preaching, in which I passionately believe, is a very down-to-earth operation.

'On another occasion I was preaching in a Trentside hamlet. The service was to begin at 6.30pm. I was in the vestry at 6.20 when the steward came in and said we could start. I said it was too early. He said it didn't matter, because everybody had arrived! That was one of my bigger congregations – about a dozen people were there.

'I passionately believe in preaching as a means of communication, but it is helpful to look at the way other media communicate. If we look at television commercials, we see very effective communication. The objective is to catch the viewer's attention, to make a point and then to invite the viewer to take action. That same process is vital to every sermon.'

On the Millennium, he says: 'I am very concerned about young people in worship, and the worrying decline we have seen over the last few years. We must address ourselves to this problem, or we will perish. We must put more resources into youth work and training. We are light years away from being able to communicate with young people. Another thing is the great ecumenical movement, which we should allow to happen from the grass roots.'

On the death of Diana, Princess of Wales, he says: 'I used the death of Diana as an illustration for what seemed to me an immense, grass-roots spiritual hunger. I felt so moved, not just by her death but by the fact that people did not know how to mourn her death. They did not know where to turn for comfort. They did not know what death meant. The Church was slow to get across its message that death is not the end. I did feel inept at the time. I and others did not seem able to get across the fact that there is great comfort in the death and resurrection of Jesus, and his going ahead to prepare a place for us. But there are great signs of hope. Diana's death vividly illustrated the desire in people for something more than the material things in life. I believe now that the pendulum in society will swing away from the material to a society that tries to find some spiritual peace. The Church can still be a doorway for people. We just have to make it accessible.'

Text: John 14:1–14.

'DID YOU see the sunset last night? It was the best I've ever
seen!'

I listen politely but I'd been in a long meeting and I didn't see it – so
I'm not convinced.

'Did you see the musical at the Haymarket? There's never been anything as good before.'

I listen politely but since I failed to get tickets, I dismiss the claim.

'We had a healing service: a man got out of his wheelchair and
walked.'

I listen politely, but I didn't see it happen. I want to believe it happened, but I start to rationalize what they describe.

Do you identify with these reactions? I guess most do. I guess most
of us at heart are like Thomas. We want to see proof. We want first-
hand experience. We question, if not out loud, in our minds. Seeing,
they say, is believing! I imagine that we all have some sympathy for
Thomas. He was missing when Jesus appeared to the other disciples.
He'd missed the moment of drama. He didn't believe what the other
disciples told him, even though he would want to believe.

He was perfectly aware that Jesus had been most horribly crucified.
He would know every detail of the events of Good Friday. He would
surely have heard of the tomb Joseph of Arimathea had provided. He
would equally have heard of the claims that Mary Magdalene and the
other women had made when they came to the tomb on the first
Easter Day and found it empty.

He would be aware that the women had believed that their Lord had
been taken away. None of them could even begin to accept the fact that
he had risen from the dead.

Surely he would have known that Jesus, in the first of his appear-
ances, spoke to Mary in the garden – or at least that was her claim. But
Thomas wasn't there and he found it impossible to believe.

I found it impossible to believe: that Sunday morning in August
when I put the radio on and heard grave voices speaking of the death
of a Princess in a tunnel in Paris.

It was a death that shocked us all. I had to put the television on and
phone a friend before I could believe. If two days later I'd been told that
she was alive, I wouldn't have believed it. Like everyone in this church
I asked the question: Why? Why her?

And none of us here are untouched by the death of a loved one.
We've all been there. I imagine we've all asked why. Why now? Why so
cruelly? Why so young? Every time I attend a funeral I give thanks that
our faith offers us the hope of eternal life. So death isn't the end – we
would claim that it is the next stage. Many would affirm that their

loved ones are still close and that in daily conversation they still communicate.

To make it clear to his followers that in a different form he would be with them for ever, Jesus was able to gently reveal himself to his followers as they could bear it. He was able to say to Thomas with such understanding 'Put your finger here and look at my hands . . . stop your doubting and believe' (John 20:27).

And, of course, he doesn't restrict his words to one of his disciples 2,000 years ago. They're equally meant for us today: 'Believe', he says and he says it to you and me. 'How happy', says Jesus, 'are those who believe without seeing me' (John 20:29).

What happens when we die?
People have given various answers. I have at least one friend who believes that's the end of us. Eternal sleep. We've had our threescore years and ten, we are no more. What a waste if that were true.

Some believe in reincarnation. Returning as a dove, or as a snail, or as a human being in a different age and in a different body.

Others believe that it is possible in a séance, or with the help of a medium, to make contact with loved ones who have died. Some will tell you that mediums have answered questions which only the deceased could have answered. I worry about such situations. About the false hopes that can be aroused. About the tampering with emotions such things represent.

Roman Catholics believe in a place called Purgatory. There, the souls of the dead who have repented of, but not fully atoned for, their sins, are purified by suffering until they are fit for heaven. It's a concept which doesn't seem to be based on any biblical evidence and with which, I have to confess, I have some difficulty.

For we believe as Christians that death is the start of a whole new episode of life – a wonderful future lived in God's presence.

Is there life after death?
As Christians we believe there is. You will all have read books describing after-death experiences. The descriptions are always attractive and pleasant. They speak of a feeling of well-being, of warmth, of security, of loveliness, of beauty and of gentle reassurance.

Friends were telling me the other day of the death of a young boy and of the things he said. Of his smile. Of his willingness to leave. Evidence, if such it is, that the next stage is something to be desired.

Jesus knew that death was about to take him. The words about his Father's house are among his last words to his followers. They were, of course, words of reassurance. He was going through death to a new kind of existence.

Because of what was going to happen to him after his death, Jesus said the same good things would be available to his followers. To describe the indescribable, Jesus used a picture full of comfort and security.

Paul, in his second letter to the Corinthians, talks about heaven being a home which God has made for us – death for him was merely going home (2 Cor 5:1).

I was as a boy a Scout and a very enthusiastic one. I learned how to lay a trail. Using natural materials we made arrows that pointed ahead, arrows that turned corners, signs that indicated a dead end and one, a circle of sticks with a stone in the middle, which meant: 'Gone home'.

When Lord Baden-Powell died, in 1941, Scouts around the world subscribed to a tomb for him. On it is a circle with a dot in the middle: 'Gone home'.

Jesus makes it clear that he goes before us to prepare a place, that he is the way and if we follow the way we shall be with him in his Father's house. Jesus not only tells us that he is the way, but he takes us there. He takes us home.

Who will go home?

Jesus spoke of division. He spoke of separation. He spoke of sheep and lambs, of bridesmaids who were not prepared when he came. He spoke of cutting out dead wood.

Does this mean some will be cast beyond God's presence? Does this mean that heaven will only be populated by those who are Christians? For we all know of saints who are not followers of Christ.

Many years ago Dr Shah, who is President of the Jain Temple near the Newark Gate in Leicester, took me to see the building, which is exquisitely decorated.

But I was more impressed with him than with the building. He exuded love and compassion. He was gentle, saintly and prayerful. If I ever get to heaven I expect to see him there.

Because Jesus' teaching on heaven and hell is far from clear, try to remove from your minds images of medieval paintings depicting hell. Creative though they may be, they are not based on any biblical truth.

There is a story that a television researcher, preparing for two satirical programmes, faxed the company's Roman Catholic consultants asking how she could get the official Catholic view on heaven and hell. The answer came back. It was brief but accurate: 'Die!'

Jesus repeatedly spoke of himself as the simple and sure way to be absolutely confident of God's welcome in eternity. I believe that. We all need to believe that in the end he will keep his promise and take us home.

How can we be certain that we'll live for ever?

Like Thomas and, I'm sure, the other disciples, we all seek that reassurance. Jesus answered his questions by saying: 'I am going where you want to go.' He promises that we will be where he is and he invites us to come along with him. I read that the form of expression Jesus used would be used by Arabs today if asked directions to a lonely, remote place: 'I am the way.' With that reassurance and his promise that we'll never be alone, death need never frighten us.

Sarah Miles, an actress, said at the funeral of her husband: 'Until we come to terms with death and the dying process, we will always be driven by fear, rather than love.'

Of course we all love life. So too did Jesus. He didn't want to die. In the Garden of Gethsemane he prayed that he might be spared the way of the cross. He loved his family and his friends. Some contemporary writers suggest that he also loved Mary Magdalene in the human sense. I don't know. But I do know that he didn't want to die.

Neither do we want loved ones to die. We don't want them to leave us. We grieve for them. However lovely a place we believe them to be in, we don't want to be without them. However faithful we are, our grieving is perfectly natural. Little did Thomas realize, as he became a follower of Jesus, that he would shortly be grieving for the Man he loved.

The unique thing about our faith is that we believe in life after death. We believe that death is neither a beginning nor an end, but a continuation of a journey. The journey is signposted, others follow the same route and we all have a guide. And our guide understands our frailty. Understands that we are all doubting Thomases. That we find it hard to believe when we haven't seen.

And he comes to each of us, in our need, and says, look Mary, look John: 'Put your finger here and look at my hands, then stretch out your hand and put it in my side. Stop your doubting and believe!'

And he wants each of us to respond as Thomas responded:

'My Lord and my God' (John 20:28).

Can we make that response?

Nothing else matters.

Comments

Kieran Conry: *'Makes good use of short sentences to produce a pithy and clear exposition. Engaging and carefully developed at the start, the development of the main theme is helpful, as are the questions asked to help guide the listener through the process.'*

Paul Walker: *'Deals with the question of life after death. The more I preach,* the more I realize that this is the big question. No easy answers here, but questions are met head on.'

Peter Graves: 'Very good introduction. Well-constructed sermon, with argument clearly developed and illustrated.'

Jonathan Romain: 'To declare that the saintly of other religions will find a place in heaven even if they do not follow the path of Jesus is admirably inclusive, but does it mean Jesus is not the only way and just one option among many?'

There is No One Holy Like the Lord

REV. PAUL WALKER

Winning sermon preached at the final of the 1997 Preacher of the Year Award at Durham Cathedral on 12 November 1997.

The Rev. Paul Walker, 35, was winner of the 1997 Preacher of the Year Award.

Mr Walker, 35, born and brought up in York, is married to Penny, a free-lance editor and proof-reader. They have two daughters.

Apart from a brief and reluctant six months in Sunday School, neither he nor any of his immediate family went to church. After a happy childhood he became, to the irritation of his family and friends, an atheist and a Marxist in adolescence. At 17 he won an essay competition organized by the York Anglo-Israeli Friendship Society and as his prize was sent on holiday to Israel.

'It was in Israel, away from my family that I first seriously encountered religion, from an Orthodox Jewish Auschwitz survivor with whom I stayed, and from so many people praying in Jerusalem. It was also here, when later staying on a kibbutz that I came across sex and drugs. Quite a heady combination for one so young.' He adds: 'As I went off to university I was still coming to terms with all this. The radical in me rejected religion, though I briefly flirted with Buddhism as it was fairly trendy. So finally, at the age of 19, I picked up a Bible, something I'd never done before. Reading the Gospels was a wonderful experience, I had never come across anything like it and in a way I fell in love with the figure of Jesus. With all the ups and downs that have followed it is a love that has never died. At the same time I had an over-whelming sense of calling to serve God in ministry, a call I rejected then. But in spite of all my best efforts to do something else, the Church agreed I had a genuine calling, and I was accepted for training for ordination.'

He spent a year as pastoral assistant at the American cathedral in Paris, three years at theological college in Sussex, and served two curacies in County Durham. For the last five years, he has been working on a series of housing estates on the edge of Sunderland, with a brief to start a new church congregation in a school. This he has now done, and St Wilfrid's, Moorside is a thriving congregation, meeting in Benedict Biscop School with a congrega-tion of about 100 youthful families, most of which have no churchgoing backgound at all. 'My aim has been to create a Church accessible to working-class families', he says.

'Winning the competition had an all-and-nothing effect on my life', he adds. 'There was a lot of media interest which was enjoyable. On the day of the final, at Durham Cathedral, it seemed to be a never-ending round of dashing from one interview to the next. I must have done eight radio and five television interviews on the day itself. In ensuing weeks I took part in a BBC Songs of Praise broadcast, did some presenting and reporting for BBC Radio Newcastle and even presented an entire mid-morning programme. I have been invited to teach and preach to Northern lay readers this year. But in some respects, nothing really changed in my life. There was a certain snobbery within the Church of England itself about the competition, which was quite irritating.'

He is clear on his views about the Millennium. 'In terms of Christianity it means little, but I am really excited about it because I love the concept of the passage of time, and it is just great to be alive at the year 2000. I have always seen Christmas as a religious festival and New Year as a secular festival. So I just want to have a good time, to have a big party. In terms of mission, I think the Christians are getting far too hot under the collar about it.'

On the question of the death of Diana, his response is more complex. In the week she died, Mr Walker suffered a close personal bereavement. 'Because of this, the whole thing more or less passed me by', he says. 'I get annoyed when I hear Christians endlessly bringing it up, as if they are trying to sound modern and relevant. In my heart of hearts, I am a bit of a republican, I think. But when she died, I did think: "What have we done?" It was nothing to do with newspapers, it was to do with all of us, with people's desire to know. I think all of us in this country know that, deep down, it was our fault. We all created her, and then we destroyed her. I think this is why so many people still feel uncomfortable with the whole thing.'

Text: 1 Samuel 2:2.

Just because this is the Preacher of the Year Final doesn't mean I've spent any longer than usual on my sermon. But did you know that the word 'holiness' appears 25 times in my Bible, while the word 'holy' comes up 586 times? You can check.

So given that holiness is my theme I picked the text 1 Samuel 2:2 'There is no one holy like the Lord', spoken by Samuel's mother Hannah when she learns that God has answered her prayer for a child, because it states simply the fact that holiness is about God. The prophet Isaiah calls God 'The Holy One', and that is a title taken up in the Gospels for Jesus. Holy is an adjective that describes the very nature of God, or put another way, holy and godly are synonymous. The more present God is, the more holy the place of his presence.

But most people hardly ever use the word 'holy' except occasionally as an expletive, sometimes linked with 'mackerel' for some reason. The

Americans link it with something even more profane but we won't go into that now. If anything, the word 'holy' is linked with a particular kind of morality. This is fair enough but that's a subsidiary meaning.

But things are still there even if we don't use the word. We still have a sense of the holy, we just call it something else. In fact we call it exactly that: 'Something else' or rather 'something'. We say that there is something about a place or person. I mean I can't be the only person who walked into this place today and felt: 'There's just something about Durham Cathedral'. There's the age of the place, the extraordinary thick pillars, the colour of the light caught in the stained glass. Whatever, but then maybe there's something more, maybe, just maybe the fact that this cathedral was built to the glory of God and has been prayed in for over 900 years might give it that extra 'something' that so many people feel when they come here. Most people would say that at times they've experienced what William James called a perception of 'something there' in his book *The Varieties of Religious Experience*, written in 1902.

Now don't get me wrong. When we say there's 'something' about a place or a person we're not only referring to holiness. The phrase can cover a multitude of euphemisms, so when somebody says to me that there's something about Andre Agassi, what they're probably referring to, if I'm being polite, are his legs (although for all I know, Andre Agassi may be a very holy person). And there are for many of us places, pictures, pieces of music which are somehow more than the sum of their parts, they seem to point us beyond ourselves to something more. We search to understand this. The New Age movement gives it the vague title of 'spirituality'.

I often wonder whether we religious people are scared to put a name to the source of this spirituality. But I think that this experience of the 'beyond' is a brush with the holy, with God. Yet God is somehow a more uncomfortable topic than a vague notion like spirituality. God makes demands. God gives us this sense of his presence but goes on to ask more of us.

And holiness would be a pretty trite thing if it were nothing more than a vaguely warm feeling. I mean if you want to feel warm, have a sauna. But there can be a deeper brush with God, with that something beyond ourselves which is deeply affecting. In his book *The Idea of the Holy*, Rudolf Otto wrote that holiness both 'overwhelms us and drives us on'. When Isaiah felt himself to be in the presence of holiness, he was shattered by a sense of his own sinfulness. The presence of holiness both changed him and also led him on to prophesy for God. Many people have just one single head-on encounter with holiness which changes them for ever. They suddenly become aware that God is not only present but that he demands something of them. They're so struck by this experience that they go further than to say they've changed, they say they have been converted.

For others the holy is something they sense in quiet. In pondering the holiness of God, people feel it to be worth pursuing above everything else. It is the pearl of great price and they give up the desire for wealth, human or sexual love, and seek a life of contemplation.

But for most Christians, holiness is something lived and experienced in ordinary life. Jesus is the holy one, but somehow not some distant ascetic figure, rather a carpenter from the north-east of Israel. Jesus didn't do what many wanted him to do: he didn't make certain things sacred and other things profane, he made ordinary things holy, like bread and wine. Jesus took God away from a temple made with human hands, away from those who said they could interpret God's law, away from those who told people what was holy and what was not, and in his human life lived as the holy one, and showed us that human life was profoundly holy *in itself.*

And that means that each one of us is capable of being holy and experiencing holiness. We don't need to be a monk or nun, we don't need to have been converted, we simply need to recognize the holy presence in our lives and in the lives of those around us. So I'd just like to share a story that once happened to me.

It happened at Victoria Station. I was at college on the south coast training to be a priest and was therefore reliant on what in those days was called Southern Region Railways – later to become Network South-East. Now that I live up north, my lack of sympathy for the plight of London's commuters is very unholy, but when I hear the words Connex South Central on travel news associated with delays, I wonder whether this could be the same piece of railway?

Anyway this particular day I was stuck at Victoria Station. I was going to be late due to trains on the line or something, so I prepared for a long wait. I refuse to buy drinks on those bars on stations which charge £5 for a pint of lemonade, so I went across to an off-licence and bought myself a can of beer, came back and went to sit down, opened it and lit a cigarette (you can see what an example of holiness I am). Then this bloke came in. You know the type you see at London stations. He was dirty and smelly, looking around in bins and talking to people. I just had that sinking feeling I knew he was going to collar me. I looked away, avoided his eyes, developed a strong fascination with the graffiti and prayed I would avoid him.

But sure enough he walked straight up to me and spoke. Here you'll have to forgive me. Because the story is true it contains one cliché, the man was Scottish. Now if I'd made it up I'd have made him posh, but there you go. 'Got a ciggie?' he asked. 'Sure', I said, hoping that would see him off. 'Can I have a swig of your beer?' Well normally I'd have said no, but I was a bit frightened. Anyway a conversation followed that went something like this:

'What do you do then?'

'I'm a student.'

'Student of what?'

'I, I'm training to be a priest.'

'Do you pray?'

Not quite what I'd expected, but yes I assured him I did.

'Really pray, I mean pray all the time?'

This was weird, but 'Yeees', I lied.

'Look at this', he said, then out of his pocket he pulled a very old broken set of rosary beads.

'I use these all the time', he said. 'You'll never achieve anything unless you pray.'

'No, I realize that', I said.

The conversation went on a while. It was all about prayer. Then at the end he reminded me God is only with us if we let him be. Then he looked me in the eyes and thanked me for the ciggie and the beer and said: 'Paul' (and I could swear I'd never told him my name), 'you never know who you've been talking to.'

And with that, he went his way.